THE HERO WITH AN
AFRICAN FACE

THE HERO WITH AN AFRICAN FACE

Mythic Wisdom of Traditional Africa

CLYDE W. FORD

BANTAM BOOKS

NEW YORK TORONTO LONDON SYDNEY AUCKLAND

THE HERO WITH AN AFRICAN FACE

A Bantam Book / January 1999

All rights reserved.
Copyright © 1999 by Clyde W. Ford

BOOK DESIGN BY TANYA PÉREZ-ROCK

Library of Congress Cataloging-in-Publication Data
Ford, Clyde W.
The hero with an african face : mythic wisdom of traditional Africa /
Clyde W. Ford.
p.   cm.
Includes bibliographical references and index.
ISBN 0-553-10544-2 (hc)
1. Mythology, African.   2. Africa—Religion.   3. Spiritual life.
I. Title.
BL2400.F67   1999
299'.6—dc21   98-24162
                                                              CIP
Published simultaneously in the United States and Canada

PRINTED IN THE UNITED STATES OF AMERICA

BVG   10 9 8 7 6 5 4 3 2 1

TABLE OF CONTENTS

PREFACE

Little dreams, say the Elgon forest dwellers of central Africa, are of no great account, but if a person has a "big dream," the entire community must be gathered and told. How then does an Elgonyi know a big dream? Upon waking there is an instinctive feeling about the significance of the dream for the community—and the thought of keeping such a dream secret never occurs. This book began as just such a "big dream" for me.

My interest in traditional African sacred wisdom, especially as it is reflected in African mythology, was an unlikely outgrowth of my efforts to understand the relationship between personal and social healing. As a chiropractor and a therapist I sought answers to how individuals and groups, particularly African Americans, might heal from long-standing trauma and pain. I knew that a turning point in the individual healing process often came when the "personal stories" of trauma shifted from litanies of victimization to legends of empowerment, and I felt that something similar must be true about social healing, though it was harder to grasp what those "social stories" might be.

When I looked at the historical experience of African Americans, I saw a series of episodes, one slowly dissolving into the next: "Capture in Africa," "Monstrous Transport Through the Middle Passage," "The Horrors of Slavery," "Whispers of Rebellion and Revolt," "Promises of Freedom Broken," "The Entrenchment of Racism," and "The Ongoing Struggle for Freedom and Justice." What I failed to see was the larger story into which these episodes might fit. It would be easy to place them in an account of victimization focusing on the atrocities of racism and oppression, and just as easy to fit them into a narrative of denial claiming that these events happened a long time ago and so should not affect us now.

But in pondering how to portray the historical and present-day experiences of African Americans in a story that transcended victimization and denial, I asked myself, "If a single person had lived through all these experiences, how would I describe that person's life?" I realized that this series of episodes reminded me of the epic journey of a hero or heroine, and it was this notion of African Americans' "heroic journey" that first pointed me toward mythology. For the heroic journey is the quintessential story of mythology throughout the ages: the quest of a hero or heroine who willingly or unwillingly ventures beyond the known boundaries of the day, meets and defeats spectacular forces, then returns with some hard-won, precious gift. "There is a balm in Gilead," says an African-American spiritual, and when the African-American experience is viewed in the heroic terms of mythology, we can find that "Gilead" where the trauma of our history may be healed.

Yet mythology seems anachronistic. In today's common parlance, the term *myth* refers to unwarranted falsifications rather than unceasing truths. The gods and goddesses, heavens and hells, devils and demons, heroes and heroines of myth have long since yielded to the microscopes, telescopes, and intellects of modern humans. Dim reminders of our mythic past flash by only occasionally now—on the motion picture screen, in recollections of our deepest dreams, or in the eyes of a child fretting over what lies waiting beneath a crib or bed. It's true that grasping the finite realm of space and time is best left to science; this has never been mythology's goal. But pursuing the infinite, timeless, spaceless realm of the human soul is where mythology shines, for the hero's public journey through myth has long been a marvelous metaphor for the soul's private journey through life. Traditionally, this public telling of myths provided an anchor for both individuals and groups. Myths *are,* in fact, the "social stories" that heal. For myths supply more than the moral tag lines we learned early on to associate with nursery rhymes and fairy tales. Properly read, myths bring us into accord with the eternal mysteries of being, help us manage the inevitable passages of our lives, and give us templates for our relationship with the societies in which we live and for the relationship of these societies to the earth we share with all life. When trauma confronts us, individually or collectively, myths are a way of reestablishing harmony in the wake of chaos.

Still, we have few guiding myths in Western civilization, whether African American or otherwise, beyond those of Judaism and Christianity, and even here we commonly read (misread?) the mythology of Western religions as historical fact, rather than mythological truth. Some African myths did survive the era of slavery and have become part of the folklore of African Americans, but these were adapted more to our survival during those brutal times than to our present-day circumstances. And so I wondered what we might reclaim from the mythology of traditional Africa that would be of use in the world today.

But the literature on African mythology is not welcoming. Western mythologists, including the late Joseph Campbell, write sparsely and often derisively about African mythology, demoting African contributions to the level of folktales rather than including them in the ranks of the "higher mythologies" reserved for oriental and occidental cultures. Campbell, in particular, is enigmatic concerning Africa. During his lifetime, he did more than any single individual to promote popular interest in mythology, yet Africa is mentioned only rarely throughout the broad range of his scholarship. Admittedly, I have been influenced by his thoughts on mythology, even though he said little about Africa's important role. Indeed, here I have applied the universal themes he spoke of to the African myths he never bothered to explore. And I have found the results astounding and profound.

Africa is the largest inhabited continent in the world, with many thousands of language and population groups; the very notion, then, of writing a single book on African mythology is somewhat pretentious. Currently, there is even serious debate over the use of the term *Africa* to describe such things as "African art," "African culture," or "African mythology." Some scholars have argued that doing so reduces the diversity of this continent to a meaningless blur, while others have countered that a vital, pan-African ethos can be found.[1] I do not wish to take up this debate in these pages, but I do want to indicate the course I navigated through this conceptual labyrinth. I believe that mythology can, and must, be investigated and understood on two principal levels: that of the elemental ideas contained in the myths and that of the local expressions of these elemental ideas.[2] So, for example, one African culture may possess a creation myth featuring a "spiderweb" that connects the earth to the heavens, while in another culture, spiders are loathsome and the creation mythology features a "central tree" that connects these two realms. Here, the "elemental idea" is of a World Axis connecting humanity and divinity; the spider's web and the central tree are two of many possible "local expressions."

This book identifies and explores those elemental ideas found throughout the mythologies of Africa while also comparing and contrasting the local expressions of these elemental ideas. For this reason, I feel justified in using the term *African mythology,* and I have attempted to go one step further by focusing on *traditional African mythology,* by which I mean those mythologies present before wide-scale contact between Africa and the Christian and Muslim worlds. For the sake of space, this volume concentrates on the mythologies of sub-Saharan Africa, excluding, for the most part, the many wonderful and important contributions from Egypt, North Africa, and the African "horn."

I have tried to include African myths that feature both men and women as the central figures, but regardless of the sex of the protagonists these heroes and heroines can speak to us all. Similarly, I have made an effort to use gender-inclusive language and nongender pronouns, but where this produced awkward sentence structure I reverted to more common usage.

In this book I make a distinction between African folktales and African myths, the former being primarily tales that entertain while the latter are tales that contain universally recognizable symbols of psychological and spiritual significance. Admittedly, the line drawn between the two is often arbitrary, so my commentary on the myths focuses on this psychological and spiritual dimension, for here is where the sacred wisdom of African mythology lies. There are many ways to approach a myth; I have sought to balance the wonder of a child confronting an engaging story with the interest of a psychologist in what myth tells us about the human mind and the yearnings of a seeker for signposts along the way to spiritual fulfillment. The interpretations of these myths are my own, and they often oppose the assessments of early collectors of these stories, who dismissed them as the ramblings of savage, primitive folk. There is a wealth of insight and sagacity in these tales; one simply needs to learn the symbolic codes in which this wisdom is cloaked. What's more, there is no one correct way to analyze or understand a myth, for myth lives in the mind of the beholder, much as dream lives in the mind of the dreamer. I have by no means exhausted all possible explanations of these myths, and I encourage you to let the myths speak for themselves. Should they sound a resonant chord in your heart or mind that differs from the thoughts I've offered, then accept this African gift from across the ages, regardless of my explanation.

You might also ask how these myths spoke to the people and cultures from which they came and whether we are justified in interpreting them now in terms of elemental ideas and universal themes. It is not easy to say with absolute certainty what these African myths meant to the mythmakers nor what they mean to present-day members of their cultures of origin. In part, this is because some of these cultures no longer exist—war or famine has savaged them—or because the myths themselves have not survived the onslaught of modern life. Some ethnologists and anthropologists have visited an African society fifty years or more after a body of mythology has been collected, only to find that no one now remembers the meanings of the "old stories." Then there is the challenge of whom within a society to rely on for such insights into this mythic wisdom; not everyone will comprehend his or her mythological traditions at the same depth.

When possible, I have turned to native African authors for their views on the mythic traditions of their cultures, and they have confirmed my belief that we are justified in analyzing these myths beyond the appeal of the story, that the mythmakers indeed intended more. In one instance, at least, the mythmakers have left us a record of their intentions, even though the myths themselves were passed along through an oral tradition. This record is found in the rock art of the San of southern Africa where engraved and painted images have reflected the group's myths and rituals for many thousands of years, well into the present day. The San, whom I discuss in chapter 6, clearly used myth, image, and ritual to explore the innermost depths of the human mind and the furthest reaches of the human spirit.

Finally, another source affirms the idea that the earliest makers and followers of African myth understood them in terms of their elemental ideas, and that source is the transformation of African mythic wisdom that occurred as the result of the Atlantic slave trade. Vital elements of the mythic traditions of the Yoruba, for example, were transferred en masse from Africa to the Caribbean and Central and South America. When slave masters prevented one of the Yoruba's traditional mythic figures, such as the hero-god Obatala, from being mentioned in the Americas, these Africans found a Christian saint whose attributes corresponded to those of the original figure. Then, they could worship their traditional gods under the guise of paying homage to Christian saints. This syncretism, as the fusing of different precepts and practices is called, was possible because these Africans understood their spirituality and recognized the deeper ground of the elemental ideas beyond the relative superficiality of local expressions.

Do not be surprised if many of the motifs in these African myths are familiar to you as well—from other mythological traditions, from your own religious and spiritual background, or even from your dreams. Observing these similar themes in myths from widely different parts of the world and from different parts of Africa, we may well ask, What is the original source of these myths? This, too, is a much-debated topic among scholars of mythology, who have put forth two main theories: that of *diffusion* and of *parallel origin*. The diffusion theory holds that a handful of myths was widely dispersed throughout the world via travel, trade, conquest, and other forms of human contact. In contrast, the theory of parallel origins says that humans in different areas developed similar myths because the basic constituents of mythology are everywhere the same: all humans are born and will die, experience a life of pleasure and pain, alternate from the darkness of night to the light of day, wonder about the sun, moon, and celestial bodies, and share the earth with other humans, animals, and plants. All these great mysteries and inevitabilities of life nourish the tales the mythmakers tell. I lean toward the latter view, though convincing evidence for both theories is found throughout African mythology; and especially among closely related geographical and language groups, there are ample signs of diffusion.

There is also the related question of how old these African myths are. This is tougher to answer. African mythology began, as all

mythology did, as an oral tradition, which by its very nature is difficult to trace back to its roots. Just as a jazz performer may improvise
on an old tune, imbuing it with his or her own unique style while re-
taining the essential characteristics of the original, so, too, those who
passed the myths along through oral performance colored them with
the unique style of their presentation. If you record the improvisa-
tion—and that is what was recorded of African mythology—how can
you figure out the age of the original? One exception to this situation
occurs with the San, whose rock art can be dated, and since this art
is a product of their mythology, the myths can also be dated in a relative way. The results, discussed later in the book, are pretty amaz-
ing, for modern scientific methods have fixed the age of some of this
rock art at thirty thousand years old. Certainly not all of the African
mythologies we will explore are this old, but some may well be, for
the mythic themes found among the San exist throughout the other
traditions we visit, as well.

The myths in this book come from numerous sources, principally
from the published transcriptions and translations of missionaries,
ethnographers, and anthropologists. We need, then, to keep in mind
the backgrounds of many of these earliest transcribers: most were
male missionaries or explorers, and most were Christian; they were
prejudiced to include or exclude aspects of African mythic wisdom
based on their own gender, cultural, and religious biases.

In presenting the myths in this book, I have often adapted them
from their previously published forms, especially where I found
translations too literal and cumbersome and the awkward language
overshadowed the light of the tale. Presenting the myths in my own
voice is in keeping with the oral tradition from which they emerged.
Where I have rewritten a myth, I have followed as closely as I could
the original sense of the tale, and the endnotes list the sources where
I found the story. But traditional scholarly standards are difficult to
maintain when it comes to African mythology. Multiple versions of a
single myth may appear in different sources without any attribution;
who, then, is to be credited with first publishing the myth? A copy-
righted work may include myths that have previously been published
in noncopyrighted form or myths that are so widely known that they
are part of the public domain among the societies where they origi-
nate; from whom, then, does an author seek permission? In these

cases, I have simply done my best to honor the traditions from which the myths arose, as well as respect other authors in this field, hoping that my attempts to treat African mythology seriously will contribute, in some small way, to its elevation among the great mythologies of the world.

GUIDELINES FOR THE PRONUNCIATION
OF AFRICAN WORDS

With several thousand African languages and dialects, it is virtually impossible to compile any comprehensive set of rules for the pronunciation of African words. Still, the following brief guidelines may help with the handful of African words found in the text.

In general, words are pronounced phonetically with all vowel and consonant sounds made. Most vowels are short. When longer vowel sounds are intended, they may be strung together, like *oo*, or have a diacritical sign, such as *ō*. The unique vocalized "clicks" of the Khoisan language family are represented by four orthographic signs, indicating from which part of the oral cavity the tongue is sharply drawn away in making the sound:

SIGN	DESCRIPTION	APPROXIMATE LOCATION
/	Dental	Back of teeth
//	Labial or lateral	Toward the cheek
!	Alveolar	Back of gums
‡	Alveo-palatal	Farther back on palate

LIST OF WATERMARKS

LIST OF ILLUSTRATIONS
AND TABLE

To the ancestors who called me on this mythic journey,

and for the guidance, support, and blessings I received

from them along the way.

1

VOICES OF
THE ANCESTORS

The truth that was lost in the morning comes home in the evening.

AFRICAN PROVERB

In the summer of 1968, on the west coast of Africa, I stood facing the Elmina slave castle, a place where countless thousands of Africans had begun their passage into a disconsolate and treacherous unknown. The Atlantic lashed the rocks around this ominous monolith of weather-beaten white stone; built by the Portuguese in 1482, it serviced the slave trade for nearly four hundred years. An African caretaker, a wizened, slightly stooped old man, emerged from the shadows carrying an oil lamp. "This way," he intoned in a high-pitched, crackling whisper, staring at me and motioning with his finger. I stepped across the threshold of this dark fortress and began my descent into the abyss.

A long, narrow passageway led down to the chamber where male slaves were held. It was dark and damp, and walking upright was out of the question. I had to crouch so low I was almost on all fours, and as the caretaker bent over, the iron handle on his oil lamp groaned. About halfway down this cramped corridor the old man paused abruptly in front of an iron-reinforced wooden door.

"When a slave died," he murmured, "this door was opened and his body was washed out to sea."

The rhythmic drone of waves surrounded us as we plunged deeper into the castle's inner vault, some fifty feet beneath the water. There the old man dimmed his lamp, and when my eyes adjusted to the darkness, I could just make out a window the size of my fist atop a small shaft leading up from the cave we were now in. Through that small opening came the only air and light allowed into this thankless pit.

As I moved around to take the measure of this awful place, I felt something under my feet and heard a crunching sound, like stepping on fallen leaves, only heavier and metallic. Unable to see, I reached down and groped in the dark until my fingers found their way over one, then two, then three links. It was a chain! I was walking on the rusted remains of slave chains. The more I moved about this Neptunian dungeon, the more I realized the rusting chains were everywhere.

At first, the caretaker said nothing. Surely he had seen this before: the sons of slaves walking on the chains of their fathers. What words could capture this scene?

"You know," he finally said in a slow, measured cadence, "your ancestors could have been in this very room."

But I was already beyond the caretaker's words, for my body had grown heavy and my feet felt shackled in place. Then I thought I heard voices. At first I was sure it was just the roar of the sea. But I listened closely and made out in my mind what sounded like the low murmur of distant conversation. The rumbling traveled closer and closer—one, then two, then three, then layer upon layer of voices; a cacophony of humans not moaning or sighing but talking among themselves. I strained even harder to hear, when suddenly a message shot forth from the darkness, ricocheting off the earthen walls, bouncing back and forth over and over again in time with the rhythm of the sea.

"Whatever you do, my son," the voices seemed to say in unison, "make your life count for us. . . . Whatever you do, my son, make your life count for us. . . . Whatever you do, my son, make your life count for us. . . ." The echo slowly trailed away.

I was covered in sweat, tears flooded my eyes, my heart was racing, and I could not make logical sense of what was happening. For all I knew I could have been riveted in place for hours, though in reality only a few moments had passed.

"Yes, I know," I uttered softly, unsure to whom I was responding. Then turning toward the caretaker, I said more deliberately, "Yes, I know."

Over the years I've pondered those voices—not so much their origin or the truth of their being as their message and whether it has been a boon or a burden for me. Whatever trauma those voices experienced still winds its way through generations far removed from their suffering. Might these wounds have been not just to dark bodies but to humanity's collective soul?

Myth and the African-American Past

The magnitude of trauma in the African-American past is daunting, even by the parameters of savagery known in the modern world—the Jewish Holocaust, the Cambodian killing fields, the "ethnic cleansing" in the Balkans, or the carnage in Rwanda. By conservative estimates, thirty to sixty million Africans were captured as slaves during the African slave trade. Of this total, one-third died in overland marches from their point of capture to the coastal staging areas, like the Elmina castle, from which they were shipped; another one-third died during or awaiting that inhuman transatlantic voyage known as the Middle Passage. By any measure, this was a holocaust of unprecedented and unspeakable proportions.[1]

The enormity of this trauma escapes my full embrace; instead, I have chosen to wrestle with a single question: If the experience of African Americans could be collapsed into a single character, how would I portray that character's life? Tragic, traumatic, sad, unique, dangerous, plaintive, triumphant? Certainly all of these would apply at different times. Yet rolling in again and again, like the timeless motion of the waves, comes the word *heroic*. At first this seems odd to me, given the feelings of immense tragedy I have about so much of our history. But thinking of my character's survival of the Middle Passage, "a dark sea journey" comes to mind; and of his suffering during slavery, "the dark night of the soul"; and did he not enter "the belly of the beast" to battle for freedom, justice, and equality in America? These phrases bespeak the journey of a hero.

Across time and throughout the world, the hero strides out of myths and legends as the one who has ventured beyond the security of the present into an uncertain future, there to claim some victory or boon for humanity left behind. For reasons not always known in advance, the hero is called, or thrust, into the full career of an adventure, pitting him against an array of fabulous forces. The stories tell of him leaving the safety of his land of origin and coming to a threshold that he must cross. Frequently that threshold is the water's edge, where a monster, such as a whale or sea dragon, jealously guards the murky depths. A battle ensues, and the hero is swallowed whole or in pieces into the monster's belly. He descends into this abyss at the bleakest hour; it is "the dark night of the soul," and the fate of the hero hangs in precarious balance. But through the remembrance of a critical oath, the power of a charm, or the help of gods and goddesses, the hero battles forth, ultimately emerging from near certain demise with a hard-won victory in hand.

How well we know these supernatural tales of larger-than-life figures. They never cease to entertain and inspire us, but are they ever to be taken seriously? If you look closely, you will find that these hero journeys do offer more than just the drama of the tale; they speak, through metaphor, of our human journey through life. The hero's challenges are our very own, the inevitable passages each of us faces in life: birth, maturation, setbacks, accomplishments, pain, pleasure, marriage, aging, and death. Then courage, cunning, wisdom, strength, determination, faith, love, compassion, and the many other traits the hero displays to answer the challenges of the quest are symbolic of those inner resources on which we too must call to meet the challenges of our life. Ultimately, the hero's quest is not along an isolated path but on one traveled by all humanity; not a victory over outside forces but over those within; not a journey to far-off worlds but to the very center of one's self.

It is moving to consider the African-American experience in these terms. Here is a way in which the history I would change or avenge and that which I would cherish and adore can become grist for the mill of my own life's journey. As a hero's journey, the African-American experience confronts me with the issues of life and death, good and evil, pain and suffering, triumph and tragedy, trauma and healing, bondage and freedom, inequity and justice—not merely as abstract concerns related to my ancestors long ago but as issues related to my life and the journey of my "hero within" right now.

Depicting the African-American experience in mythological terms may seem surprising at first. Sadly, modern society has lost touch with the power of myth. We now use the word as a synonym for falsehood rather than as an expression of eternal truth.

Read one way, myths are phantasmagoric tales of gods and demons, exaggerated humans, improbable animals, impossible places, and unbelievable series of serendipitous events—engaging, to be sure, but at face value simply untrue. Modern science assures us of the falsehood of myths: even at the speed of light, we could travel 3.5 billion years yet never reach the heaven of the gods nor the hell of demons, for we would still be within the known universe. Archaeologists and molecular biologists have found compelling fossil and genetic evidence linking us not to an extraterrestrial race of deities come to earth but to much more mundane primate stock. And astrophysicists are rapidly converging on an understanding of the origin of the universe itself, not molded from clay by a divine being but extruded from a nuclear explosion some four to five billion years ago.

Yet read another way, myths are absolutely true: not as fact but as metaphor; not as physics but as metaphysics. For mythological insight starts where scientific inquiry stalls. Mythology is interested in the timeless questions of humanity: What is the relationship of human life to the great mystery of being behind all life? How are we to understand our relationship to the earth we inhabit and to the cosmos in which we find ourselves? How am I to pass through the stages of my life? And how is my life coordinated with the life of the society I live in? These questions do not yield to the telescope or microscope; their answers are best lived, then passed along to those who follow—and that is the mythic route. Mythology, then, was traditionally a means of healing self and society by helping people bring the circumstances of their lives into harmony with these larger, more abiding concerns. And it is just this sort of healing that may be gained from considering the African-American experience in mythological terms.

To this day the BaKongo[2], for example, tell a story of the fate of their brethren captured and sold to white men in ships. The slaves are said to have been taken first to the realm of Mputu and from there, cast away "to an island where there was a forest with no food in it, and the sea on every side."[3] Now *Mputu* is a word of mythic import for the BaKongo, referring to Europeans but also to the land of the dead; and death here does not simply mean one's physical demise but the underground realm of unconscious powers and invisible causes we will encounter again and again throughout our tour of African mythology. The word is a contraction of *Mputuleezo,* which is itself a KiKongo variation of "Portuguese," though it means "agitated water" as well, an allusion both to the Atlantic surf out of which Europeans appeared and into which Africans disappeared and to the mythic waters that separate the realm of waking consciousness from that of the unconscious, the light world of the everyday from the spirit world whose voices may be heard in the crashing sounds of breaking waves.[4] Mputu is also the realm to which hero-figures in the myths of this region of Africa travel, there battling magical beings and bizarre forces in pursuit of treasured gifts or boons with which to return. And according to BaKongo wisdom, the journey of the human soul inevitably carries it into Mputu after life, to be reborn from there into a continuing cycle of life, death, and rebirth (see Chapter 10 for a more detailed account of BaKongo mythic wisdom).

So in the hearts and minds of their BaKongo kin, slaves were heroes, thrust into the bleak landscape of Mputu to confront the dark powers there. Eventually, the myth tells us, these forlorn heroes were assisted by divine intervention: "God gave them civilization . . . and food . . . and every needful thing."[5] And even today, the BaKongo consider African Americans to be hero-souls of ancestors departed to Mputu who will return home again, as all heroes must. "We're waiting for them," said an old man in Kinshasa, "this is nobody's country but theirs."[6] Here is mythology used to heal the trauma of slaves ripped away from their society of origin.

Language, Mythology, and Race

There is a poignant moment in the film *Malcolm X* when Malcolm, while in prison, has a dictionary opened for him to the definition of the word *black.* One senses his instant recognition of the immense burden borne by African Americans simply from the relationship between language and belief; every definition of *black* is negative, while every corresponding definition of *white* is positive. Substitute any dictionary definition for *black* in the phrase "black people" and you will get some idea of the power behind the language we use to refer to ourselves and to others. But we, like Malcolm, then close the dictionary with definitions accepted, failing to ask why it is that *black* and *white* should hold such sway.

In the refusal of this question, we deny ourselves the opportunity to penetrate beyond the history of race, beyond even the politics, economics, sociology, or psychology of race, for the origins and power of these two words are best understood in mythological terms, and mythology has rarely, if ever, entered the modern discourse on race. This is unfortunate, as mythology has the potential to indicate from what ancient depths these racial issues emerge—and then to equip us with Promethean responses.

In mythological terms, the modern usage of *black* and *white* can be traced back at least to the Middle East in the sixth century B.C.E.* In olden Persia (Iran of today), Zoroastrianism made the separation and combat between black and white a cornerstone of its mythology. Zarathustra, the founder of this doctrine, held that there are essentially two forces operating in the world: Ahura Mazda and the good gods of light; and Angra Mainyu and the evil gods of darkness (also called devs). These two forces have been locked in conflict from the beginning of creation, but the god of light will ultimately triumph over the god of darkness, and it is the task of the virtuous to identify roundly and completely with the forces of light.[7]

These powerful ideas about the inevitable conflict between good and evil came to influence the mythology underlying all the religions of the children of Abraham—the "Big Three" religions of Western civilization: Christianity, Judaism, and Islam. The *Avesta,* the sacred text of Zoroastrianism, painted this conflict in black and white.[8] By the time more extensive contacts between Europe and Africa began in the fifteenth and sixteenth centuries, a European mythology of deification and demonization was already well established: gods wore white skins, devils wore black skins, and it was the duty of the gods to vanquish the devils. So much of the history of the West is embodied in this simple but devastating mythology that pits people with

---

*Throughout the text, I will use B.C.E. (before the common era) and C.E. (common era) to indicate dates formerly labeled B.C. and A.D.

white skins against those with dark skins—a cultural mythology that plagues us to this very day and remains inscribed, as Malcolm discovered, even in the dictionary's pages.

Thankfully, however, the story does not stop here, for I was amazed to discover more authentic origins of the word *black*. *Webster's Dictionary* finds no derivation beyond the Old High German word *blah*, meaning the color black, but suggests a relationship to the Latin *flagare* and Greek *phlegein*, both meaning "to burn." But other linguists have traced the word for the color black through the Greek root *melan*, from which we derive the modern word *melanin* (the skin pigment predominant in people of color).[9] Melantho, the Greek goddess, for example, is identified with the blackness of the fertile earth. But then comes a surprise, for these terms involving the root word *melan* can be further derived from an Egyptian word spelled *M3nw*, which simply means the "Mountain in the West."[10]

Now, the sun disappears in the west, sinking behind the western mountains and so slipping into the mythic darkness of the underworld. This is a well-established motif in the mythologies of many cultures worldwide. In Buddhist mythology, for instance, Amitabha, the much-favored Buddha of Immeasurable Radiance, is allied with this western direction of the setting sun; he manifests infinite compassion toward all life, and he is incarnated on earth as the Dalai Lama. The underworld journey of the sun is, then, specifically related to the cycles of death and renewal in life: the daily round of human consciousness from the light world of day to the dark world of dream and back again; the planting of seeds in the fertile darkness of the earth, or the female womb; or the journey the human soul must take on its way to realizing its own divine nature.

In the mythology from which this derivation of *black* originates, Nut, the Egyptian goddess of the sky, symbolically swallows the sun in the west every evening, bearing it as a pregnancy throughout the night, then giving rebirth to the sun at dawn in the east (see Figure 1). Egyptian mythology was also extremely concerned with the underworld journey of the soul on its route to divinity, and the *Egyptian Book of the Dead* is devoted primarily to the successful negotiation of this passage. Even African-American slaves described their furtive, heroic passages to freedom as riding the "Underground Railroad." We will find this theme of the underworld journey repeated throughout the mythology of the African hero.

Figure 1. The Egyptian goddess Nut swallowing the sun in the west in the evening, giving birth to it in the east at dawn. Her rays shine on Hathor, a symbol of life and love.

The point is that when viewed through the eyes of African mythology, as well as other non-Western mythologies, *black* has no intrinsically negative connotation; in fact, just the opposite is true, for the underworld realm is seen as a source of dynamic potential for the light world above. Once more, substitute these new meanings for the word *black* into the phrase "black people," and what do you have now? People of the mountains of the west; people of the setting sun; people of the dream time; people of the seeded earth; people of the fertile womb; people on the underground journey toward God-realization; people of immeasurable radiance; people of infinite compassion.

Still there is more. *Niger* is yet another root word meaning black, not Greek but Latin, from which we derive the word *negro*. Here, too, mythology reveals a word whose grace, power, and beauty have long since been lost. The name once referred to the Nigretai, a fearsome tribe of charioteers from Libya, admired for their beautiful black skins. But the origin of all these words is a vowelless Semitic root, *ngr*, with the poetic meaning "water to flow into sand."[11] It specifically refers to the Niger River, whose strange U-shaped course must have convinced early travelers that the river simply terminated in the desert sands.[12] So, to this list of new meanings for the word *black* let us now add the word *negro,* people of the water flowing into sand—a wonderful image of the transformative power of water to bring life to a desolate land.

Then, most surprisingly, from the deep reaches of occidental mythology, a similar connotation of the significance and power of *black* breaks through, confirmed by the alchemical texts of medieval Europe. There we learn that the essential first step of alchemy was called either *melanosis* or *nigredo*—in either case, a blackening. Now, alchemy was an elaborate metaphor built around the mysteries of chemistry but actually meant to address the mysteries of human transformation; the refinement of a base metal (like lead) into gold was symbolic of the transformation of baser human concerns into the higher pursuits of the human spirit. But the first moment of this transformation was a blackening through fire that reduced the base metal to a more primal substance; only from this primal matter could the refinement to gold occur.

If we interpret this alchemy in terms of human psychology, as alchemy was always meant to be, melanosis or nigredo identified the process of moving from the world of ordinary conscious activity to the deeper, primary layers of the human unconscious, there to resolve the base concerns of ordinary existence and finally to emerge transformed. Anyone who has ever faced a vexing life issue, gone to sleep and in the depths of dreaming received insight into the matter, then awakened with resolution in hand, intimately knows this process of blackening prior to transformation. And since *black* was originally defined as the direction of the setting sun, symbolic of the movement of human consciousness into dream and the realm of the unconscious, or as the life-giving waters that flow into the barren sands, we come here full circle from Africa to Europe in this wholly different sense of black as a potent symbol of renewal and transformation.

What is the myth you are living?" psychologist Carl Jung often asked. In other words, what are the symbols, images, metaphors, and stories that speak to you most deeply and passionately, that inform your life? To which I would now answer, "This reclaimed mythology of black."

We need just such symbols and stories today. After the publication of my book *We Can All Get Along: 50 Steps You Can Take to Help End Racism,* I was asked what I would do about the intraracial violence plaguing young people in so many African-American communities. "Tell them a good story," I replied to my interviewer.

"A story?" she said quizzically. "But aren't most of these young people beyond the age where they are read to before going to bed?"

"Tell them a story," I persisted, "something other than the stories they are told through television scripts and advertisements—that the worth of human life is judged by the possession and consumption of consumer goods; that the American measure of one's soul is proportional to the dollars in one's pocket."

Tell them a story, I then thought to myself, that they too are heroes and heroines capable of following in the footsteps of the heroes and heroines of all times, even when faced with the relentless monsters of hunger, poverty, injustice, and racism. Better yet, tell them a story with heroes and heroines linked to them through history and heritage.

It takes a village to raise a child, says an African proverb now made famous by Hillary Clinton. But there is a more profound African maxim that speaks not only to the raising of children but also to the relationship of each individual with society. It states simply, *I am because we are, we are because I am.*[13] This message, widespread through African mythology and spirituality, ought to be the basis of the stories we tell the young heroes and heroines in our midst. For when I see that my existence is predicated on others' and their existence is predicated on mine, then I must also see that doing violence to others is doing violence to myself.

The Roots of African Mythology

With a deepened interest in mythology and especially in the hero's journey, I was excited to turn to the contributions Africa has made to world mythology. But what a surprise it was to consult *The Hero with a Thousand Faces* by the late Joseph Campbell, perhaps the most famous modern text on mythology, and read this opening phrase:

> Whether we listen with aloof amusement to the dreamlike mumbo jumbo of some red-eyed witch doctor of the Congo, or read with cultivated rapture thin translations from the sonnets of the mystic Lao-tse . . .[14]

These words were my Symplegades—the ominous clashing rocks through which the Greek hero Jason had to pass before reaching the Sea of Wonders en route to recapturing the Golden Fleece. I closed the book with a heavy heart.

But if the hero has a thousand faces, many must be African, though the hero with an African face is seldom seen. Several months passed before I mustered the courage to challenge Campbell again; this time I held fast to the idea that if mythological insights were indeed universal, as Campbell claimed, then they would necessarily extend to African mythology even though he had dismissed African contributions as "mumbo jumbo." I was rewarded for my persistence. Campbell's shortsightedness about Africa could not obliterate his immense contributions to mythology, and his omission gave me an opportunity to explore African mythology in a novel and meaningful way.

African mythology ought to begin with human prehistory, for Africa holds a compelling place in the ancient record of humanity. Archaeologists, paleontologists, and molecular biologists have amassed overwhelming fossil and genetic evidence that Africa is indeed the sole birthplace of humankind. As the womb of humanity, Africa literally gave birth to the first human heroes and heroines; the first hero journeys happened there. These early heroes risked the greatest adventure of all alone, for their quest was nothing less than the birth of humanity.

Diaspora is the word frequently used to describe the massive, forceful displacement of millions of Africans from their homeland over the four hundred years of the Atlantic slave trade. It literally means to sow seeds through scattering, and it is a poetic description of the heroic journey of African people. Yet slavery was not the first or the only African diaspora; the others were perhaps of even greater mythic significance. Two million years ago, our human predecessors ventured out of Africa through the "horn"—the northeast land bridge between Africa and the Near East. The heroes of this first African diaspora journeyed to Europe and Asia to plant the first seeds of humanity there, but this quest ultimately ended in failure; their stock died out. At least two additional waves of humanity made their exodus from Africa to Europe and Asia over the next 1.8 million years, among them the Neanderthals, but their fate was also extinction. Perseverance, one lesson of the hero's journey, was not lacking in this evolutionary process. So, one hundred thousand years ago another hero's journey began from Africa, following in the footsteps of those who had gone before. These *Homo sapiens* out of Africa succeeded in their quest. They reached Europe, Asia, the Americas, and beyond; the scions of the human family tree that they planted during this African diaspora took root and thrived, and to this stock everyone alive today can trace their heritage.[15]

Then five hundred years ago, with the beginning of the slave trade, Africa again answered the call of the hero's journey—not willingly this time but through force—and these scattered human seeds too have taken hold even in the most forbidding and unfriendly ground. If in the spirit of the medieval alchemists, every human alive today were to undergo a "genetic" melanosis or nigredo, they would resolve their genetic heritage to a common, primal source from Africa. Ultimately, we are all the transformed gold of the prime matter of Africa—all children of some African diaspora—and to these African heroes and heroines, we all owe our lives.

But Africa gave birth to more than just a new form of life called *Homo sapiens;* a new form of consciousness came into being with this creature as well. Over the two million years from the emergence of the earliest human precursors to the emergence of *Homo sapiens,* brain size doubled, and this increase resulted in a profound transformation in consciousness. Our human consciousness is unique in its ability to contemplate its own origins. We humans, then, were the first creatures able to tackle such profound issues as the relationship of our life to the mysterious source from which all life emerges and back into which all life dies. In such contemplation lies the basis of mythology and the beginnings of sacred wisdom.

Keepers of the Flame

The mythic wisdom of Africa encompasses a wide terrain. Here are epics as grand as Gilgamesh, heroes as hardy as Hercules, heroines as vexing as Venus, adventurers as outstanding as Odysseus, and gods and goddesses as prolific as the pantheons of India and ancient Greece.

What's more, within the body of traditional African mythology lie themes whose harmonies we know well even today. Here are tales of the miraculous creation of the world, intimations of the virgin birth, lessons of the fall, accounts of the death and resurrection of a spiritual hero, reports of the flood, records of the ark's voyage, and symbols of the chalice, blade, and cross. But don't be misled; all this is not the evidence of some early Christianization of Africa's soul. These themes appeared in Africa long before the advent of Christianity, and they are found throughout the world's great mythologies as well, although some Christians might wish us to believe their faith has sole possession.

yes!

Christianity has been a good friend to African Americans. It sustained us through the dark night of slavery, and it has been the pulpit from which many a heroic battle for freedom and justice has been launched. But I also find Christianity inelegantly rigid and awkwardly blind on matters of the human spirit. Much of Christianity dogmatically insists on a literal interpretation of its mythology. We are to believe, for example, that the miraculous creation of the world, the virgin birth of its spiritual hero, and his ultimate death, resurrection, and ascension to heaven actually took place. Now these same themes appear in African mythology, but the emphasis is on their metaphorical rather than their literal interpretation. African mythology allows me to approach my own spirituality without an attitude of "the Bible says it, that settles it." In fact, African mythology has even helped me better understand and appreciate Christianity.

Not long ago I was sitting in a Baptist church in Seattle listening to a friend perform traditional African-American spirituals in a well-honed, operatic baritone. Throughout most of the concert I found myself in rapture, staring at the huge wooden cross behind the pulpit. I kept turning over the West African Bambara notion that the center of the cross is symbolically the *kuru* (God-point); here, the Bambara say, life emerges from divinity through birth and merges back into divinity through death, and through this cyclical transformation, we achieve immortality. What a wonderful image to meditate on while hearing Tony sing of a world savior dying on the cross. I felt the radiance of the human spirit as traditional African mythology delivered a sermon, even set to song, more powerful than any I had witnessed; and after all, the same message lies at the heart of Christianity, only it is often buried deep under layers of dogmatic belief.

Still, in an age where technology allows for the instantaneous transfer of information anyplace on earth, why bother with African mythology, coming as it does from an era when information flowed simply from the storyteller's mouth to a small audience? A very short creation story from the Bulu people of Cameroon offers one answer[16]:

◎◎ Zambe, son of the supreme god Mebe'e, created a chimpanzee, a gorilla, an elephant, and two men—a European and an African—each of whom was named Zambe as well. To these creatures, Zambe gave the tools of survival—fire, water, food, weapons, and a book. In time, Zambe returned to check on the earth. "All the tools you were given for survival," he asked each creature, "where are they now?"

The chimpanzee and the gorilla had discarded all but the fruit, and Zambe banished them to the forest forever. The elephant could not remember what he'd done with his possessions. The European kept the book but discarded the fire, while the African discarded the book but kept the fire. Thus, Europeans remained keepers of the book, but Africans keepers of the flame. ◎◎

The book is symbolic of human efforts to control the natural world, and humanity within it, through reason and intellect; this is the course Western civilization has taken. Fire, on the other hand, is a portion of the sun brought down to earth, an earthly representative of the sun god, giver of life. Fire, then, is symbolic of that undying cosmic energy which informs all life; it represents the sacred power that brings forth life through creation, sustains it, then consumes it in the flames of destruction; and it is symbolic of the sacred wisdom that sees beyond the created world of humanity to the divine mystery which is its source. Fire signifies the passionate burning of the light of the human soul.

To control the mundane, the myth tells us, Europeans sacrificed the sacred. To hold on to the sacred, Africans sacrificed the mundane. And now, as we are poised at the millennium, we cannot hope that all personal and social conundrums will be solved by turning the next page in the book of intellect and reason alone; there must also be turnings of the soul, and here the mythic wisdom of Africa keeps a flame that may help light the way.

2

THE HERO WITH AN AFRICAN FACE

We have not even to risk the adventure alone; for the heroes of all time have gone before us; the labyrinth is thoroughly known; we have only to follow the thread of the hero-path.

JOSEPH CAMPBELL

The fire of mythology is not easily extinguished, as its flame is fueled from the inexhaustible well of the human psyche. Though we modern humans pay scant heed to the call of myth, we are nonetheless moved by its power. We have only to close our eyes to sleep and there in the nether land of the unconscious, we may be visited nightly by the potent forms and forces of the mythic realm. Myth is a collective dream, dream a personal myth. If you have ever been swayed by a deeply meaningful or powerful dream, then you have tasted the intoxicating nectar of this realm just beyond the grasp of your waking consciousness. And if you have ever longed to bring back into your daily life the insights, feelings, and accomplishments of a dream, then you have been initiated into the quest of the hero or heroine who ventures into the darkness of the unknown, to return with the unique gift that would completely reinvigorate self or society.

There are other times when we need not even seek sleep to find myth. In the clinic, for example, with the doctor as a guide, the patient may cross over the threshold of wakeful awareness into the mythic realm. Then, doctor and patient, now guide and traveler, may find themselves in the midst of an extraordinary journey. Trained as a chiropractor and psychotherapist, I have known such journeys.

Walter was a forty-two-year-old endocrinologist. After nearly a year of unsuccessful treatment through conventional medicine, his daughter pleaded with him to seek nontraditional therapy for his nagging back pain. As a medical doctor, he was obviously skeptical about seeing a chiropractor. However, after an initial examination, X rays, and a thorough grilling about my medical knowledge, Walter agreed to undergo a period of treatment.

The first session was unassuming; I used my standard array of techniques for treating lower back pain, and Walter left feeling extremely relaxed, remarking that his pain had eased. At our next session, while I gently applied traction and manipulated his lower back, I also asked him to focus on this area as though it were a place. Five minutes of silence elapsed, and then I inquired where he was.

"I'm in a cave," he said, "a cave with multicolored walls."

Walter walked around this cave, touched the walls, and remarked how little light there was inside. When asked if there were a way for him to leave, he paused for a minute or so, and informed me that there was a hole in the floor of the cave.

"I'm going to go through it," he said almost gleefully, "I'm going through it."

For Walter, going through the cave floor was like Alice going through the looking glass. His experience immediately intensified, and in staccato bursts he reported what was taking place.

"I don't believe it," he blurted out. "I'm flying, I'm flying!"

He then lapsed into silence for nearly twenty minutes while I proceeded to work my way up his spine. His body moved continuously, sometimes gently and other times wildly. Every now and then he would punctuate the silence with an exclamation: "This is incredible, just incredible!"

My hands supported Walter's upper chest and upper back as his inner journey was about to conclude. His body stopped moving, his breathing changed, and he uttered a sigh.

"I'm at the entry to the cave again," he said, "but I'm not sure that I want to go back in."

The session concluded five minutes later with Walter still sitting outside the cave pondering whether he should go in. When I saw him next, he was very clear about the meaning of this session.

"I was out of my body flying," he said with amazement. "I've heard about experiences like this, but I never really gave them much credence. Yet I truly felt out of my body. I could see myself lying on your table and I could see you, but I was hovering overhead.

"The cave represented my life now," he offered in a sad tone. "I've lost a lot in the years since entering medical school. I love what I'm doing, but I'm constantly under stress. Moreover, I've given up things that were very dear to me, like painting, music, and reading.

"The hole in the cave floor was the passageway back to my real self," he observed, "and the out-of-body experience was an opportunity for me to feel reconnected with my soul. My ambivalence about reentering the cave was a true expression of my inner conflict over continuing my life feeling stressed and spiritually unconnected."

Walter then went on to inform me that after our sessions he had made up his mind to reclaim those parts of himself that had been set aside for his career. He had already started painting, reading, and finding time to play the violin again. Walter came from an Asian-Pacific culture with deep spiritual roots, and though he had often heard his elders talking about spirituality, he had never paid much attention. After our sessions, those familiar conversations took on a different meaning for him.

"Now I know what my ancestors meant by connecting with one's Spirit," he stated. "This is just the beginning of that process for me."

Here, then, is the call of myth answered not in the depths of sleep but in the light of conscious attention. Here, too, is the power of myth to part the seas of ordinary experience and illuminate a new path.

The Quest for the African Hero

The hero with an African face has much in common with the heroes of all ages and all lands, for the hero quest is not predicated on the particularities of place and time. Simply stated, the hero quest is orchestrated in three movements: a hero is called to venture forth from familiar lands into territory previously unknown; there the hero encounters marvelous forces and with magical assistance wins a decisive victory over the hindering powers of the unknown; then, with boon in hand, the hero returns to the land of his origin.[1] Departure, fulfillment, return—evidence of these three movements is uncovered in all African hero adventures. African mythology then shades the hero's career in colors of its own.

On this journey, the hero with an African face might aid us in navigating the vicissitudes of life: helping us to find strength and courage where we had thought only to find weakness and fear; to venture deeply within ourselves where we had thought only to pass lightly through our lives; to wake our gods where we had thought only to wrestle our demons.

The Call of Destiny

◎◎ Uncama dug a millet garden, but when the millet had begun to ripen, a porcupine continually wasted it. No matter how early Uncama rose, when he arrived in his garden the porcupine had already devoured the millet. At length he waited for a day on which there was an abundance of dew. On that day, he arose and said, "Today then I can follow it well, if it has eaten in the garden, for where it has gone the dew will be brushed off. At length I may discover where it has gone into its hole." ◎◎

Thus begins a Zulu tale of Uncama's journey to the underworld.[2]

Whether in life or in myth, the hero quest commences with some call or lure that wakes the hero to his destiny: an unforeseen illness may arise; a monster may appear to terrorize the countryside; a chance encounter may open a life-changing path; an unexpected animal appears whose trail the hero follows to great adventure, as in the opening of this Zulu myth.

◎◎ So Uncama, with weapons in hand, embarked along the marauding porcupine's trail of dew, and upon discovering its hole, he pressed ahead, down into the depths, without further hesitation, saying, "I will go till I reach it, and kill it." Once inside the hole, Uncama passed through to the underground realm, crossing over to the land of departed souls. ◎◎

Zulus are among the southernmost members of the extensive Bantu language family, which shares many beliefs, including belief in the special potency and sacred power of the subterranean realm Uncama visited. This is the spirit world of departed souls referred to among the Bantu as *mosima,* which originally meant "the abyss" but has since devolved to mean simply "a hole in the ground," "a den," or "the hole of a wild animal"—hence the obvious relationship in this myth between the porcupine's hole and Uncama's arrival in this spirit land.[3]

Uncama's curiosity and his determination to punish this animal lead him on until finally he comes to a village. He has entered a kind of purgatory, a world inhabited by departed souls yet fashioned in the image of the world of the living.

◎◎ "Ho! What place is this?" he said. "I am following the porcupine, yet I have come upon a dwelling."

At this point Uncama became fearful and he began to retreat, walking backward along the path he had thus far traversed, anxiously pondering his fate with the thought: "Let me not go to these people, for I do not know them; perhaps they will kill me." ◎◎

Alas, this erstwhile traveler returns home, back through the animal portal of his adventure, to a surprised wife and community, for they had already burned his clothes and possessions, taking him for dead. And to these assembled, astonished folk he tells his tale:

◎◎ "I have come from a great distance—from those who live underground. I followed a porcupine; I came to a village and heard dogs baying, children crying; I saw people moving around, the smoke from their cooking fires was rising. So I came back. I was afraid, I thought they would kill me. *And it is because I feared and returned that you see me this day.*" ◎◎

Mythological journeys of descent into the underworld of the dead are symbolic of movement from the light world of ordinary reality to the dark world of the unconscious; there, just as when we fall asleep, we die to the world of wakeful consciousness and awake to the marvelous world of evanescent forms and symbols within. The challenge met by those who successfully travel these corridors of the psyche is to claim some boon or gift from this inner realm: an insight or revelation that will release the energies pent up in the labyrinths of personal or social crises; the marker of a new direction that offers reinvigoration where old ways have grown stale. But Uncama's journey, interrupted as it was by his own fear, is marked by failure of this quest; he follows the lure of the porcupine to the underworld, only to become frightened and then return.

I am reminded of a personal dream some years ago: I was fortunate to have grown up knowing my great-grandfather, with whom I was very close. He died when I was twenty, and shortly afterward I was in that half-asleep, half-awake state called hypnagogic, when I felt his presence in my bedroom and believed I could also make out his form. It scared me, and in this semiconscious state I told him to leave, which he did. It was many years before he appeared in any of my dreams again.

In the mythic realm, the terrain always rises to meet the traveler— this is the built-in safeguard of the mythic way, even for unsuspecting and unprepared wayfarers like Uncama. The adventure the hero gets is precisely the one he or she is ready for. The kingdom is spread in front of Uncama, but he is unable to meet the requirements for entry because he has followed the porcupine's trail out of mere curiosity and anger. The hero's journey is not for the faint-hearted wanderer, curious but not serious about where the journey leads, nor is it a journey to be taken in the throes of anger, but one to be relished in the spirit of high adventure.

Uncama's journey to the underworld, motivated by anger, is splendidly contrasted with the Ashanti tale of Kwasi Benefo's journey to Asamando, the Ashanti world of departed souls. Here is the story of a hero whose quest is motivated out of love, suffering, and great compassion[4]:

◎◎ A young man was living among the Ashanti. His name was Kwasi Benefo. His fields flourished, he had many cattle. He lacked only a wife to bear children for him, to care for his household, and when the time should come, to mourn his death. Kwasi Benefo went looking. In his village he found a young woman who greatly pleased him. They married. They were content with each other. But soon the young woman faded, and death took her. Kwasi Benefo grieved. He bought her an *amoasie,* a piece of silk-cotton cloth to cover her genitals, and beads to go around her waist, and in these things she was buried.

Kwasi Benefo could not forget her. He looked for her in his house, but she was not there. His heart was not with the living anymore. His brothers spoke to him, his uncle spoke to him, his friends spoke to him, saying, "Kwasi, put it from your mind. This is the way it is in the world. Find yourself another wife."

At last Kwasi Benefo comforted himself. He went to another village. He found a young woman there and made arrangements. He brought her home. Again he became contented with living. The woman had a good character. She took good care of the household. She tried in every way to please her husband. Kwasi Benefo said, "Yes, living is worthwhile." But after she had been pregnant for some time, the young woman became ill. She grew gaunt. Death took her. Kwasi Benefo's heart hurt him. This wife, too, was buried in her *amoasie* and beads.

Kwasi Benefo could not be consoled. He sat in his house. He would not come out. People said to him, "People have died before. Arise, come out of your house. Mingle with your friends as you used to do." But Kwasi Benefo did not desire life anymore. He remained in his house.

The family of the young woman who had died heard about Kwasi Benefo's grief. They said, "He is suffering too much. This man loved our daughter. Let us give him another wife." They sent messengers to Kwasi Benefo, and they brought him to their village. They said to him, "One must grieve, yes, but you cannot give your life to it. We have another daughter, she will make a good wife for you. Take her. This way you will not be alone. What is past is past, one cannot go there anymore. What a man has loved is in his heart, it does not go away. Let the dead live with the dead, and the living with the living." ◎◎

Embedded in these words of consolation to a distraught Kwasi Benefo are references to Akan (the language family of the Ashanti) sacred wisdom. Just as with the Bantu, the Ashanti believe that the dead inhabit a world that is a mirror image of the world of the living, only underground; in this world, death happens in stages over several generations. As long as the name of a departed ancestor can be called, that ancestor is not dead in some final sense of the word. These unseen ancestors (called *nsamanfo* in Akan) can, then, be forces in the lives of the living, and in dreams or states of deep reverie, the spirit of a living individual (*sunsum*) can convene with these *nsamanfo*.[5]

Kwasi Benefo felt the presence of his wife who had passed into the world of the ancestors:

◎◎ "Now, how can I take another wife when the one who has died calls to me?"

They answered, "Yes, that is the way a person feels. But in time it will be different."

In time it was different for Kwasi Benefo, who returned to his home and his fields; eventually the pain of his wife's death lessened, and he went back to the village of her family seeking the daughter whose hand in marriage they had so graciously offered him. The two were wedded, and she bore a fine son whose birth was feted throughout Kwasi Benefo's village.

"My life is good," Kwasi Benefo told his wife and friends. "When has it ever been so good?"

One day while Kwasi Benefo was tending his crops, some village women hurried to him with news that a tree had fallen.

"Who cries over a falling tree?" he thought. Then darkness covered his spirit. He said, "Is there something left unspoken?"

They said, "Your wife was coming back from the river. She sat beneath the tree to rest. A spirit of the woods weakened the roots, and the tree fell on her." Kwasi Benefo ran to the village. He went to his house. His wife lay upon her mat without life in her body. Kwasi Benefo cried out. He threw himself on the ground and lay there as if life had departed from him also. He heard nothing, felt nothing. People said, "Kwasi Benefo is dead." The medicine men came. They said, "No, he is not dead. He lingers between here and there." They worked on Kwasi Benefo. They revived him. He stood up. He made the arrangements that were necessary. There was a wake, and the next day his wife was buried in her *amoasie* and beads.

After this Kwasi Benefo plunged into deep despair. What evil fate had visited his life? What woman would want to be married to him? What family would entrust their daughter to him? Even his friends began to look at him with suspicion. His cattle, his crops, even his son—what meaning did they have for him after all this tragedy and loss?

He abandoned his house, he abandoned his farm. He carried his son to the place where his wife's family lived and left him there. He went out into the bush. He walked for many days, not caring where he was. He arrived at a distant village, but he departed from it at once and went deeper into the bush. At last, at a wild place, he stopped. He said, "This place, far from people, I will stay here." He built a crude house. He gathered roots and seeds to eat. He made traps for small game. Thus he lived. His clothing turned to rags, and he began to wear the skins of animals. In time he almost forgot that his name was Kwasi Benefo and that he had once been a prosperous farmer. His life was wretched, but he did not care. This is the way it was with Kwasi Benefo. ◎◎

These were the "forest years" of Kwasi Benefo's self-enforced exile. This earnest man has misread the signposts of his life, interpret-

ing his great pain and suffering as a direction to quit the world, re-
nounce all material possessions, and retreat to the life of an ascetic
recluse. But this hero's journey does not end here:

◎◎ After several years passed, Kwasi Benefo reemerged from his forest
seclusion and traveled to a distant village where he was unknown; there
he began to farm again and married for a fourth time. But when his
fourth wife fell ill and died, Kwasi Benefo's will was broken.

"How can I go on living?" He abandoned his farm, his house, and
his cattle, and he journeyed back to the village where he was born. People were surprised because they had thought he was dead. His family and
his friends gathered to celebrate his return, but Kwasi Benefo said, "No,
there is to be no celebration. I have come back only to die in my own village and be buried here near the graves of my ancestors." ◎◎

This is the turning point of the whole adventure, for once Kwasi
Benefo lets go of willing how his life should unfold, a way opens for
him to receive a great boon, born of the pain and suffering he has so
desperately wished to escape.

◎◎ One night as he lay sleepless, the thought came to him that he
should go to Asamando, the land of the dead, and see the four young
women who had shared his life. He arose. He went out of his house and
departed from his village. He went to the forest place called
Nsamandow, where the dead were buried. He reached it; he went on.
There were no paths to follow. There was no light. All was darkness. He
passed through the forest and came to a place of dim light. No one was
living there. There were no sounds in the air. No voices of people, no
birds, no animals broke the stillness. Kwasi Benefo went on, until he
came at last to a river. He tried to ford the river, but he could not do it,
for the water was too deep and it was running too fast. He thought,
"Here my journey comes to an end." ◎◎

Kwasi Benefo followed the lure of his own pain and suffering into
a new, uncharted, and potentially dangerous realm where there were
"no paths to follow," where "no one was living," where "all was
darkness." This is the first step for one who has been called to an authentic life of self-realization beyond the pale of social or personal ex-
pectations and demands; here, actually, is the true beginning of Kwasi
Benefo's hero quest for which his suffering and exile have been but

preparation. Here, too, we should hasten to understand this myth in symbolic terms, for like the underworld, forests are symbolic of the human unconscious, and so the myth points to the inward journey beyond the pain and suffering of human life.

Unsure of how to continue on his path, Kwasi Benefo sits by the river's edge—the first great threshold of this African hero's adventure. On the far shore is the object of his quest, but to get there he must first find a way to cross over.

◎◎ At this moment he felt the splash of water on his face, and he looked up. Sitting on the far bank was an old woman with a brass pan at her side. The pan was full of women's loincloths and beads. By this sign, Kwasi Benefo knew her to be Amokye, the person who welcomed the souls of dead women to Asamando, and took from each of them her *amoasie* and beads. This was why women prepared for burial were dressed as they were, so that each could give her *amoasie* and beads to Amokye at the river crossing.

Amokye said to Kwasi Benefo, "Why are you here?"

And he answered, "I have come to see my wives. I cannot live any longer, because every woman who stays in my house, death takes her. I cannot sleep, I cannot eat, I want nothing that the living world has for the living."

Amokye said to him, "Oh, you must be Kwasi Benefo. Yes, I have heard of you. Many persons who came through here have spoken of your misfortune. But you are not a soul, you are a living man, therefore you cannot cross over."

Kwasi Benefo said, "Then I will remain here until I die and become a soul."

Amokye, the guardian at the river, felt compassion for Kwasi Benefo. She said, "Because of your suffering I will let you come across." She caused the water to run slowly. She caused it to become shallow. She said, "Go that way. There you will find them. But they are like the air; you will not be able to see them, though they will know you have come."
◎◎

Crossing such a threshold is often the hero's first challenge, and just as often the threshold guardian is not as benevolent as Amokye. Many African myths symbolize her as an old woman who when not the compassionate crone, is the heinous hag out to frustrate and impede the hero's progress. Other African myths, and much of the world's mythology, depict this threshold guardian as an ogre or monster who if not mastered, threatens the hero's demise.

In personal terms, the threshold guardian represents those forces of our psyche that bar access to the deeper and more dangerous realms of insight, revelation, and self-discovery—the "yonder shore" of our inner quest. This is the part of our personality we often encounter when we embark, or are thrust, on an adventure of life-changing significance, a time in our life when we must, like Kwasi Benefo, cross over the river into our personal land of the dead. Ask anyone who has ever changed a career, ended a long-standing relationship, or recovered from a serious illness or injury; they will tell you it is like a death, a dying of one's former self so that a new self may be born in its stead. Fear, like that of Uncama's in the preceding myth, may hinder the crossing of the threshold, but so too may low self-esteem, lack of confidence in one's abilities, or the abandonment of hope and faith. Self-revelation itself can cause us to suffer—it is not always easy to learn how we may have contributed to our own pain; it may be difficult admitting what we must do to change. Yet passing such thresholds and facing such challenges and discoveries are the essence of the inner hero's journey.

This theme of crossing over into the land of the dead was picked up by Nigerian writer Amos Tutuola in his groundbreaking 1952 novel, *The Palm-Wine Drinkard*, often hailed as marking the beginning of the modern era of African literature. Tutuola's protagonist embarks on a heroic quest in search of his palm-wine tapster who has died; this leads him through a series of adventures to Dead's Town where the threshold guardian tells him "alives" are forbidden to enter, just as Amokye first cautions Kwasi Benefo. The palm-wine drinkard then begins walking backward slowly, retracing his steps as did Uncama, but he finally convinces the guardian to let

Figure 2. A Kwa Ba (Akua'ba). An Ashanti symbol of the feminine power, which Kwasi Benefo encounters on his mythic journey.

him stay and goes to meet his former tapster, much as Kwasi Benefo goes to meet his wives. Similar direct references to African mythology are the foundation of the works of many modern-day African writers like Chinua Achebe, Wole Soyinka, and Ben Okri, and it would be difficult to appreciate fully the depths of modern African literature without recourse to the mythology on which it is built.

Though Kwasi Benefo is an "alive," he, too, was able to enter the land of the "deads":

◎◎ Kwasi Benefo crossed the river, and he went on. Now he was in Asamando. He came to a house; he entered. Outside the house he heard the sounds of village activities. He heard people calling to one another. He heard hoeing in the fields, the clearing of brush, and grain being pounded in mortars.

A bucket of water appeared, and washcloths suddenly came into view before him. He washed off the dust of his journey. Outside the house now, he heard his wives singing a song of welcome. The bucket and washcloths disappeared, and in their place he saw a gourd dish of food and a jug of water. While he ate, the voices of his wives went on singing Kwasi's praises. They told of what a kind husband he had been in the land of the living; they spoke of his gentleness. When he was through eating, the dish and the jug disappeared, and then there was a sleeping mat for Kwasi. His wives invited him to rest. He lay down on the mat. His wives sang again, and in their song they told Kwasi to continue living until his natural death, when his soul would come to Asamando unencumbered by a body. When this time arrived, they said, they would be waiting for him. Meanwhile, they said, Kwasi should marry again, and this time his wife would not die.

Hearing these sweet words from the women he loved, Kwasi Benefo fell into a deep sleep. When at last he awoke he was no longer in Asamando but back in the forest. He arose. He made his way back to his house in the village. He called on his friends to come and help him build a new house. When that was done, he sent messengers to the people who belonged to his fraternal society, saying that on such and such a day there would be a clearing of his fields. The men gathered on that day. They cleared and burned his fields; they began the hoeing. Kwasi Benefo planted. He began to farm and his crops grew. Again he mingled among people. In time he found a wife. They had children. They lived on. That is the story of Kwasi Benefo. The old people told it that way. ◎◎

So Kwasi Benefo passes through the portal to the underworld unafraid, and receives the redeeming, life-affirming words of the wives who have gone there before him. With this sublime gift, he returns to the light world of ordinary mortals renewed, a living witness to the redemptive, transforming power of suffering, compassion, and love.

We can hear echoes of this hero myth in the words of Martin Luther King Jr., a modern-day hero, who in his "I Have a Dream" speech encouraged his listeners "to work with the faith that unearned suffering is redemptive." With these words, King, a Baptist preacher, expressed the Christian symbolism of Jesus' willing crucifixion in social and political terms. The principal themes of this Ashanti myth, then, converge with similar themes about pain and suffering found in Christianity, Buddhism, and spiritual traditions worldwide that point the way to a path through and beyond the inevitable sorrows of life.

The Heroes of Myths and Nations

"Culture heroes" offer insight into the soul of the societies that give birth to them. Through their lives, or through mythological tales about them, we find history interpreted, values transmitted, and aspirations molded. Simply ask who are the culture heroes of the present age—wealthy athletes? wealthier media stars? even wealthier entrepreneurs of high technology?—and you quickly discover what is most coveted and valued in modern culture. The culture heroes of yore were vested with larger responsibilities than entertaining an audience or amassing a fortune, and myths of their lives communicated more than a sense of how one might discover the path to fame and fortune.

Kimanaueze is just such a culture hero for the Ambundu people of Angola, featured in a cycle of myths recorded and translated in the late nineteenth century by the linguist and business agent Héli Chatelain. As with most African myths transmitted orally over many generations, it is virtually impossible to determine the true source for this story or the facts surrounding its principal hero. But it is highly unlikely that an actual person named Kimanaueze ever lived. It is more probable that this mythic figure has come down to us from many sources, amalgamated over many years. The cycle of myths surrounding Kimanaueze, then, is both rich and unique; through him, his son, and grandsons we can trace aspects of Ambundu mythic wisdom and culture from the creation of the world through the colonial occupation of Angola by the Portuguese beginning in the sixteenth and seventeenth centuries. The following myth, adapted and abridged from Chatelain's original translation, comes from the midpoint in this cycle of myths and speaks of Kimanaueze's grandson, Sudika-mbambi, the Wonder Child.[6]

◎◎ Let us tell of Kimanaueze the senior, favorite among friends, who begat a son, Kimanaueze the junior. One day, the elder Kimanaueze said, "My son, I wish you to go to Luanda to do business there."

"Just now, Father?" queried the younger. "Why, only recently have I brought home a wife."

"Go!" commanded the father, and the younger Kimanaueze left for Luanda to do his father's business.

While the son was away, the Makishi arrived and sacked the family's home.* When he returned from Luanda, the younger Kimanaueze found no one there—his family had been killed—but off in the distance he saw a woman roaming aimlessly through the fields. He called to her, and as she approached, Kimanaueze recognized her as his wife. He cried out, asking what terrible fate had befallen his family. And she tearfully informed him that only she had escaped the Makishi's raid.

Alone, without other family, Kimanaueze and his wife struggled on. Eventually she became pregnant and when the day of her birthing came, she heard sounds from within her belly:

> *Mother, my sword, here it comes.*
> *Mother, my knife, here it comes.*
> *Mother, my* kilembe,[†] *here it comes.*
> *Mother, my staff, here it comes.*
> *Mother, steady yourself, for I am coming now.*

Able to speak at birth, the child entered the world with these words: "I am Sudika-mbambi. On the ground I set my staff. In the sky I set an antelope."

Still the wife of Kimanaueze heard more words coming from her belly:

---

* *Makishi* is the plural of *Kishi*, a Bantu word for a monster or ogre that eats people, sometimes described as many-headed with the capacity to regenerate its severed heads.

† A *kilembe* is a mythical plant, a "life tree," brought into existence with the birth of an individual; the growth and fate of a *kilembe* is a reflection of the individual life with which it is associated.

Mother, my sword, here it comes;
My knife, here it comes;
My staff, here it comes;
My kilembe, *here it comes.*
Mother, sit well; I am coming now.

And a second son was born speaking: "I am Kabundungulu."

Sudika-mbambi then said, "My *kilembe*, plant it at the back of the house." Then turning to his mother he asked, "Mother, why do you look at me so?"

"You are the baby I just gave birth to and already you are speaking. How can this be?" she replied.

"Do not wonder," Sudika-mbambi assured her. "You will see all the miraculous things I am going to do."

Then he spoke to his brother. "Let us go to cut poles, so we may build houses for our parents."

The twin sons took up swords and went into the bush to cut house poles. As soon as Sudika-mbambi had cut one pole, the other poles cut themselves. And the younger brother too, after cutting just one pole, the other poles cut themselves. The brothers bound the poles together and brought them to the clearing where they would erect their parents' house. Then they went back to the bush to cut grass for the thatched roof.

When the building materials were assembled, Sudika-mbambi began to erect the hut poles. As soon as he erected one pole, the entire house erected itself. He tied one cord around the poles, and all the cords tied themselves. He thatched one grass stalk; the roof became thatched of its own accord. The house was complete.

"Now, enter the house I have built for you," he said to his mother and father. "And you, Kabundungulu, my younger brother, stay with our parents while I go to fight the Makishi." Turning to his family, Sudika-mbambi reminded them, "Watch my *kilembe*. If you see it has withered, then you will know I have died." ◎◎

Sudika-mbambi's miraculous birth and childhood portend his power; mighty gods and legendary world saviors are foretold from such beginnings. Hercules, while still a baby, kills a snake sent against him by the angry goddess Hera. Siegfried, the Nordic culture hero, grows quickly from birth to enormous stature and, as a young boy, slays the dragon Regin. Krishna, the beloved child-incarnation of the supreme Hindu god Vishnu, just after birth subdues a monster in the guise of a wet nurse whose breasts are full of poison. Just as Sudika-mbambi's mother hears sounds from the child of destiny in her womb, so too Mary hears the angel heralding the child destined to enter her womb: "Thou shalt conceive in thy womb, and bring forth a son, and shalt call him Jesus. He shall be great and shall be called the Son of the Highest." Born from his mother's side, the Buddha is placed on the ground by the gods, covered in a golden cloth; then, taking seven eastward steps, he points up with his right hand, down with his left, proclaiming, "Worlds above, worlds below, behold, I am the master of all worlds!"

Tutuola also visits this theme of the miraculous birth in *The Palm-Wine Drinkard;* his nameless main character spends some years in a town along the way of his quest, where we learn:

> I noticed that the left hand thumb of my wife was swelling out as if it was a buoy, but it did not pain her. One day, she followed me to the farm in which I was tapping the palm-wine, and to my surprise when the thumb that swelled out touched a palm-tree thorn, the thumb burst out suddenly and there we saw a male child came out of it and at the same time that the child came out from the thumb, he began to talk to us as if he was ten years of age.
>
> Within the hour that he came down from the thumb he grew up to the height of about three feet and some inches and his voice by that time was as plain as if somebody strikes an anvil with a steel hammer. Then the first thing that he did, he asked his mother:— "Do you know my name?"[7] . . .

The human creators of such superhuman legends are not striving to provide a plausible biography for the mythic hero. The fantastic details of the hero's birth, like all the elemental ideas found in myths, are not designed for the eye of reason but rather for the eye of introspection. And the hero's life is not given solely for us to emulate but to use as a meditation on our own. The hero's miraculous birth, then, becomes a reflection of the extraordinary, latent capacities dwelling within us all, and his achievements symbolize the fulfillment of our own human potential.

The Angolan adventure continues:

◎◎ So Sudika-mbambi set out to meet the Makishi. While walking along the road, he met four Kipalendes,* each of whom boasted of its magical powers. Sudika-mbambi welcomed them to meet the Makishi in battle with him.

Sudika-mbambi and the four Kipalendes set up camp in the midst of the bush.

In the morning, he gathered the Kipalendes together, commanding one to stay and guard the camp while the other three accompanied him to engage the Makishi.

While the others were off fighting the Makishi,[8] an old woman and her beautiful granddaughter appeared in front of the Kipalende who guarded the camp.

"Let us fight," she crowed. "If you beat me, then you shall marry my granddaughter."

But the Kipalende was no match for the old woman, who trounced him soundly. Upon leaving, she lifted a heavy stone and placed it on top of him so he was unable to move. Meanwhile, Sudika-mbambi, with his gift of clairvoyance, saw the Kipalende under the stone. "Come, we must return," he said to the others abruptly. "Your friend is in trouble; he is trapped under a stone."

"You are lying, Sudika-mbambi," they replied. "We are far away from him. How could you know this?"

"This I know," commanded Sudika-mbambi.

So Sudika-mbambi and the Kipalendes stopped attacking the Makishi and returned to their camp to find their comrade still under the stone.

"But who has done this to you?" they questioned their compatriot.

"An old woman came with her granddaughter, saying, 'Let us fight! If you beat me, you shall marry my granddaughter.' I fought with her, but she has beaten me."

"An old woman has beaten you?" the others laughed, before going to sleep.

For the next three days the very same thing took place. Each morning Sudika-mbambi left with three Kipalendes to fight the Makishi, while one Kipalende guarded the camp. Each morning the old woman appeared with her granddaughter, challenging the Kipalende on watch, beating him, and weighing him down under a stone.

---

* *Kipalendes* are supernatural beings.

Finally, on the morning of the fifth day, Sudika-mbambi told the Kipalendes, "You four, today you shall go to fight the Makishi while I stay behind to meet this old woman."

Soon after the Kipalendes left, the old woman appeared.

"Let us fight," she crowed. "If you beat me, then you shall marry my granddaughter."

Sudika-mbambi and the crone fought, only this time he prevailed, killing the hag and taking her granddaughter for his own.

"Today I have received life," the young woman rejoiced. "For my grandmother used to shut me up in a house of stone so I would not go about. But today I am freed by Sudika-mbambi whom I wish only to marry."

Sudika-mbambi granted her wish. And when the Kipalendes returned from fighting they announced, "Today the Makishi are finished; they no longer exist to cause mischief and harm."

Surveying all that had happened, Sudika-mbambi, son of Kimanaueze the younger, turned to his new wife and the Kipalendes, saying only, "Today all is well." ◎◎

Sudika-mbambi's ultimate battle comes not with the Makishi, as expected, but with the old woman who guards her young granddaughter possessively. This familiar triangular affair involving a beautiful young princess, a wicked mother or stepmother, and a young prince who comes to the princess's rescue appears in folktales and myths throughout the world; the hero's consummate deed, of course, is to win the hand of the beautiful maiden. In contrast to the benevolent old women we encountered in the myth of Kwasi Benefo, here the hag jealously guards the vitality of which she can no longer partake—just as the withering forces of our own personality frustrate access to our dynamic potential. In Sudika-mbambi's winning of the hand of the young woman, we may find the possibility of our own triumph over the restrictive forces within ourselves, and the release of our own dammed vitality.

As a college student I worked summers in New York City teaching African-American high school youths who had failed the previous year and were labeled "problem students." One summer, I began a geometry course without a single math book; instead, each student had a copy of the speeches of Malcolm X. My reasoning was that first these young people ought to learn how to state a case and then construct a logical proof—something Malcolm X was extremely gifted at, something most "streetwise" kids know well how to do, and, after all, is the essence of high school geometry. "Rap" geometry, it might be called.

Initially, they were spellbound, then a little rebellious during the first two weeks of the eight-week course. Interspersed with the joy of reading Malcolm's speeches were youthful protests of "Maybe you don't know anything about geometry 'cause this ain't no geometry class."

"How would you know?" I'd gleefully reply. "You flunked geometry anyway!"

About the time I started drawing the connection between Malcolm's logic and the business of proving two triangles symmetrical, a young student named Victor came up to me and said softly, "Mr. Ford, I think I understand what you're getting at. Can I try teaching the next class?"

I was floored! Here was this student, deemed "unteachable" by the educational system, asking to teach my class. I told Victor what I had in mind for the next lesson and coached him on the main points I wanted the students to get. The next day I watched in awe as he taught this class in geometry more cogently than I ever could—for Victor was on fire with a newfound gift of understanding. I taught only a handful of classes for the remainder of that summer, yielding often to the flame of knowledge kindled in this remarkable young man. From the humblest of surroundings, heroes with miraculous powers may be born.

3

MYTHS OF DEATH AND RESURRECTION

*It is said that when he died, his heart went out and escaped
to become a bird.*

EPITAPH FOR A BASUTO HERO

There comes a time in the hero's career when his powers wither in
the face of some consuming monster of the abyss; a whale, a dragon,
or a man-eating ogre rises to swallow him whole or in pieces. This
symbolic descent into the belly of the beast is the pivotal moment of
the hero's adventure; this is the womb of his rebirth, the crucible of
his transformation, the time of his reinvention. By whatever means he
finds himself in this foreboding place, should he manage to escape, he
will emerge forever changed.

This motif of the hero's death and resurrection is found with great
regularity in the mythic traditions of Africa, no doubt reflecting the
countless opportunities life affords to witness this pattern. Crops die,
only to be reborn annually; women shed a portion of their body
monthly only to be renewed; the moon sheds its shadow also to be reborn in light each month; human consciousness dies to the light world
of day, is reborn to the night world of dream, and then is resurrected
to the light world again. And so it comes really as no surprise that
African mythic wisdom holds that human life corresponds to this end-

less round of nature, measuring life not linearly from birth to death but cyclically from the world of the living, to the world of the ancestors, to the world of the not yet born, to the world of the living again.

In the next adventure, Lituolone, a Basuto hero-figure, enters the belly of the shapeless monster Kammapa to save humanity[1]:

◎◎ There was a time when a huge, shapeless monster, Kammapa, spread terror everywhere. With a never-ending appetite for humans, he devoured every person living on earth save one, an old woman who had gone into hiding. She was the only person left on earth, and without the aid of a man, she gave birth to a child born wearing sacred amulets. The old woman knew this child was special, and she named him Lituolone, a name befitting a god. By the evening of his birth the child had already grown into a strong man who uttered words of great wisdom.

"Mother," said Lituolone, "is there no one else but you and I on the earth?"

"My child," replied the woman, trembling, "not long ago the valleys and mountains were covered with people, but the beast whose voice makes the rocks tremble has devoured them all."

Upon hearing this, Lituolone took up a knife and went in search of the monster, deaf to the entreaties of his mother. The two met in battle, but it was an uneven affair—Kammapa overwhelmed Lituolone, swallowing him whole. Still, even inside the great beast, Lituolone was not dead, and he struck out, tearing apart the monster's entrails and releasing himself and all the rest of humanity from the beast's belly.

Having freed himself and the others, Lituolone became the chief of the society, but people were not grateful to him, for they feared the power of one born only of a woman, one who had seen no childhood, one who had conquered the great formless monster Kammapa. So it was decided that Lituolone should be killed by being thrown into a deep pit. But Lituolone avoided it. Then his detractors built a great fire in the center of the village, intending to throw him in. But in the frenzy to capture Lituolone, another man was seized and thrown in the fire instead. Still Lituolone's pursuers would not relent; next they sought to push him over a high precipice. Once again Lituolone was spared when madness gripped his attackers and they pushed one of their own party over the cliff; this time Lituolone restored the poor man to life. So it was decided that a great hunt should be organized, which meant that the hunting party, with Lituolone as its chief, would be absent from the village for several days. One night, while the party prepared to sleep in a cave, Lituolone was persuaded to take a position far-thest from the entrance. When the others thought the chief was asleep, they stole out and kindled a great fire at the cave's mouth. But when they looked around, they found Lituolone standing among them gazing at the blaze.

Finally, Lituolone realized that nothing would ameliorate this deep hatred for him, and he grew weary of countering these attempts to do him harm. So he offered himself without resistance, allowing himself to be killed. It is said that when he died, his heart went out and escaped to become a bird. ◎◎

I once asked a filmmaker friend, as we left a movie theater, how she views a film. She told me she sees a film at least three times: "the first time to enjoy the story; the second time to analyze the actors and their direction; and the third time to observe what camera angles the director chose for the final cut."

I approach a myth in a similar way: the first time I read it to en-joy the story; the second time to look for significant symbols; and the third time to reflect on the myth's relationship to my own life's jour-ney. This Basuto hero myth rewards such an approach, for despite its brevity, the story is rich with the universal symbols of the hero's jour-ney, cloaked here in African hues: the world cries for a savior to res-cue humanity from Kammapa, the consuming monster, the guardian and master of the dark abyss; an extraordinary man-god appearing through virgin birth to answer humanity's call; the hero engaging the monster in combat only to be swallowed whole into the belly of the beast; the hero's victory releasing the rest of humanity from the mon-ster; and the hero returning to society—not as the welcomed savior but as a branded outcast.

In the virgin birth of Lituolone, we find the highest form of the hero's miraculous birth, signaling the awakening of the human spirit. Spiritual awakening is necessarily "virgin," since it is a birth not from another but from oneself, from one mode of self-awareness to an-other. Those who have "heard the call" of the spiritual life and have been "reborn" include not just "born-again" Christians but anyone who has heeded a deeply significant inner striving and found himself or herself reborn into a new life calling. This is a virgin birth.

Now, the monster Kammapa in this tale is symbolic of all that holds back most of humanity from hearing or answering the call to adventure in their lives; this is the chaotic "fog" of the average person. At nineteen, I went to work as a systems engineer for IBM, then the largest computer company in the world. At twenty-six I was inspired to leave this corporate behemoth to pursue an education and new career as a chiropractor. All my managers and many of my colleagues tried to dissuade me from this course. When it became obvious that I was leaving, I received a very different response. On my last day at work, in an exit interview with my first-level manager, I was amazed to hear him say, "Clyde, I envy you; all I ever wanted to do in life was open a bookstore." Then in a similar interview with my second-level manager I heard, "I look forward to following your career. I always dreamed of moving to Texas and becoming a wildcat oilman." Back at my desk for the last time, I turned to say good-bye to a colleague, a young woman just a few years older than me. "I wish I could leave," she cried, "but the money I make here is too good and I'm trapped." These were the lamentations of humanity devoured and caught in the belly of the "Big Blue" beast.*

Willingly or otherwise, the hero, too, must enter the belly of the beast, not to lament but to blaze a trail out. An amusing Thonga variant on this theme tells of an ogre who swallowed a shepherd boy. The lad was apparently indigestible, and the ogre was made so uncomfortable that he asked his fellow ogres to cut him open, releasing the lad along with the other people and livestock he had devoured.[2] A Zulu myth tells of a heroine in search of her children who were swallowed by an elephant; she too was swallowed by the pachyderm. Once inside "she saw large forests and great rivers and many high lands; on one side there were many rocks; and there were many people who had built their villages there, and many dogs and many cattle; all were there inside the elephant; she saw, too, her own children sitting there."[3] So she cut out and roasted the elephant's liver for them all to eat, killing the beast and liberating all the life that had been trapped inside. These are critical moments of death yielding to rebirth—passages through which the heroes, and the lives they touch, come forth renewed.

"Oppressed people cannot remain oppressed forever," wrote Martin Luther King Jr. in *Letter from the Birmingham Jail*. He had gone to Birmingham, Alabama, in 1963 to challenge that violently segregated city where cannons fired water against waves of black

---

* "Big Blue" is a corporate nickname for IBM.

bodies while the jaws of police dogs snarled and snapped at their limbs. He sat in jail, in the belly of the beast, brandishing the spear of nonviolence against the monster of racism and oppression. "Nonviolent direct action," he wrote from his cell, "seeks to create such a crisis and establish such creative tension that a community . . . is forced to confront the issue."[4]

Ultimately King emerged from the beast's belly, and though the monster of injustice was not slain, some preliminary victories were won through the courage of this modern-day hero. King was a Nobel laureate, but he was not a universally welcomed hero. His tireless message that freedom and justice for all Americans were inextricably linked to freedom and justice for black Americans did not always fall on receptive ears.

When a killer arose from the ranks of those deaf to his message, a weary King, like Lituolone, seemed to yield willingly. "I don't know what will happen now. We have got difficult days ahead," he prophetically told an audience in Memphis, Tennessee, hours before his death. "But it doesn't matter with me," he continued. "I am happy tonight; I am not worried about anything. I'm not fearing any man."[5] Some might say that when he died his heart, too, escaped like a bird and galvanized the hearts of many who continued to walk his heroic path.

And so the symbols revealed in ancient myths are still valid for the concerns of modern life, not only for the lives of modern-day heroes but for the life of the hero within every modern-day person. When we read the myth of Lituolone, we can ask of ourselves: What is the monster consuming my humanity? The impersonal demands of an unrewarding career? The emotional drain of an unfulfilling relationship? The psychic pain of an unresolved trauma? The emptiness of an unrealized dream? An unacceptable social illness like racism, violence, poverty, or homelessness? And we may ponder our own virgin birth: To what hero part of myself must I give birth to meet this monster in battle? Courage? Fearlessness? Faith? Hope? An end to denial? A belief in my own worthiness? And then we might question: Am I prepared to enter the belly of my beast to wrest whatever victory is mine? What parts of myself am I willing to sacrifice in this life-challenging effort? Am I ready to face possible ridicule and scorn from those who would not understand my hero quest? In these questions lie the personal challenges and rewards of the African hero's death and resurrection.

Rescue in the Spirit World

Not even Sudika-mbambi, the hero-child of legendary prowess, could escape the belly of the beast or the trials of the hero's death and resurrection. Winning a bride from the jealous hag was only the start of his hero journey, as we learn when his saga continues:

◎◎ The Kipalendes were actually jealous of Sudika-mbambi. "A mere child has bested us," they complained. "We must kill him, but how?" They plotted Sudika-mbambi's death by digging a hole in the ground and covering it with a mat spread on top. "Come, Sudika-mbambi, have a seat here," they said. When Sudika-mbambi sat down he dropped into the hole and the Kipalendes quickly covered the hole with dirt. They took the young woman for their own.

When Kabundungulu went to check the *kilembe* of his elder brother, he noticed the life tree had begun to wither. He lamented to himself, "My brother is going to die." Still, he poured water on the tree and it began to turn green again.

Meanwhile, at the bottom of the hole, a road leading to Kalunga-ngombe, the king of death, opened up for Sudika-mbambi. Along the road he happened on an old woman who was hoeing. "How are you, Grandmother?" Sudika-mbambi greeted her, then asked if she would show him the road from there.

"Two paths lead from here," she uttered, "a wide path and a narrow path. Take the narrow path; do not take the wide path or you will go astray. And when you finally arrive outside Kalunga-ngombe's, you must carry a jug of red pepper and a jug of wisdom." ◎◎

Here we arrive at a crucial juncture, not only in the telling of the tale but in understanding the implications of African mythic wisdom. Kalunga-ngombe is a mythical king presiding over the realm of Kalunga, viewed alternately as either underground or underwater. Kalunga is also the threshold, symbolized by the ocean, that separates the ordinary world from the mythical ground of Mputu, the world to which captured African slaves passed, according to the Kongolese society they left behind. So Sudika-mbambi, his capture by the Kipalendes, and his transit to Kalunga can also be read as a metaphor for the capture of African slaves and their transit to the Americas through the Middle Passage.

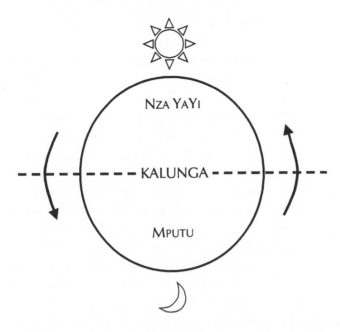

Figure 3. Kongo cosmogram showing relationship between Nza YaYi (the ordinary world), Mputu (the land of the dead), and Kalunga. See Chapter 10 for further description of this and similar cosmograms. After Mac-Gaffey (1983).

In fact, there is every reason to believe that African slaves who came from societies where tales of Kalunga flourished understood their capture and travails in just such mythic terms. "[T]he sea-passage of slaves," observes ethnographer Wyatt MacGaffey, "is not fully distinguished from the passage of souls, the slave trader from the witch, the geographical America from the land of the dead."[6]

This myth of Sudika-mbambi, then, not only informed the Ambundu society from which it originated but also the lives of those Africans torn away from this society through the horrors of the Atlantic slave trade. And the sacred circle that began with the struggles of the mythical hero Sudika-mbambi continues unbroken, with the real-life struggles of African-American heroes and heroines for freedom and justice in America to this day.

The Kipalendes' attempts to bring about Sudika-mbambi's demise actually bring him to the real challenge of his quest, which takes place in the underworld of Kalunga, the land of the dead. His progress there is monitored through his *kilembe*, which remains in the light world above. Here the tree represents the hero's psychological center, a personal manifestation of yet another universal mythic symbol: the Cosmic Tree, the World Tree, or the Tree of Life. A tree, after all, is a compact representation of the threefold mythic stage on which the drama of the hero quest unfolds: a tree's roots sink deep into the earth and coincide with the lower kingdom of the underground and underworld, the recesses of the human unconscious; its prominent trunk represents the middle kingdom of the earth, the realm of ordinary, wakeful awareness; and its leaves, turning toward the light, reflect the upper kingdom of the heavens, the enlightened domain of the human spirit.

We each need to find or form our own *kilembe*, that measuring tape of our vitality in these three kingdoms, since the measures provided by society often fail to address the deeper stirrings of our soul. Perhaps wealth is not the most important yardstick of our journey in the middle kingdom of the everyday; maybe fear thwarts the potential rewards of penetrating the underworld of our unconscious; and there might be a better way of allowing the radiance of human spirituality to shine through our lives than unquestioning adherence to dogma and doctrine. Certainly each *kilembe* would be as unique and beautiful as the individual life whose vital essence it mirrors.

Sudika-mbambi's *kilembe* withers momentarily when he is first snared by the Kipalendes' trap, but then it springs back to life as a path opens for him to travel to the underworld—the same path to the unconscious opened to Uncama, to Kwasi Benefo, and to Walter, the traveler in my clinic. Sudika-mbambi is greeted and assisted at the threshold of the underworld by a now-familiar figure, the old woman of the way, who warns him of the direction he must take and the magical objects he will need to secure his safety. Upon arriving at Kalunga-ngombe's, Sudika-mbambi asks for his daughter in marriage—a symbol of the hero's desire for knowledge of and union with all that is to be found in this realm of the unconscious.

◎◎ "Well," said the Lord of Death, "you shall marry my daughter, but only if you possess a jug of red pepper and a jug of wisdom."

When Sudika-mbambi produced the required items, Kalunga-ngombe covered his surprise with laughter and ordered the celebration to continue. But the next morning, he backed off, saying, "If you want my daughter, then first you will have to rescue her from the great serpent, Kinioka kia Tumba!"

When Sudika-mbambi arrived at Kinioka's abode, he found the great serpent away, so he sat down to wait. Kinioka, unwilling to yield, sent swarms of insects against Sudika-mbambi: first a legion of driver ants, then red ants, then bees, then wasps. Each time Sudika-mbambi fought them off. Then came a head of Kinioka, hissing with fangs bared; Sudika-mbambi cut off that head, but another head appeared in its place, and Sudika-mbambi cut off that head too.

He returned with Kalunga-ngombe's daughter, but Kalunga-ngombe wanted to test Sudika-mbambi still further. He was challenged to kill Kimbiji kia Malenda, the crocodile, master of the underworld abyss. Sudika-mbambi fished for Kimbiji with a suckling pig as bait, but the crocodile was too strong for him and pulled Sudika-mbambi into the water where he was swallowed whole. ◎◎

Sudika-mbambi's tests by Kalunga-ngombe are reminiscent of Hercules' battle with the many-headed serpentine monster, Hydra of Lerna. But when faced with the reptilian beast, Sudika-mbambi's powers fail for the first time. This is the crisis point of the entire saga, for he is pulled into the beast's belly and his *kilembe* goes limp; he is now the dead hero consumed by the monstrous forces of the unknown.

Must we, too, not die continually to be reborn? Dying first to the dark womb of our creation to be reborn to the light world outside; next to our childhood dependency, to be reborn a self-responsible adult; and again to our singly responsible self, seeking rebirth as a mutually responsible partner, mate, or parent; then again and again in the never-ending cycle of death and rebirth throughout all aspects of our life until finally we die to life itself, to be reborn back into the transcendent mystery from which we first emerged. We cannot hold on if we are to be born anew. We must let go and, when necessary, allow ourselves to be pulled into the jaws of death—death of an outmoded manner of thought; death of a burdensome set of beliefs; death of a restrictive frame of awareness; death of our personal status quo. Only then is there hope for our resurrection.

◎◎ Sudika-mbambi's only hope lay at home with his younger brother, Kabundungulu, who noticed Sudika-mbambi's life tree was dry. No longer content with staying put, this time Kabundungulu vowed to discover his brother's true fate. He retraced Sudika-mbambi's footsteps, eventually arriving at the Kipalendes campsite; they, of course, feigned ignorance of the elder brother's whereabouts.

"Liars," cried Kabundungulu. "You have killed him. Uncover the grave."

Kabundungulu forced the Kipalendes to uncover Sudika-mbambi's grave; then he jumped in and struck out on the road his brother had taken to the realm of Kalunga-ngombe. He met the old woman, who showed him the way to Kalunga-ngombe's abode, and there he demanded of the Lord of Death to know his brother's condition.

Kalunga-ngombe informed the younger hero that his elder brother had been swallowed by Kimbiji. So Kabundungulu fished the monstrous crocodile out of the water with a pig as bait, took his knife, and cut Kimbiji open. There he found the bones of Sudika-mbambi, which he gathered together, uttering, "My elder brother, arise!"

Sudika-mbambi was thus resurrected, and to him Kalunga-ngombe finally gave his daughter.

Taking the path back from the land of Kalunga, the two brothers returned through the hole where Sudika-mbambi had been trapped and concluded their unfinished business with the four Kipalendes, whom they drove away, reclaiming the first wife of Sudika-mbambi. Finally arriving home, the younger brother said, "My elder brother, give me one wife, for you have two, and I have none."

But Sudika-mbambi took offense at such a suggestion and told his younger brother never to mention it to him again. Kabundungulu persisted, not with his brother but with his wives, and on those days when Sudika-mbambi went hunting, Kabundungulu entered his house to couple with them. Eventually, one of Sudika-mbambi's wives complained to Sudika-mbambi that Kabundungulu continually sought the pleasures of her bed. This greatly angered Sudika-mbambi, and he immediately confronted Kabundungulu. The two began to quarrel, striking each other with the intention to kill, but neither one's powers were stronger than the other's. Finally they grew weary of fighting and agreed to part ways—the elder brother, Sudika-mbambi, heading east; his younger brother, Kabundungulu, traveling west.

Now, when a storm comes, the thunderclap that sounds from the east is Sudika-mbambi; the thunder echo that responds is Kabundungulu, his younger brother, who went west. ◎◎

In a final graceful stroke, this myth anchors the tale in the heaven of mortals by identifying Sudika-mbambi with the thunderclap and Kabundungulu with its echo. Just as the bell of the Angelus tolls to remind Roman Catholics of the divine mystery of the world savior

ROBE, T R 4430

Friday, September 25, 2020

who died and was resurrected, so, too, the thunderclap may recall for its Ambundu listener the mystery quest of the hero-god Sudika-mbambi who also died and was resurrected. Each boom from this thunder god then becomes a boon, announcing that the quest of this hero with an African face is no one else's but our very own.

A Fire Offering to the Gods

The Chaga, a Bantu people who inhabit the slopes of Mount Kili-manjaro in Tanzania, tell of Murile, another hero-god who dies and is resurrected[7]:

◎◎ A man and his wife living in the Chaga country had three sons, of whom Murile was the eldest. One day he went out with his mother to dig up taro root, and noticing a particularly fine tuber among those that were set aside for seed, he said, "Why, this one is as beautiful as my little brother!" His mother laughed at the notion of comparing a taro tuber with a baby; but he hid the root, and later, when no one was looking, put it away in a hollow tree and sang a magic song over it. Next day he went to look and found that the root had turned into a child. From then on, at every meal he secretly kept back some food, and whenever he could do so without being seen, he carried it to the tree and fed the baby, which grew and flourished from day to day.

But Murile's mother became very anxious when she saw how thin the boy was growing, and though she questioned him, she could get no satisfaction. Then one day his younger brothers noticed that when his portion of food was handed to him, instead of eating it at once, he put it aside. They told their mother, and she bade them follow him when he went away after dinner, and see what he did with it. They did, and saw him feeding the baby in the hollow tree, and came back and told her. She went at once to the spot and strangled the child who was starving her son.

When Murile came back next day and found the child dead, he was overcome with grief. He went home and sat down in the hut, crying bitterly. His mother asked him why he was crying, and he said it was because the smoke hurt his eyes. So she told him to go and sit on the other side of the fireplace. But as he still wept and complained of the smoke, they said he had better take his father's stool and sit outside. He picked up the stool, went out into the courtyard, and sat down. ◎◎

Strange as it may seem to compare a yam root with a child, the Chaga would easily understand such a comparison. Four days after birth, a Chaga infant's withered umbilical cord is severed from its body by a senior midwife, who places it in a gourd filled with Eleusine grain (African millet) where it is to be left undisturbed for several months until the infant is taken from the family hut by the midwife and ceremoniously presented to the local banana grove. There, if the child is male, the remains of the umbilical cord, along with a few kernels of the grain with which it has been stored, are placed on the tubers of a yam; if it is a female child, similar contents are placed on the roots of a certain banana plant. The plant, made sacred by the rite, is forever after known as the "root" of that child, and the fruits of that plant are not allowed for general consumption.

The sense of this African rite is evident even in the European descriptor of the grain, for *Eleusine* refers back to the principal mystery rites of ancient Greece conducted at the sacred temple in the town of Eleusis. Centuries ago, novices there were initiated into the great mystery of life through ritual enactment of the myth of Demeter, the goddess of fertile earth, and Persephone, Demeter's daughter who died and was resurrected, symbolizing the vital energies underneath the earth that manifest themselves in the cycles of planting (death) and of harvesting new growth (resurrection). This entire mystery school, which the Greek historian Herodotus attributed to a cultural borrowing from ancient Egypt, was then symbolized in rites which involved the drinking of a fermented barley brew. The barley seed, transformed into a drink, was symbolic of the goddess who died and was resurrected. It was used to remind participants in this rite of the importance of death and resurrection in their lives, as the millet seed was used in the lives of the Chaga. We can also observe a similar theme in the Christian sacraments of Holy Communion, where a wheat seed transformed into bread is consumed symbolically as the body of the dead and resurrected savior.

Thus, the Chaga midwife performs rites equaling those of the mysteries at Eleusis and of the Roman Catholic mass. A modern-day liturgy to accompany the combining of the child's umbilical cord and the millet grain might go something like this:

As this grain is the harvest of the body of the earth, which dies at the end of each planting season only to bring forth new life at the season's next beginning, so are you (child) the harvest of the body of your mother (symbolized by the wasted birth cord), which died each month (her menses) to bring forth new life in you.

Then the smearing of both grain and birth cord on a plant tuber might be expressed in these words:

As these roots reach deep to the mystery from which this plant arises to bear fruit, may you also reach roots deep to the mystery from which your life arises to bear fruit. Let this plant and root serve to remind you throughout your life of your connection to and participation in the great mystery cycle of life yielding to death yielding to life again and again, from this moment of your birth until you are planted, through death, back into this abiding mystery.

Using an idea already familiar to us through the Ambundu saga of Sudika-mbambi, we can say that through this rite Chaga society has supplied each child with its very own *kilembe,* its own life tree.

So with these key symbols opened in this manner, we might predict that the theme of death and resurrection will figure prominently throughout this myth, and the remainder of the account bears out this prediction. In the name of a protective mother's love and nurturance, Murile is cut off from the "root" of his life, and this propels him on a journey of self-discovery.

◎◎ Then he said, "Stool, go up on high, as my father's rope does when he hangs up his beehive in the forest!" And the stool rose up with him into the air and stuck fast in the branches of a tree. He repeated the words a second time, and again the stool moved upward. Just then his brothers happened to come out of the hut, and when they saw him, they ran back and said to their mother, "Murile is going up into the sky!"

Murile's mother did not believe her children and ran outside to see for herself, whereupon she began singing to her son to come back. The rest of Murile's family similarly called to him to return to the earth, but to no avail, for Murile continued upward, responding to everyone he had left behind, "No, no, I will never come back."

The stool carried him up till he felt solid ground beneath his feet, and then he looked around and found himself in the heaven country. He walked on till he came to some people gathering wood. He asked them the way to the Moon-chief's village, and they said, "Just pick up some sticks for us, and then we will tell you." He collected a bundle of sticks, and they directed him to go on till he should come to some people cut-ting grass. He did so, and greeted the grass cutters when he came to them.

After helping the grass cutters, Murile was directed forward until he came to some herd boys, then some women gathering beans, some peo-ple reaping millet, others gathering banana leaves, and girls fetching wa-ter. He helped each of them, and they steered him closer and closer to the Moon-chief's village.

The water carriers said, "Just go on in this direction till you come to a house where the people are eating." He found the house and called out, "Greeting, house owners! Please show me the way to the Moon-chief's village." They promised to do so if he would sit down and eat with them, which he did. At last, following their instructions, he reached his desti-nation and found the people eating their food raw. He asked them why they did not use fire to cook with and was surprised to learn they did not know what fire was.

"If I prepare nice food for you by means of fire, what will you give me?" asked Murile.

"We will give you cattle and goats and sheep," the Moon-chief replied.

"Go, then," Murile commanded the villagers, "bring me plenty of wood."

When the villagers returned with the wood, Murile and the Moon-chief went behind the house where the other people could not see them. Murile took his knife and cut two pieces of wood, one flat and the other pointed, and twirled the pointed stick till he got some sparks, with which he lit a bunch of dry grass and so kindled a fire. When it burned, he got the chief to send for some green plantains, which he roasted and offered to him. Then he cooked some meat and various other foods. The Moon-chief was delighted when he tasted them, and at once called all the peo-ple together, and said to them, "Here is a wonderful doctor come from a far country! We shall have to repay him for his fire." ◎◎

Meet the Moon-chief, or Moon-king, a deity well known in both primal and present-day mythologies, for this leader or savior person-ifies the mystery of death and resurrection, after the celestial body for which he is named. In traditional African hunting societies, for in-stance, this Moon deity manifested himself in the sacred covenant be-tween the hunter and his prey: animals were killed (death) in the belief that their departed spirits would return (resurrection) as future game for the nourishment of humankind. Likewise, in traditional African agricultural societies, this Moon deity manifested himself in the sacred covenant between the farmer and the land: reaping one crop (death) prepared the land to bring forth new crops (resurrection). Kings, the earthbound personifications of this lunar divinity (in Africa and elsewhere) were often sacrificed as part of a ritual reenactment and reinforcement of this cycle of death and resurrection.

Writing at the beginning of the twentieth century, Leo Frobenius, a prominent German scholar on Africa, identified a zone of such ritual regicide encompassing most of Bantu-speaking Africa and extending eastward to the Persian Gulf, the southern Indian subcontinent, the Andaman Islands, and northern portions of Indonesia. "In the South African 'Eritrean' zone [Mozambique, Angola, and Rhodesia]," Frobenius wrote,

> . . . the king representing the great godhead even bore the name "Moon"; while his second wife was the Moon's beloved, the planet Venus. And when the time arrived for the death of the god, the king and his Venus-spouse were strangled and their remains placed in a burial cave in a mountain, from which they were supposed then to be resurrected. . . .[8]

Later, the sacrifice of bulls, oxen, or other animals with horns shaped like the crescent moon replaced such regicide, and the flesh or blood of these animals was eaten to symbolize this fundamental cycle of life.

In the heaven land, Murile's saga also portrays an exceptional reversal of roles, for the hero offers a "fire gift" to the Moon-chief, and this is in sharp contrast to the accustomed episode of a "fire theft" from the gods for the sake of humankind. When the Greek god Prometheus stole fire from heaven, for example, Zeus was angered because fire—symbolic of the eternal energy of the sun and immortality of the gods—was supposed to belong to no one but the gods. With Murile's story, however, we now have two different mythologies, two contrasting metaphors, about the relationship between humanity and divinity. The Promethean way holds that humankind is not by nature divine and must receive the gift of divinity, the immortal flame, from the gods. The Chaga way holds that humanity *is* by nature divine, created with the spark of that immortal flame already within a mortal frame. Two choices for the soul's high adventure are, then, presented to us: If we follow the path of Prometheus, then our spiritual quest will lead us to those special places from which we may "steal" our spiritual identity—a god, a church, a doctrine, a book, a guru. But if we take Murile's path, we will find our sacredness in the midst of our everyday life, for we already have the spark of divinity within us; we need only recognize that this is so. And in return for this fire gift:

◎◎ "What must be paid to him?" the villagers asked.

"Let one man bring a cow, another a goat, another whatever he may have in his storehouse," the Moon-chief declared.

So the villagers went to fetch all these things, and Murile became a rich man. He stayed for some years at the Moon-chief's great village and married wives and had children, and his flocks and herds increased greatly. But in the end a longing for his home came over him.

So Murile dispatched birds as messengers to sing to his family of the impending return of their prodigal son. Then he took leave of his friends and of his wives, who were to stay with their own people, but his cattle and his boys came with him.

It was a long march to the place of descent from the heaven land to the earth, and Murile began to grow very tired. Now, there was a fine bull in the herd, who walked beside Murile all the way. Suddenly he spoke, saying, "As you are so weary, what will you do for me if I let you ride me? If I take you on my back, will you eat my flesh when they kill me?"

"No!" Murile answered. "I will never eat you."

So the bull let him get on his back and carried him home. And Murile sang as he rode along.

So he came home. And his father and mother ran out to meet him and anointed him with mutton fat, as is the custom when a loved one comes home from distant parts. And his brothers and everyone rejoiced and wondered greatly when they saw the cattle. But Murile showed his father the great bull that had carried him and said, "This bull must be fed and cared for till he is old. And even if you kill him when he is old, I will never eat of his flesh." So they lived quite happily for a time.

But when the bull had become very old, Murile's father slaughtered him. The mother foolishly thought it such a pity that her son, who had always taken so much trouble over the beast, should have none of the beef when everyone else was eating it. So she took a piece of fat and hid it in a pot. When she knew that all the meat was finished, she ground some grain and cooked the fat with the meal and gave it to her son. As soon as he had tasted it, the fat spoke and said to him. "Do you dare to eat me, who carried you on my back? You shall be eaten, as you are eating me!"

Then Murile sang, "Oh, my mother, I said to you, 'Do not give me to eat of the bull's flesh!' " He took a second taste, and his foot sank into the ground. He sang the same words again, while continuing to eat the food his mother had given him. As soon as he had swallowed the food, the ground opened further to swallow Murile, and he disappeared. ◎◎

To the astonished delight of his family, Murile returns from apparent death, riding the bull of heaven, symbolic of the dead and resurrected god of which he himself has now become the personification. The bull's question to Murile, "Will you eat my flesh when they kill me?" is both an invitation and a warning, like that given to Adam and Eve about the forbidden fruit or that posed by Pandora's box. Of course the fruit will be eaten, the box opened, and the bull's flesh consumed. For there is no knowledge to be gained, no adventure undertaken if the injunction is obeyed. Partaking of his first, and last, sacramental meal, Murile, the man-god, is swallowed whole by the earth, replanted deep in the mystery from which his birth plant arose. The living fruit and presence of divinity are now removed to the underworld of their roots, the further reaches of the human unconscious, where like a jewel in a closed lotus, this divine presence sits awaiting our recognition and its recovery.

4

THE SOUL'S
HIGH ADVENTURE

The world invisible is viewed,
the world intangible touched,
the world unknown known,
and the world inapprehensible clutched.

E. B. IDOWU

Once the lure of the quest has been followed, the guardians of the threshold toppled, the ogres and obstacles of the way overcome, the belly of the beast braved—once all these extraordinary challenges have been met and mastered, the African hero's greatest journey still lies ahead. Until this point the hero's aims have been chiefly on the earth and underground or underwater. Symbolically, this means that we, as the hero, have awakened to our life's adventure; we have encountered and surpassed the hindrances on our way; and we have gone into the dim recesses of our own unconscious for the rebirth of courage from fear, hope from despair, and faith from misgivings. To what more can we aspire? African mythology reminds us that while we have thus valiantly conquered the kingdoms of the earth and the underworlds, we have still neglected the celestial sphere. This home of the gods is the apex of the hero's journey, a metaphor for the province of human spirituality—the site of the soul's highest adventure.

The ultimate journey of the African hero, like the heroes of all times, is a spiritual quest. Myth, of course, represents this quest as an outward journey to a far-off heavenly realm, populated by a single great god or by a constellation of gods and goddesses amidst whom the spiritual hero seeks his fate. But in truth, there is no heaven "out there;" the kingdom of heaven is "in here," within each human being, and the task of the true spiritual hero is to find it by traveling deep within. Nor are there any larger-than-life men and women stepping lightly above the clouds, keeping track of every human move; the many gods and goddesses of myth are "in here," too, as different aspects of our own divine nature. The task of the spiritual hero is to meet these gods and goddesses and realize that divinity within.

The Solar and Lunar Voyages

The human spirit can be described as the ultimate source of our being, everlasting and indestructible, beyond the limits of space, time, and mortality to which our body and mind are bound. The search for this ultimate source is a common theme of African myths, where it is often depicted as a hero's journey to one of the two most immediate objects of the heavens—the sun or the moon.

Every twenty-eight days the moon goes through a cycle of waxing and waning, its reflected light dying and being reborn; the moon, then, is the *mortal* celestial orb that reflects the light of an *immortal* sun. Journey to the sun, and you symbolically venture to the light of the eternal mystery of being; journey to the moon, and the symbolism takes you to the reflection of this eternal light in a body that dies and is resurrected.

A Chaga myth, for instance, tells of Kyazimba, a poor man who journeyed to the sun to seek his fate[1]:

◎◎ A very poor man named Kyazimba set out in desperation for the land where the sun rises. And he had traveled long and grown tired and was simply standing, looking hopelessly in the direction of his search, when he heard someone approaching from behind. He turned and saw a decrepit little woman. She came up and wished to know his business. When he had told her, she wrapped her garment around him, and soaring from the earth, transported him to the zenith, where the sun pauses in the middle of the day. Then with a mighty din a great company of men came from the east to that place, and in the midst of them was a brilliant chieftain who, when he had arrived, slaughtered an ox and sat down to feast. The old woman asked his help for Kyazimba. The chieftain blessed the man and sent him home. And it is recorded that he lived in prosperity ever after. ◎◎

Kyazimba is a hero at the nadir of his quest, tired and lost, but he is assisted by the familiar crone who provides magical aid for his passage to the abode of the sun and then intercedes on his behalf with the sun chieftain. As a result, Kyazimba reaches his goal and receives the highest spiritual boon: direct knowledge of the divine presence, and nourishment and blessing at his side. He returns, a renewed and rewarded man.

Despite his poverty, the ease of Kyazimba's passage to the sun is indicative of his fitness and readiness for such a reward. The hero who reaches for such heights prematurely or inappropriately may be rewarded less amply. Another Chaga myth, for instance, tells of a poor man armed with a bow and arrow, who sets off to shoot the sun, depicted here as a king, named Iruwa.[2] The man is angry over the death of his children, which he blames on Iruwa, the sun. Hunted down by Iruwa's lieutenants, the fellow is brought before the shining king, who dares him to let fly his arrow. He wisely makes the opposite choice, bowing in sorrow, instead; only then does Iruwa allow him to return to earth and over the years grants him other children and good fortune.

Sacred Union

Figure 4. A seated couple from the Dogon of Mali, symbolic of the first ancestors from whom all of creation flowed.

Union with the infinite source of being, enlightenment through direct experience of the godhead—these are the pinnacles of the soul's high adventure, captured symbolically in the spiritual hero's journey. African mythology frequently depicts this spiritual union in sexual terms as the marriage between a hero and a goddess or between a heroine and a god. Females and males symbolize all the pairs of opposites—light and dark, good and evil, positive and negative, north and south, east and west—that came into being with the created universe. The hero's union with the goddess or the heroine's with the god, then, represents a passage beyond these limiting forms of the ordinary world to the inseparable unity that is their source.

The "Unwanted Suitor" is a familiar, worldwide form of this story of the sacred union, told here in a myth from the Rwanda of East Africa.[3]

◎◎ There was a certain woman of Rwanda, the wife of Kwisaba. Her husband went away to the wars and was absent for many months. One day while she was all alone in the hut, she fell ill and found herself too weak and wretched to get up and make a fire, which would have been done for her at once had anyone been present. She cried out, talking wildly in her despair: "Oh, what shall I do? If only I had someone to split the kindling wood and build the fire! I shall die of cold if no one comes! Oh, if someone would but come—if it were the very Thunder of heaven himself."

So the woman spoke, scarcely knowing what she said, and presently a little cloud appeared in the sky. She could not see it, but very soon it spread; other clouds collected, till the sky was quite overcast. It grew dark as night inside the hut, and she heard thunder rumbling in the distance. Then there came a flash of lightning close by, and she saw the Thunder standing before her in the likeness of a man, with a little bright ax in his hand. He fell to and had split all the wood in a twinkling; then he built it up and lit it just with a touch of his hand, as if his fingers had been torches. When the blaze leapt up he turned to the woman and said, "Now, O wife of Kwisaba, what will you give me?" She was quite paralyzed with fright and could not utter a word. He gave her a little time to recover, and then went on, "When your baby is born, if it is a girl, will you give her to me for a wife?" Trembling all over, the poor woman could only stammer out, "Yes!" and the Thunder vanished.

Not long after this a baby girl was born, who grew into a fine healthy child and was given the name of Miseke. When Kwisaba came home from the wars, the women met him with the news that he had a little daughter, and he was delighted, partly perhaps with the thought of the cattle he would get as her bride-price when she was old enough to be married. But when his wife told him about the Thunder, he looked very serious and said, "When she grows older, you must never on any account let her go outside the house, or we shall have the Thunder carrying her off." ◎◎

The beginnings of this tale hint at a virgin birth, suggested by Kwisaba's long absence, the appearance of the Thunder god as a man "with a little bright ax in his hand," the mother's desire for someone to "light her fire," and the birth of a girl-child, Miseke, capable of miraculous feats, as we next see, not long after the Thunder god's retreat. Here the father's principal concern is with the bride-price his daughter will eventually bring, while the mother has already committed her daughter to the spiritual life she herself has tasted, however briefly, through her miraculous visit with the Thunder god. One approach to this myth, then, is to look at how it sets up the competing aims of a spiritually fulfilled and a worldly fulfilled life, with the young child symbolic of a soul torn between the dominant voice of worldly aims (the father) and the quieter, acquiescent voice of spiritual intentions (the mother). The story proceeds:

◎◎ So as long as Miseke was quite little, she was allowed to play outdoors with the other children, but the time came all too soon when she had to be shut up inside the hut. One day some of the other girls came running to Miseke's mother in great excitement. "Miseke is dropping beads out of her mouth! We thought she had put them in on purpose, but they come dropping out every time she laughs." Sure enough, the mother found that it was so, and not only did Miseke produce beads of the kinds most valued, but beautiful brass and copper bangles. Miseke's father was greatly troubled when they told him of this. He said it must be the Thunder who sent the beads in this extraordinary way as the presents that a man always has to send to his betrothed while she is growing up. So Miseke had always to stay indoors and amuse herself as best she could—when she was not helping in the housework—by plaiting mats and making baskets. Sometimes her old playmates came to see her, but they too did not care to be shut up for long in a dark, stuffy hut. ◎◎

Mythologies throughout the world never tire of the tale of the lovely maiden unwillingly sequestered in her castle by a tyrannical parent, awaiting rescue by a soon-to-arrive prince or god. This Rwandan tale varies little from these other plots but is simply fabricated in an African design. If the maiden is worthy, she will find release from this false imprisonment, for the walls of her incarceration—be they the stone slabs of a castle or the thin thatching of a hut—stand for the false views we hold of ourself, blocking access to the more ennobling aspects of our soul. Miseke's emancipation comes when she is fifteen and she succumbs to the entreaties of her girlfriends, who are on their way to dig potting clay in a riverbed:

◎◎ The temptation was too great, and she slipped out very quietly and went with them to the river where the white clay was to be found. So many people had gone there at different times for the same purpose that quite a large pit had been dug out. The girls got into it and fell to work, laughing and chattering, when suddenly they became aware that it was growing dark, and looking up, they saw a great black cloud gathering overhead.

Instantly, the figure of a man stood before them, and he called out in a great voice, "Where is Miseke, daughter of Kwisaba?" One girl came out of the clay pit and said, "I am not Miseke, daughter of Kwisaba. When Miseke laughs, beads and bangles drop from her lips." The Thunder said, "Well, then, laugh, and let me see." She laughed, and nothing happened. "No, I see you are not she." So one after another was questioned and sent on her way. Miseke herself came last and tried to pass, repeating the same words that the others had said, but the Thunder insisted on her laughing, and a shower of beads fell on the ground. So the Thunder caught her up, carried her off to the sky, and married her.

Of course she was terribly frightened, but the Thunder proved a kind husband, and she settled down quite happily, in due time bearing three children, two boys and a girl. When the baby girl was a few weeks old, Miseke told her husband that she would like to go home and see her parents. He not only consented but provided her with cattle, beer (as provision for the journey), presents for her family, and carriers for her hammock, sending her down to earth with this parting advice: "Keep to the high road; do not turn aside into any unfrequented bypath." ◎◎

On one level, this myth is an initiatory tale about the feminine passage from childhood into womanhood and motherhood. Here we notice that the important Rwandan signs and symbols of this passage are relevant to many African cultures: the arrangement of a marriage while the woman is still an infant; the seclusion of a menstruating woman in a hut; the importance of the dowry (bride-price); the terror of womanhood yielding to the joys and gifts of motherhood.

Yet we would miss the true mythic wisdom within this tale if we read it only in this way, for it merits a spiritual reading as well. As a pubescent girl, Miseke reveals herself to the god, despite the precautions of her parents, and he spirits her off in matrimony to his abode. If the heroine (or hero) of the spiritual quest is fully capable of assimilating the powers of the transcendent realm to which she has passed, then the marriage will bestow bliss; if, however, she has risen too quickly to these heights—through guile, impudence, vanity, or zeal—then the marriage will be fiendish, and the god will turn into a demon, a sorcerer, or a brute. The Chaga, for example, tell of a girl who refused to marry, until her eyes caught sight of a beautiful young man at a village sword dance, "wearing a broad ring like a halo round his head, who drew all eyes by his grace and nobility."[4] She ultimately was betrothed to this handsome lad, only to discover on leaving sight of her village with him that he was a *rimu* (werewolf). Miseke's marriage was congenial despite its frightful start. Still, an adventure awaited her, for she did not "Keep to the high road."

◎◎ Being unacquainted with the country, Miseke's carriers soon strayed from the main track. After they had gone for some distance along the wrong road, they found the path barred by a strange monster called an *igikoko,* who demanded something to eat. Miseke told the servants to give him the beer they were carrying, and he drank all the pots dry in no time. Then he seized one of the carriers and ate him, then a second—in short, he devoured them all, as well as the cattle, till no one was left but Miseke and her children. The ogre then demanded a child. Seeing no help for it, Miseke gave him the younger boy and then, driven to the extreme, the baby she was nursing, but while he was thus engaged, she contrived to send off the older boy, whispering to him to run till he came to a house. "If you see an old man sitting on the ash heap in the front yard, that will be your grandfather; if you see some young men shooting arrows at a mark, they will be your uncles; the boys herding the cows are your cousins; and you will find your grandmother inside the hut. Tell them to come and help us."

The boy set off, while his mother kept off the ogre as best she could. He arrived at his grandfather's homestead and told them what had happened. Immediately, they left in search of Miseke. When they found her, the young men rushed in and killed the ogre with their spears. Before he died he said, "If you cut off my big toe you will get back everything belonging to you." They did so, and behold! Out came the carriers and the cattle, the servants and the children, none of them any the worse. ◎◎

Miseke returns to a great welcome at her parents' house, but the time passes quickly and soon she begins to think of returning to the god realm from which she has come:

◎◎ The old people sent out for cattle and all sorts of presents, as is the custom when a guest is going to leave. Everything was gotten together outside the village, and her brothers were ready to escort her when they saw the clouds gathering, and behold! All of a sudden Miseke, her children, her servants, her cattle, and her porters, with their loads, were all taken up into the air and disappeared. The family was struck with awe, and they never saw Miseke on earth again. ◎◎

Miseke must bring the fruits of her accomplishment, the gifts of her ascension to the realm of divinity, symbolized by her children, back to the ordinary world. She encounters and conquers the same kinds of challenges on this return journey that are ordinarily found at the beginning of the heroic quest: the threshold guardian is vanquished, the belly of the beast split open, and the gifts delivered to a waiting people. But Miseke's fate is not to dwell in the ordinary world forever; she is destined to return to the heaven land.

Miseke's return journey represents the challenge faced by anyone who has received the boon of a penetrating insight, life-changing revelation, deeply significant dream, or profound personal experience: how do you now return with this gift to your everyday world?

I have completed several silent, ten-day Buddhist retreats where the daily schedule involves nearly twelve hours of sitting in meditation. With the pain from sore knees, a mind clamoring for release from what sometimes seems like endless monotony, the troubling personal insights that arise, and all these punctuated by periods of utter tranquillity, equanimity, and release, such retreats are a kind of heroic inner journey complete with threshold guardians, the beast's belly, major battles to be fought, and indescribable episodes of rapture and bliss. The final day of the retreat is transitional, with optional meditation periods and talking permitted, and I am often seized with anger as I feel the world I left slowly engulfing the splendor I have found. Driving away, I have more than once pulled over to the side of the road and cried with remorse at the prospect of giving up the miracle-child of my labors to the ogre of an insane world awaiting me at home. And once home, I have watched—first with regret, then with resignation—as the sacred gift slowly decays to a fraction of what it was, and I, like Miseke, long again for the heaven country, promising myself that next time I will do better to shield my child of wonder from the gluttonous clutches of the world.

Sex Roles and Mythology

Mythology allots different roles to the sexes. Simply stated, the mythological assignment of the female is to surrender to the energies of nature that inform all life and that she herself manifests through her body and being, best exemplified in the form of her monthly menses. The mythological problem of the male, however, is to acquire knowledge and experience of these source energies of life, which he does not naturally command through his body. So, when confronted with a sacred union in mythology, heroines are found struggling *with* the gods they acquire (surrender), while heroes are found struggling *for* the goddesses they desire (acquisition).

This difference between the male and female is clearly indicated in the Dagara practice of "speaking" to a child in the womb—a ritual performed to welcome the new soul into the world and determine its name.[5] Male children are addressed in utero three times, but female children are spoken to four times. The first question to both determines the sex of the child; the next two questions ascertain what former soul is making its reentrance into the world and what life purpose this soul now carries; but the fourth question, reserved only for a female child, is addressed to the additional body of life she carries in her being, the potential for bringing new life into the world when she is of age.

Acquiring the goddess as a symbolic form of spiritual union is the theme of one of a cycle of myths about Kintu, a legendary culture hero of the Baganda people of Uganda and an important figure in that country's history. Prior to him, it is said, the land was populated only by a handful of isolated, autonomous clans whom Kintu subdued and brought together into a nation. Well into the twentieth century, the royal family of Uganda traced their lineage back more than a thousand years to Kintu. In the story that follows, the supreme god, Gulu, tests Kintu's worthiness to marry his daughter.[6]

◎◎ When Kintu first came to Uganda, there were no food sources to be found, and he brought with him only one cow off which he lived. In time, Nambi, the daughter of Gulu, descended to earth and fell in love with Kintu, whom she wished to marry. Gulu was suspicious of the idea of his daughter marrying this earth man and determined to judge for himself Kintu's worthiness. So he ordered Kintu's food cow stolen, and the hero nearly starved to death until his beloved Nambi showed him what herbs he could substitute for food. Though she returned to heaven with her suitor, Gulu ordered a further test, so food enough for a hundred people was prepared and brought to Kintu, who was told that unless he ate it all, he would meet his death. Failure to consume the prodigious portion would prove that he was not the great Kintu and thus was not worthy of the goddess's hand. Initially at a loss to meet this challenge, Kintu soon discovered a deep hole in the floor of his guesthouse; there he dumped all the prepared feast, then covered his ruse with dirt; once again Gulu was thwarted.

But Gulu still would not relent. Handing Kintu a copper ax, Gulu ordered him to chop firewood from a rock, for the god remarked that he used no ordinary manner of kindling. Kintu examined the rock closely and discovered Gulu's trick. Hitting the rock with an ax would only produce sparks, but gently flaking off pieces would satisfy his inquisitor's request. With each successful test Gulu became more determined, so then he ordered Kintu to fill his water pot not from a well but from dew only; this too the equally determined hero accomplished.

"You are a wonderful being," said Gulu. "Go pick out of my herd the cow I took from you, and you can then marry my daughter."

This task, however, proved more difficult than all the rest, for in Gulu's vast herd there were many cows that looked like Kintu's. But Kintu unexpectedly received help from a bee who whispered in his ear, "When you see me alight on the horns of a cow, you will know it to be yours."

In this way, Kintu correctly chose his cow from all the others, and an incredulous Gulu finally yielded, saying, "You are truly Kintu, a clever man whom no one can ever deceive or rob. Take my daughter who loves you, marry her and carry her back to earth." ◎◎

Kintu's trials illustrate the difference between the hero and heroine on the sacred journey, for Kintu must struggle with Gulu's tests of his fitness for the sacred bride. A similar fate awaits the son of Kimanaueze in the Ambundu tale that follows. As we have seen, there are two Kimanauezes in Ambundu legend, father and son; the one described here is the junior, the father of Sudika-mbambi whose escapades we followed in Chapter 3.[7]

◎◎ I often tell of Kimanaueze, who begat a male child. The child grew up, and he came to the age of marrying. His father said, "Marry." He said, "I will not marry a woman of the earth."

His father asked, "Then whom will you marry?"

He answered, "If it must be, I shall marry the daughter of Lord Sun and Lady Moon."

But everyone asked, "Who can go to the sky where the daughter of Lord Sun and Lady Moon lives?"

He simply said, "I, indeed, I want her. If it is anyone on earth, I will not marry her." ◎◎

The sun, we recall, is symbolic of the eternal light of the godhead, while the moon is symbolic of the reflection of this eternal flame in a body that is born and dies. A child of this parentage, then, is fully conscious of both its eternity and its destiny, its sacredness and its profaneness, its immortality and its mortality, its humanity and its divinity; and he who weds this child will also become one with this unified consciousness. Of course, such a union is not easily won; the sages and saints of all ages have labored mightily to achieve this realization of divinity while still within the human form. Kimanaueze's first challenge is to discover how to communicate his love to a goddess who lives in heaven, and he undertakes to do this in a letter to the Sun King and Moon Queen, expressing his intentions. Getting the letter to heaven is another matter. He gives it to Antelope, who says:

◎◎ "I cannot go to the sky." He gave the letter to Hawk. Hawk, too, said, "I cannot go to the sky." He gave it to Vulture, but Vulture said, "I can go halfway to the sky, but all the way I cannot go."

Finally the young man said, "How shall I do it?" He put the letter away and was quiet.

One day Frog came and sought out the son of Kimanaueze and spoke to him.

"Young master," he said, "give me the letter that I may take it."

But the young master said, "Begone! If those who have wings gave up, how can you say, 'I will go there'? How can you get there?"

Frog said, "Young master, I am equal to the task."

So the son of Kimanaueze gave Frog the letter, saying, "If you cannot get there and you return with it, I shall give you a thrashing." ◎◎

Do we not hear in the early stanzas of this tale a familiar theme found also in European lore: how a lowly frog emerged from the murky depths of its accustomed existence, not to raise a golden ball for a princess, as the brothers Grimm told it in "The Frog Prince," but to raise a golden letter for a prince? Like crocodiles, sea monsters, water snakes, or other denizens of the watery abyss, frogs symbolize the dynamism of this underwater-unconscious realm—but unlike their monstrous kin, frogs are benign, and when their force is trusted by the willing heroine or hero, she is led to her prince and he to his queen. As amphibious creatures, frogs also represent transformation: from the solid ground of the familiar (marrying someone in the usual way) to the fluid realm of adventure (seeking union with one's highest ideal). The frog in this tale functions as a Paraclete—a mediator between body and spirit, a messenger between the realms of humanity and divinity, a guide for the soul's great adventure.

◎◎ Frog knew that the people of the Sun and Moon's kingdom daily fetched water from a certain earthly well. So he put young Kimanaueze's letter in his mouth, hopped into this well, and floated there quietly, awaiting the heavenly water carriers. When their water jug was dipped into the well, Frog plopped into the jug, and the water carriers were none the wiser. Thus, Frog arrived in heaven, and when the jug was laid down inside a room of water jugs in the royal household, he jumped free and spat out the letter conspicuously on a nearby table.

After some time, the Sun King himself wandered into the water room and, noticing the letter on the table, inquired of the people of this realm whence it had come. But not one of his subjects knew. So he opened the letter and began to read:

> I, the son of Na Kimanaueze Kia-Tumb'a Ndala, a man of earth, want to marry the daughter of Lord Sun and Lady Moon. . . .

Lord Sun thought in his heart, "Na Kimanaueze lives on earth; I am a man who lives in the sky. Who came here with this letter, then?" He put the letter into his box and said nothing.

Frog, meanwhile, had been hiding in a corner, and once the Sun King completed reading the letter he hopped back into the jug again. In due course, the water was emptied from this jug, and the water carriers took it back to earth to be refilled. When the empty jug was lowered into the well, Frog promptly dove back under the water, hiding there until the water carriers concluded their rounds.

Then Frog came out of the water and went back to his home, where he kept quiet and said nothing. When many days had passed, the son of Kimanaueze asked Frog, "My friend, where did you take the letter, and how?"

Frog answered, "Master, I delivered the letter, but they have not yet returned an answer."

The son of Kimanaueze said, "O man, you are telling a lie; you did not go there."

Frog said, "Master, I did travel there, you shall see."

After six days, the son of Kimanaueze again wrote a letter, saying, "I wrote to you, Lord Sun and Lady Moon. My letter was delivered but you returned no answer whatsoever to me." He sealed the letter, and gave it to Frog. Frog put the letter into his mouth, got back into the water, and squatted on the bottom.

Once again he was transported via the water carriers to the kingdom of Lord Sun and Lady Moon, and as before he spat out Kimanaueze's letter on the table for Lord Sun.

Lord Sun asked the water carriers if they had carried the letter with them.

"No, master," they replied.

Then doubt possessed Lord Sun. He laid the letter down and wrote to the son of Kimanaueze, saying:

> You who send me letters about marrying my daughter: I agree, on condition you appear in person, with your wooing present, so that I may know you.

When he finished writing, he folded the letter, laid it on the table, and went away. Frog now came out of the corner and took the letter. He put it in his mouth and entered the jug. Again, the water carriers descended to earth by climbing down the cord of Spider. Frog delivered the letter to the young master. ◉◉

Here a symbol that is particularly significant in African mythology has been quietly slipped into the plot—namely, the "cord of Spider." The spider figures in many African myths, and its web, like the World Tree, is frequently the connecting link between earth and heaven, the conveyance by which humanity ascends to divinity and divinity descends to humanity. The water carriers of this tale use this celestial spiderweb for traveling to and from the earthly water well; the water they collect thus represents the Water of Life, here meaning spiritual life, and the well symbolizes the World Axis, that central point of contact between the realm of the spirit and that of the flesh, as Bethlehem is for Christians, Jerusalem for Jews, Mecca for Muslims, and the Bodhi tree in Bodhgaya for Buddhists.

Now, our Frog, you will recall, has just returned from Lord Sun with the first real message for young Kimanaueze, who is pleased to learn of the Sun's response to his supplications. Next follows a series of negotiations over the bride-price to be paid for the daughter of the Sun and Moon, with the discussions mediated always by the "shuttle diplomacy" of Frog. The Sun dropped his request for Kimanaueze to appear before him, for he knew that eventually he would meet his daughter's suitor when the young man came to take her home. When the expected gifts have been given and the required bride-price paid, Frog reports to young Kimanaueze:

◎◎ "Young master, I gave them the wooing present, and they accepted it. They cooked me a young hog, and I ate it. Now, you yourself shall choose the day to fetch the bride home."

The son of Kimanaueze said, "Very well." Then twelve days elapsed.

Now the son of Kimanaueze spoke to Frog: "I need people to fetch the bride for me, but I cannot find them. All those to whom I speak say, 'We cannot go to the sky.' Now what shall I do, Frog?"

Frog said, "My young master, rest easily; I shall find a way to go and bring her home for you."

But the son of Kimanaueze said, "You cannot do that. You could indeed carry the letters, but bring the bride home—that you are unable to do."

But Frog again said, "Young master, be at ease; do not be troubled for I will be able to go and bring her home. Do not despair."

Frog soon arrived at the well, where he hid. After a while, the water carriers appeared and dipped their jugs in the water. When they had filled them, they went back to the Sun's house unknowingly carrying Frog with them. When the sun had set and it was evening, Frog left the room of the water jugs and went in search of the Sun's daughter. He found her asleep, so quickly, he first took out one of her eyes and then the other. These he tied up in a handkerchief and went back to the room where the jugs were.

In the morning, all the people got up, but not the daughter of Lord Sun.

"My eyes are closed," she told her parents; "I cannot see."

So Lord Sun called for two messengers and said to them, "Go to Ngombo the diviner to find out why my child cannot see."

Now the messengers did not tell Ngombo anything about the situation; they simply said, "We have come for a divination."

Ngombo looked into his paraphernalia and said, "Disease has brought you; a young woman is sick. She cannot see."

The messengers said, "This is true; now tell us what caused the ailment."

Ngombo looked again and said, "She is not yet married. She is only chosen. The one who would wed her has sent a spell, saying, 'My wife, let her come; if she does not come, she shall die.' You, who came for my divination, go, bring her to her husband, that she may escape death."

The messengers agreed and went immediately to Lord Sun with Ngombo's words.

"All right," said Lord Sun. "Let us sleep. Tomorrow evening they shall take her down to the earth."

Frog, still hiding in the water room, heard all that was said.

The next morning, Frog got into a jug and let the water carriers transport him to earth in the usual manner. Upon his arrival he hurried to find the son of Kimanaueze. "O young master!" said Frog. "Your bride will come to you today."

The son of Kimanaueze said, "Begone, man, you are a liar."

Frog answered, "Master, this is the truth itself. This evening I will bring her to you."

Meanwhile, the Sun told Spider, "Weave a large web down to earth, for today my daughter will be taken there." As the sun began to set, the Sun had his daughter taken down to the earth. His ministers left her at the well and then returned to the sky.

Frog found the young woman at the well and said to her, "I will be your guide. Let us go immediately so that I can bring you to your husband." Then Frog returned her eyes to her, and they started toward the house of the son of Kimanaueze. When they got there, Frog exclaimed, "O young master! Your bride's here."

The son of Kimanaueze said, "Mainu the Frog, I should never have doubted you."

And so the son of Kimanaueze married the daughter of Lord Sun and Lady Moon, and they lived on. ◎◎

At the conclusion of this tale, divinity has been enticed to descend down the World Axis to meet humanity. The goddess, with her eyes removed, is, so to speak, blinded by love. She, then, comes to the son of Kimanaueze out of love for his humanity, while he reaches for her out of love for her divinity; and the two marry, thus becoming whole. The symbolism of such a marriage is plain: the most sacred union is that which brings the seeker (the younger Kimanaueze) into oneness with both his immortality and his mortality (the daughter of the Sun and Moon). But the implications are profound: in the midst of the vicissitudes of ordinary life, you must wed yourself to what is eternal. And this quest for the eternal, this spiritual journey, the African myth tells us, does not mean leaving one's humanity but going fully and deeply into it. "God's place" is not to be found in a faraway land at a faraway time but here, now, within the human condition. Divinity will come to the earnest seeker: through the window of the ordinary, look out on the transcendent; amidst the profane, discover the sacred; through mortality, reach immortality; look without or within and find God. This is the enduring legacy of the soul's high adventure, as read in African mythology, and this is the promise of the soul's great reward.

5

THE HEART OF THE
SACRED WARRIOR

I have seen in the sky things unseen which I could not divulge.

MWINDO, THE NYAŊGA WARRIOR

Warriors march along the razor's edge. They tread a treacherous path between the considered use of deadly force and the indiscriminate slaughter of lives; between destroying obstacles to the well-being of self and society and raging berserk in the midst of battle; between fearlessness in the face of death and recklessness for life itself. The noble warrior also answers a call that neither begins nor ends with the bugle of the battlefield but is the trumpet of the soul, sounding a higher note of loyalty to an ideal, a cause, a god, or a nation.

Yet in today's world, the warrior spirit is largely scorned, for too often we have seen the dark side of its force. From the violence of nationalism, to terrorism, to abuse perpetrated in even the most elegant homes, the bells toll for those caught in the rampage of the warrior spirit gone amok.

Some claim the warrior spirit is a bastard of patriarchy, an aberration of masculinity, and they would emasculate both its swagger and sway. Yet this may be neither possible nor desirable, for the roots of the warrior spirit run deeper than the politics of gender, and it may not be ours to eradicate of our own choosing. If you've ever seen a lion stalking its prey, an eagle diving for a salmon, an orca hunting a seal, or even looked under a microscope and seen the killer T cells of the human immune system attacking a foreign organism, then you have glimpsed the warrior spirit. Similar actions occur millions of times each moment on an infinite number of levels in the natural world, and each action brings about death in the service of life. This is where the warrior spirit moves, in the inescapable dance of death yielding to life yielding to death again. This is where that spirit is rooted: in the primal law that everywhere, without exception, life is sustained by consuming other life. The warrior does not turn away in denial or disgust from this essential vulgarity and violence; instead, the warrior marches in harmony with this eternal rhythm of life.

The Thonga of Mozambique, for example, ask their warriors and hunters to align deeply with this elemental cycle of life before departing for the battle or the hunt. Just as menstruating women are set apart, both warrior and hunter are separated from the rest of society and undergo ritual transformations, allowing them to establish a sacred covenant with the wild animals they either wish to emulate (warriors) or to kill (hunters). Once returned, the warrior and hunter are not considered normal; instead, they are "hot" beings, still living in the accelerated time of the pursuit and the kill. In order to reenter everyday society, warriors and hunters must first undergo a "cooling-off" period that involves additional rites and further seclusion.[1]

We long ago ceased hearing the call of the ancient warrior spirit amidst the din of ever-expanding civilization. Supermarkets now stamp and date the products of a mechanized hunt and kill, packaging them for our consumption but making it even harder to contemplate our participation in the cycle of death nourishing life. Similarly, mass media now stamp and date the exploits of the modern warrior, packaging them for our consumption in such sanitizing terms as *body counts, surgical strikes,* and *collateral damage.* Perhaps it is because we are so alienated from the true warrior spirit that the decisive use of force has now become the mindless, mind-boggling violence seen daily in the world. Our young men and women have few models to emulate, even fewer rites or myths to fall back on, save those of the television and motion-picture screen where the message of the sacred cycle of death and life is more often a banal litany of gratuitous violence in order to advance a plot. In this vacuum, African mythology of the sacred warrior might be of some aid, for through absorbing tales of the warrior's remarkable deeds and of his agonizing struggles with life and death, we might find a way back to the warrior spirit within ourselves. Then we might come to understand, as this mythology so clearly shows, that the warrior's greatest battle is not with forces outside himself but with those within.

Epic of a Sacred Warrior

Epics like those of Homer are counted among the oldest treasures of the Western canon, yet when the literary tide turns toward Africa, few imagine that equivalent forms exist. In fact, African mythology presents many rich epics through which we may explore the ways of the sacred warrior. Almost all these epics come from transcriptions of live performances by African griots, the bards charged with remembering and passing along a society's history and tradition through story and song. The *Epic of Sundiata,* for example, the mythological saga of a warrior-king of the ancient West African kingdom of Mali, is probably the most widely known of these performance epics. Less

well known is *The Mwindo Epic* from the Nyanga of the Democratic Republic of Congo (formerly Zaire). The version of this epic transcribed and translated by Daniel Biebuyck and Kahombo Matene is a book unto itself—a long, marvelously intricate story of the warrior-hero Mwindo and of his deeds and adventures in the realm of ordinary life, in the underworld of death, and in the heaven of the gods. Rarely does a single myth offer such a rich collection of motifs or such a robust telling of the tale. And throughout this epic, presented here abridged and adapted from the original, we follow the warrior's classic struggle between his power to destroy life and his desire to renew life[2]:

Figure 5. Bronze and iron statue of a seated warrior, from Mali.

The Mwindo Epic

EPISODE I:
THE BIRTH OF THE SACRED WARRIOR

A long time ago in the state of Ihimbi, there lived a king named Shemwindo who ruled the village of Tubondo. Shemwindo married seven women, after which he summoned together a council of all his people. There, in the midst of this assembly of juniors and seniors, advisers, counselors, and nobles, Shemwindo decreed, "You my wives must all give birth to girls. Any among you who shall bear a boy, I will kill that child." Then the assembly was dismissed, and Shemwindo hurriedly visited the house of each of his seven wives, planting his seed into each one as they lay together. After several weeks it became known to all that Shemwindo's wives got pregnant from the king's first visit to them.

Now Shemwindo was famed throughout the country, and the birth of his children was eagerly awaited by the villagers of Tubondo. After many months had passed, six of Shemwindo's seven wives gave birth to female children all on the same day. But Nyamwindo, the seventh wife and preferred one, remained inexplicably pregnant and worried what her long gestation might portend.

Then suddenly, strange things began to happen: cut firewood magically appeared at her doorstep; a water jar seemed to fill itself; and raw vegetables turned up on her table. In each case, Nyamwindo felt it was the child still in her womb who was performing these miraculous deeds, but she had no idea how. Meanwhile, the inhabitants of Tubondo began to disdain Nyamwindo for failing to deliver her child. But the child dwelling in the womb of the preferred one meditated to itself: I do not wish to come out the birth canal of my mother, for then others may not understand that I am no ordinary man.

When the pains of childbirth began, old midwives, wives of the counselors, arrived at Nyamwindo's house. But the child dwelling in her womb climbed up into her belly, then farther up toward her shoulder, descending down her arm where it was born through the preferred one's middle finger.

Seeing him wailing on the ground, the old midwives were astonished. "What kind of child is this?" they asked. Others answered in a somber tone, "It's a male child." Then some of the old midwives said that they should announce to the village that a male child was born. Many thought this unwise because Shemwindo would surely kill the baby.

Shemwindo, sitting together with his counselors, heard of the preferred one's delivery and demanded to know, "What child is born there?" But the old midwives, sitting in the house with the child, kept silent. They gave him the name Mwindo, because he was the first male child who followed only female children in order of birth.

Mwindo was born laughing, speaking, and walking, holding a conga-scepter in his right hand and an ax in his left. He was born wearing a little bag of the spirit of Kahindo, the goddess of good fortune, slung across the left side of his back, and in that little bag there was a long rope.*

In the house where the child was born, there was a little cricket perched on the wall. When the cricket heard that the midwives were unwilling to give Shemwindo an answer, it went to Shemwindo and said, "A male child was born to the preferred one today; his name is Mwindo; that is why no one has answered you."

Shemwindo was enraged upon hearing this news. He sharpened his spear on a whetstone and immediately left for the birth hut. But the moment he prepared to throw the spear into the hut, the child shouted from within, "Each time you throw a spear may it end up at the bottom of the house pole; may it never reach me, these old midwives, or my mother."

Shemwindo threw the spear into the house six times, and each time it fell short of its mark. Failing to kill Mwindo, Shemwindo became exhausted and told his counselors they should dig a grave and throw Mwindo into it. The counselors dug the grave, then went to fetch the child. But after being placed in the grave, Mwindo howled, saying, "O my father, this is the death that you will die, but first you will suffer many sorrows." Shemwindo heard the sound of the little castaway and scolded his people, telling them to cover the grave immediately. Fallen plantain stems were fetched and placed over Mwindo; on top of these stems mounds of soil were heaped. Yet as evening fell, a light as bright as the sun shone from Mwindo's grave. Those still sitting outdoors rushed to tell Shemwindo's counselors what they beheld. The counselors returned, but the great heat, like a fire burning from where Mwindo lay, forced them to stand back. Throughout the night they took turns keep-

---

* The *conga-scepter* is a ceremonial switch made from the tail hairs of a buffalo or antelope; in the epic it serves as the hero's magical *bâton de commandement*. Nyanga children use a small ax to cut shrubs and small trees; it is also a symbol associated with male circumcision rites. A magical rope is found throughout African mythology as a symbol connecting the ordinary world of humans with the realm of the gods.

ing a vigil over the child's grave. During the first watch, when the rest of Tubondo was already asleep, Mwindo got out of his grave and crept silently into the house of his mother.

Shemwindo, who was awakened by the sound of a child wailing in the house of the preferred one, crept to her hut and questioned his wife: "Where does this child come from? Did you have another one in your womb?"

"No," she replied, "this child is Mwindo."

Shemwindo left at once to wake up his counselors. "Tomorrow," he ordered, "you will cut a piece from the trunk of a tree; you will carve from it the body of a drum; you will then put the skin of an antelope in the river to soften for the drumhead. You will place this miracle child, Mwindo, in the drum and seal it tightly."

When dawn came, the counselors went to the forest to cut a piece of wood for the shell of the drum. They hollowed the wood, and when they had finished, they went to fetch Mwindo once more. They stuck him into the body of the drum and glued the antelope hide on top.

Shemwindo then summoned two expert divers to throw this drum into the pool where nothing moves, as the entire village looked on. The swimmers entered the pool, and in the middle they released the drum, which quickly sank into the watery depths. ◎◎

The significance of Mwindo's life is announced by the special circumstances of his birth. As with all heroes of great stature, and especially those of spiritual import, Mwindo's legendary life begins with a virgin birth. Not wishing to be identified as the child of a woman, he is born from his mother's middle finger. Now, the Buddha was born from his mother's side; Athena, the patroness of Greek heroes, was born from the head of Zeus; and Dionysus, the god of death and transformation, emerged from Zeus's thigh. Nigerian novelist Tutuola wove this theme into *The Palm-Wine Drinkard* when the protagonist's wife gave birth to a "miracle child" through her thumb.

In these cases, as in all forms of virgin birth, the event marks not the inception of natural human life but the nascence of human spiritual life. This is further confirmed by the appellation Mwindo will soon use in reference to himself, "the little-one-just-born-he-walked." Once again, we find similar childhood résumés for other great spiritual heroes: the Buddha took seven steps at his birth; Abraham, deserted by his mother in a cave, was fed by the angel Gabriel for ten days, whereupon he arose and walked about; and Sudika-mbambi, the Ambundu hero, emerged from his mother's womb talking and walking. Mwindo, the hero-child, is not young physically, but he is young spiritually, for he is just at the beginning of his spiritual odyssey. In sum, then, we can read of Mwindo's birth and ask ourselves, "Am I ready to be born into my spiritual life?" Here, "spiritual life" is not restricted to a series of dogmas, set of beliefs, or suite of actions; rather, it refers to a life in continual alignment with a source of renewal and revivification.

Mwindo is also born under the cloud of his father's edict that all male newborns will be killed. This is a familiar Judeo-Christian theme: Abraham, common patriarch of Muslims, Jews, and Christians, was born under an injunction by the astrologer-king Nimrod to kill all male children, and Moses, after him, was born at the time of a similar pharaonic decree to kill all male Hebrew children. But legends of the jealous king or father mandating the death of potential newborn male challengers to his sovereignty spread wider still: from Babylonia, one of the oldest recorded hero myths concerns the birth of Sargon the First, who was placed as an infant in a vessel of reeds, sealed with pitch, and set adrift down the Tigris, while the great Hindu epic *The Mahabharata* tells of the hero Karni, placed by a fearful mother in a basket of reeds sealed with wax. Otto Rank, the Freudian psychologist, in his 1909 book entitled *The Myth of the Birth of the Hero,* cites no fewer than twenty myths worldwide that turn on this theme of the castigation and banishment of the child-hero.[3] But let us return to Mwindo, sealed in a drum by his jealous and fearful father, then set upon the river:

◎◎ Mwindo moaned inside the drum, stuck his ear to the drumhead, listened attentively, and said resolutely to himself, "I would not be Mwindo if I simply floated. My father, and the others, they will hear the sound of my voice again." And with those words, the drum arose unassisted from the sandy river bottom and floated to the surface of the water, remaining fixed at one point in the middle of the pool where nothing moves.

When a group of maidens came to draw water from the river, they saw Mwindo's drum turning round and round in the middle of the pool, and they heard him singing of his father's perfidy. The frightened women scurried up the riverbank and ran back to the village. When news of the sighting reached Shemwindo, he too was in disbelief; he again assembled all his people, who headed for the river armed with spears, arrows, and fire torches. Mwindo waited until the residents of Tubondo had gathered along the river's edge, then he threw sweet words of song into his mouth:

> I am saying farewell to Shemwindo—
> oh, you ungrateful people, do you think I shall die?
> The counselors abandoned Shemwindo.
> He who appears to die but actually will be safe,
> he is going to encounter Iyangura.

When Mwindo finished this ode of farewell, the drum sank once more below the surface of the pool, and Shemwindo and the other villagers returned to Tubondo with an overwhelming sense of dread.

Iyangura, Shemwindo's sister, had married one Mukiti, a huge underwater serpent, described in the epic as the master of the unfathomable realm. Yet it is she whom Mwindo turns to for help with his rescue. Iyangura, the hero's aunt, represents the benign, compassionate Mother, a humanizing, life-affirming force in the warrior's life that is in sharp contrast to Shemwindo, the Father of destruction and cruelty. We will see the hero-warrior oscillate between these two poles of cruelty and compassion throughout this tale—but first the trapped Mwindo must be set free.

◎◎

EPISODE 2:

RESCUE BY THE MOTHER

Mwindo's drum headed upstream, for he was not sure where Iyangura lived and thought to begin his journey at the river's source. From Kahungu the Hawk, Mwindo learned that she inhabited an unfathomable realm of the river even deeper than he had ventured so far. Thus began Mwindo's voyage down into the river's depths to meet his aunt Iyangura. He sang to all who might impede his quest:

> Get out of my way!
> You are impotent against Mwindo,
> Mwindo is the little-one-just-born-he-walked.
> I am going to meet Iyangura.
> He who will go up against me, it is he who will die on the way.

Now Mukiti, master of the unfathomable realm and husband of Iyangura, had placed his younger sister Musoka* as a guardian at the portal of his domain. When she saw Mwindo, she dispatched an envoy to Mukiti who, by return messenger, ordered her to keep Mwindo far away, for Mwindo was a threat to him. Musoka tried to block Mwindo's progress, but to no avail; he dove with his drum even farther into the watery depths, burying himself deep within the bottom sand. There he dug a tunnel around Musoka and surfaced farther downstream.

When Mukiti heard Mwindo calling for his aunt and challenging him in song, he began to stir, asking who had just mentioned his wife. He shook heaven and earth.

"I, Mwindo, I spoke of your wife," Mwindo defiantly answered. "We shall meet in battle today," he continued, "for I, Mwindo, am being denied access to my aunt!"

When Mukiti finally saw Mwindo he exclaimed, "You are not the one I expected to see! You are a child inside a drum! Who are you?"

Mwindo referred to himself as the little-one-just-born-he-walked, nephew of Iyangura, who was on his way to meet his aunt.

"Do not even dare to dream that you, of all people, are capable of besting me, Mukiti, lord of the unfathomable realm; you will not pass beyond my guard."

These harsh words were overheard by some of Iyangura's maidens who had come to Mukiti's pool to fetch water. At this mention of their mistress's name, they grew frightened and ran to Iyangura, saying, "There is a little man inside a drum insisting that Mukiti should release him, that he is Mwindo, going to encounter Iyangura, his paternal aunt."

"That is my child," she exclaimed, "let me go to him."* Iyangura made her way to the water hole. She slashed the drumhead, removing the hide, and there beheld the multiple rays of the rising sun and the moon—the radiant beauty of the child Mwindo. Mwindo got out of the drum, still holding his conga-scepter, his ax, and the little bag with rope in it. ◎◎

Mwindo takes his place in a long history of mythic heroes who have been rescued by a benevolent maternal figure. And, not surprisingly, these are many of the same hero-figures who had a mirac-

---

* "Child" here is the figurative expression Iyangura uses for her nephew.

ulous birth after which they were exiled by a jealous patriarch: In an original inscription in his own hand, Sargon I, the founder of ancient Babylonia, tells how, after being set upon the Tigris (circa 2800 B.C.E.), he was rescued by Akki, the water carrier, then raised under favor of the goddess Ishtar. Moses, abandoned to the Nile, was rescued and raised by Pharaoh's daughter. And Karni, of Hindu myth, was plucked out of the Ganges by the barren goddess Radha. What, then, are we to make of this nearly universal mythic theme of the exposed male-child rescued by a charitable woman? Traditional psychoanalysts, for whom all mythology is nothing but the expression of unresolved infantile crises, inform us that here we have the essential, trilateral "family romance," fantasized by all male children: they are set in opposition to a monstrous father (the figure who consigns them to exile) and are ever seeking a return to their primary, blissful union with an all-loving mother (the figure who rescues them from exile).

After rescue from exile, these child-heroes become warrior-heroes and embark on a "father quest" to confront their paternal antagonist, to discover the reasons for their initial rebuke, and to lay claim to an empire that is rightfully theirs. This quest leads them through great dangers, for just as often the father figure, himself a warrior, has succumbed to the temptations of the darker side of the warrior spirit. In the popular motion-picture epic *Star Wars*, for instance, this is precisely the situation young Luke Skywalker finds himself in with re-

Figure 6. Northern African rock art image of a warrior.

spect to Darth Vader, who turns out to be his warrior-father, gone over to the "dark side of the Force."

Yet true as this infantile engima may be, it is not the last word on the mythological symbolism of Mwindo's ordeals. For the drama offers an understanding not only of the treacherous nature of birth into the world of flesh but also of the equally perilous nature of birth into the world of spirit. In this view, the father figure Shemwindo represents the highest, though corrupted, ideals of material society: avarice and the desire for power. The river of Mwindo's exile is, in fact, the canal of his rebirth into a spiritual quest of which his aunt is the midwife who pulls him through; he must then confront, as all heroes and heroines must, the threshold guardians symbolized here by Mukiti, the master of the unfathomable realm—the dynamic and dangerous powers of the deep unconscious mind. As we might expect, Mwindo's next episode is a battle with these dark powers.

EPISODE 3:
BATTLING THE FORCES OF THE UNFATHOMABLE REALM

When Kahungu the Hawk observed Mwindo meeting with his aunt, he flew to Kasiyembe, whom Mukiti had given the task of keeping watch over his wife.

"Kasiyembe," Kahungu cried, "it is not merely a little man who converses with Iyangura; he is a man of many great feats. Perhaps you have more trouble than you think."

"Go tell this Mwindo he should not even try to venture past the area I guard," proclaimed the brazen Kasiyembe. "Otherwise I will tear out his spinal column. I am already setting traps, pits, pointed sticks, and razors in the ground, so he will be unable to step anywhere."

Now, Katee the Hedgehog overheard this talk between Kahungu and Kasiyembe and immediately sought out Mwindo. "Mwindo," said Katee, "Kahungu and Kasiyembe are holding secret council against you; they are even preparing pit traps against you, with pointed sticks and razors. But I am Katee, a hedgehog," he continued. "I am going to dig a tunnel for you, a road that begins right here and comes out inside the house of your aunt."

Mwindo then told his aunt Iyangura to return to her home where he would join her shortly. "And tell your bodyguard, Kasiyembe, to be careful," he warned.

When Katee's tunnel was complete, Mwindo followed it until he came out in Iyangura's house, to the astonishment of Kasiyembe. Meanwhile Mwindo was also receiving unseen help at the hands of Master Spider who had been watching Kasiyembe build the pits.

"As far as I am concerned," Master Spider said to himself, "Mwindo will not perish." So the spider began building bridges over the top of the pits he knew Mwindo would have to cross.

When Iyangura saw that her nephew Mwindo had arrived, she said to him, "My son, don't eat food yet; come, first let us dance to the rhythm of the drum."

Mwindo stepped outside with Iyangura and told her that if he danced without food he might faint.

"What shall we do then?" pleaded Iyangura. "Kasiyembe is demanding that you dance." Mwindo understood he was dancing into a trap laid by Kasiyembe, but still he agreed. And dance he did: round and round the middle of the pits, with his body bent over them; with glee, he danced everywhere that traps had been set for him, and he remained uninjured, thanks to Master Spider. And all the while Mwindo waved his conga-scepter and taunted Kasiyembe's impotence against him. ◎◎

Mwindo, we see, has a full complement of magical aid upon which to draw in order to overcome the dangers of his passage to the unfathomable realm. When the United States Army drafted young men from the Navaho reservation into service during World War II, Jeff King, an octogenarian Navaho who had served in the army from 1870 to 1911, prepared these inductees with the centuries-old spiritual initiation of the Navaho warrior.[4] It consisted of singing an epic, much like the bards of Africa, of the adventures of the original Navaho hero-warriors: two child-heroes who, like the child-hero Mwindo, set off in search of their father—in this case, the sun. These child-heroes, twins known as Monster Slayer and Child Born of Water (appellations that Mwindo could also rightfully claim), had miraculous births and walked when but four days old. And on their way to the house of their father, they came upon the old woman of the way who was curiously called Spider Woman. She assisted them in crossing a field of razor-sharp reeds that cut, cattails that stabbed, and rocks that clapped together; her main boon came in the form of an eagle-feather charm for each twin, analogous to Mwindo's conga-scepter. The symbols in these myths of the sacred warrior from two disparate cultures are not only similar in content but also in intent: to recall the sacred warrior back to that mythic wisdom which will transform his participation in battle from the fields of outer conquest to those of inner victory.

Returning now to Mwindo, we find him in a pitched battle with Kasiyembe, who refuses to submit to a "boy from inside a drum." Kasiyembe calls on the god Nkuba, the lightning hurler, to send a bolt that will strike Mwindo down. But Mwindo turns this threat aside by reminding the god that it is he, Mwindo, whom he will harm. Then, Mwindo points skyward to Nkuba and says, "You too will meet a terrible fate if you try to harm me."

◎◎ Instead Nkuba sent down seven bolts of lightning that missed Mwindo intentionally each time. Now angered by Kasiyembe's intransigence, Mwindo cast an eye in his direction, and suddenly the guard's hair flared up in flames. People went to fetch water in jars to extinguish the fire, but when they arrived, the jars were empty; the water had magically evaporated.

"Kasiyembe is about to die," they intoned. "Let us go to his master, Mukiti, for help." But they were too late. Mwindo, in his anger, had also dried up the pool where Mukiti lived.

When Iyangura saw that Mwindo had killed both Mukiti and Kasiyembe she begged of her nephew, "Widen your heart, my child. Did you come here to attack us? Set your heart down; untie your anger; undo my husband and his guardian Kasiyembe; heal them without harboring further resentment."

Mwindo was moved by his aunt's compassionate request; he opened his heart, waking first Kasiyembe by waving his conga-scepter above him. Suddenly, Kasiyembe returned to life, water returned to the jars, the river was full again, and Mukiti awoke from death. Everyone who witnessed Mwindo's feat was astonished. "Lo! Mwindo, he too is a great man," they said. Even Kasiyembe gave Mwindo a salute: "Hail! Hail, Mwindo!"

After Mwindo had accomplished this great deed, he announced to his aunt that tomorrow he would be going to Tubondo alone to fight with his father.

"Don't go alone," she implored her nephew. "The lonely path is never nice."

But Mwindo refused to listen, and when she realized that her appeals had fallen on deaf ears, she said only, "I do not wish you, my young man, to go fight with your father, but if you persist on going, then I shall go with you to witness this terrible event."

We humans are born into knowledge of our mother, but we must grow into knowledge of our father. In the symbolic language of mythology, Father represents the totality of the Unknown. From the cribside, the father figure is a mysterious, intruding Other, encroaching on our primary relationship with Mother. Freudian analysts have long ago worked out the details of the psychic conflict this imposes on our young minds, basing their understanding in part on mythological themes expressed in the Greek dramas of Oedipus and Electra. Suffice it to say, Father is seen as an ogre (literally, in myth and folktales) who threatens our principal connection with Mother and who sees in his offspring the seeds of his eventual demise. Here, the psychoanalysts tell us, is the basis for the recurring theme of the vengeful father or king in myths like that of Moses or Mwindo; here, too, is the basis for the warrior's "father quest" and ultimate battle to dethrone this father-king, in order to become the father-king himself.

◎◎

EPISODE 4:

THE FATHER QUEST

Mwindo, his aunt, and her servants set off on a war march to Tubondo. Along the way they enlisted recruits. The fighting began shortly after they arrived on the outskirts of the city. Mwindo's forces were badly beaten, so he called on Nkuba to help, and the lightning hurler unleashed seven bolts against Tubondo, turning to dust the village and all who lived there. But after entering the devastated city, Mwindo soon learned that Shemwindo, his father, had fled before the holocaust, escaping to the underworld realm of Muisa, "the place where no one ever gathers around the fire."

Again his aunt Iyangura tried to dissuade him from pursuing his father, but Mwindo paid her no heed. He told her to remain in Tubondo, holding one end of his birth rope. If the rope became still, then she could assume he was dead.

Suddenly, Sparrow appeared to Mwindo with these words: "Come here for me to show you the path that your father took upon entering the underground realm of Muisa at the base of the root of the *kikoka* fern." * When Mwindo arrived at the *kikoka* fern, he pulled the plant out of the ground and entered the underworld realm.

Mwindo was met by Kahindo,† the daughter of Muisa and guardian of the entrance to the underworld, whose repulsive body was covered from head to foot with yaws.‡ She cautioned him against going farther: "No one ever gets through Muisa's village," she warned. "Do you think you with all your pride will succeed?"

But Mwindo persisted, and Kahindo then supplied him with the oaths and knowledge needed to procure his safe passage: "When you arrive in the village meeting place, you will see a very tall, very big man, curled up in the ashes near the hearth," she informed Mwindo. "That is Muisa, and if he greets you, 'Blessing be with you, my father,' you too will answer, 'Yes, my father.' Then he will offer you a stool, but you must refuse it.

"Next," Kahindo continued, "he will offer you some banana beer to drink; you must refuse that too. Finally, Muisa will invite you to have some gruel to eat; that, Mwindo, you must also refuse."

Mwindo's heart reached out to the disfigured Kahindo, and he realized he could not leave without washing her scabs. He cleansed and soothed the lesions, then healed her entirely of her yaws before taking leave.

Mwindo headed on to Muisa's village. On seeing him, Muisa greeted Mwindo, "Blessing be with you, my father." Mwindo answered, "Yes, my father." Muisa then offered Mwindo a stool on which to sit, some banana beer to drink, and some gruel to eat, all of which Mwindo refused. Seeing Mwindo escape these ordeals, Muisa suggested that he might like to go back and rest at his daughter's house for a while.

So he went back to Kahindo's, who in the meantime had made herself like the "anus of a snail"§: dressing up, then rubbing herself with red powder and castor oil. Mwindo was taken aback by her radiant beauty. "Come in, Mwindo," Kahindo exclaimed, "please, come in."

---

*Muisa is the Nyangan deity of the subterranean underworld, symbolically represented as an aardvark, which the Nyanga consider a sacred animal. This is in contrast to Mukiti, the fish, who rules the subaquatic underworld.

† Kahindo is the Nyangan female deity of good luck, whose charm Mwindo was born with and wore around his neck.

‡ Yaws is a nonvenereal syphilislike disease of the tropics, characterized by raised lesions over the skin surface.

§ A Nyangan symbol of cleanliness and neatness.

"Oh, my sister," he replied, "I would harm myself if I stayed outside."

Kahindo went to prepare some food, but Muisa, who had observed her tender behavior toward Mwindo, quickly intervened. Before giving him his father, Muisa told Mwindo he would have to face a series of challenges to prove his worth.

"Tomorrow you will start cultivating a new banana grove for me," Muisa ordered. "You must first cut leaves, then plant the banana trees, then fell the trees; then cut the newly grown weeds, then prune the banana trees, then prop them up, then bring ripe bananas. After you have performed all these tasks," Muisa concluded, "I shall give you your father."

In the morning Mwindo left to accomplish the tasks. He laid out his tools on the ground; then all by themselves the tools went to work: first, they cut the grasses; then the tools having cut the grasses, the banana trees planted themselves; the banana trees having planted themselves, Mwindo sent a bunch of axes to fell the trees; when the axes finished their work, he sent many weeding tools that went across the banana grove cutting the newly grown weeds. After his weeding tools had finished, his other tools now cut supporting staffs; the staffs themselves propped up the banana trees. The staffs having finished sustaining the trees, the banana stems were ripe. In one day, Mwindo cleared, planted, and cultivated an entire field of bananas.

While Mwindo was harvesting his crop, an astonished informant told Muisa of these miraculous events. Muisa then determined to send his *karemba* belt against Mwindo, for he never intended to hand over Mwindo's father. "You, my *karemba,* you are going to fight Mwindo," he said. "When you see him, you will bend him, then smash him against the ground."

Karemba, having heard the instructions of its master, went to the banana grove. When it saw Mwindo, the belt fell upon him, making him

Figure 7. A belt made of cowrie shells, like Muisa's *karemba.*

scream. Muisa's belt crushed him; it planted his mouth against the ground and froth came out. Mwindo could neither breathe nor could he control his bladder and bowels. Then, seeing its master with no way out, Mwindo's conga awoke to its duty; it wagged itself above his head, and he succeeded in taking a short breath, then a sneeze; and finally he opened his eyes and gazed about.

All the while, Mwindo's birth rope was quiet, and his aunt in the upperworld began crying, "Mwindo is dead! His rope has become still. He must escape this terrible fate," she implored the divinities, "he is my child."

Mwindo remembered his aunt and communicated to her through the power of his thoughts: "My aunt there in Tubondo, my rope did not move because Muisa had trapped me; he wrapped me up like a bunch of bananas in his *karemba*; but don't worry now, I am saved; my conga has rescued me."

Mwindo then sent his conga-scepter to attack Muisa. "You, my conga," he commanded, "when you arrive at Muisa's, you will smash him with force; you must plant his mouth to the ground; his tongue must penetrate the earth; do not release him until I return."

Whirling through the air, the conga went on its way, and arriving at Muisa's, it did smash him; it planted his mouth to the ground; his tongue dug into the earth; his bladder and bowels left him; and his breath was cut off.

Mwindo remained in the banana grove, preparing a load of green and ripe bananas. When he returned to the village, he cast his eyes at Muisa and saw foam oozing out of his mouth and nostrils. "Now give me my father," he said to Kahindo, who met him as he moved toward Muisa, "so I may go home with him."

Figure 8. A conga-scepter similar to that described in the Mwindo epic.

"Begin first by healing my

father," she pleaded, "so I may find out where your father is and give him to you."

Mwindo sang while awakening Muisa:

> He who went to sleep wakes up.
> Muisa, you are powerless against Mwindo,
> because Mwindo is the little-one-just-born-he-walked.

Mwindo went on singing like that while beating Muisa incessantly on the head with his conga in order to wake him up. When Muisa was revived, he pointed to a tree some distance from where he stood and said, "Mwindo, if you want to get your father, go tomorrow and extract honey for me from that tree."

That evening Kahindo cooked for Mwindo, and after eating, she put her leg across him* and they slept. When daylight came, Mwindo, equipped with his ax and with fire, went into the forest to extract the honey. He arrived at the base of the tree and climbed up high to where the honey was. But Muisa did not mean for Mwindo to succeed at this task either. Once again he sent his *karemba* belt after Mwindo; it smashed Mwindo on the tree; it planted his mouth into the trunk of the tree; he could not breathe; his bladder and bowels left him.

Once again Mwindo's aunt felt his birth rope grow still, and she feared the end had come. But Mwindo's conga, lying on the ground at the base of the tree, realized that its master was dying. It climbed up the tree to where he was and began to beat and beat Mwindo about his head. Mwindo sneezed, lifted his eyes slightly, and a bit of breath came out.

When Nkuba, the lightning hurler, heard the cry of his friend Mwindo, he unleashed a lightning bolt that split the tree into pieces. Mwindo got down from the tree without a single wound. He then went back with a basket of honey and set it down before Muisa, demanding to be given his father. Muisa, pretending to comply with Mwindo's demand, sent a boy to fetch Shemwindo from his hiding place. But the boy arrived and found Shemwindo was no longer there.

Suddenly, Kahungu the Hawk, who had previously abetted Muisa, swooped down from the sky squawking, "Muisa lies; he has warned your father to flee, saying that you were too tough an opponent."

---

*A Nyangan euphemism for sexual intercourse.

Now Mwindo was furious. "Give me my father immediately, you scoundrel! Make him come out from where you have hidden him so that I may return to the upperworld with him. You said that when I cultivated a field for you, when I extracted honey for you, you would then give me my father. You lied! I want him right now; don't let your saliva dry up before giving him to me."

Muisa did not bring his father out, and Mwindo gave up on polite words. He beat Muisa on the top of his head with his conga; Muisa lost control of his bladder and bowels; he fainted and froth came out of his nose, his eyes, and his mouth; he tossed his feet up into the air; he stiffened like a dead snake.

"Stay like that, you dog," Mwindo yelled. "I will heal you when I have finally caught my father."

Meanwhile Shemwindo had sought refuge with the god Sheburungu,* and Mwindo followed him there, wrapped in his hatred.

"Oh, Mwindo," Sheburungu shouted, "let us play *wiki* together first."†

Mwindo accepted Sheburungu's challenge to play; if he won, he could then retrieve his father. Through superior play, Sheburungu won everything Mwindo had—his money, his possessions, his aunt, even his claim to the village of Tubondo. In desperation Mwindo wagered his conga against the god, and finally his fortune turned; ultimately he won everything the god possessed—people, cattle, goats—and most important, the ability to capture his fugitive father.

"Mwindo, come quickly," sang Kahungu the Hawk, "your father wants to flee again." Mwindo hastily abandoned the *wiki* game and headed off to intercept his father in a banana grove.

Seeing Shemwindo, Mwindo inquired sarcastically, "O my father, is it you here?"

Shemwindo answered meekly, "Here I am."

After seizing his father, Mwindo returned to Sheburungu's, telling the god he did not want any of the things he had won during the game. Then Mwindo bid farewell to Sheburungu and tugged on the rope to remind his aunt he was still alive. On his return home he went into Muisa's house, where Kahindo came running. "You see my father here, his bones fill a basket; what shall I do then? It is befitting that you heal my father; please don't leave him like that; wake him up; he is the chief of all these people."

---

*Sheburungu is another name for the Nyanga creator-god, Ongo.
†*Wiki* is a game of chance where one player must guess the number of seeds being held by another player.

Mwindo resurrected Muisa once more, striking him with his conga, telling him, "You have offended me in vain; you have tried to equal Mwindo. But only I am Mwindo, the little-one-just-born-he-walked, the little one who does not eat earthly foods; and the day he was born, he did not drink at the breasts of his mother."

Mwindo tugged on the rope again, and this time Iyangura knew that he was on his way home with his father.

In time, the Oedipal crisis of the cradle shifts to reveal yet another dimension of the Father as Unknown, for the hero-warrior's striking out in search of his father is also a quest to discover his own character and career. Will he simply step into the shoes of his father, or will he meet and then better his father's calling? Mwindo displays a ferocity and ruthlessness toward his opponents reminiscent of that displayed by his father toward him, reminding us that the "sins of the father" are revisited on the son and that a thin line separates the life-affirming and life-denying aspects of the sacred warrior spirit. It is Iyangura and Kahindo, the feminine powers of this tale, who intercede to recall Mwindo to his humanity, pleading that he display compassion to those he has vanquished and resurrect them from the dead.

Returning from the underworld with his captured father, Mwindo faces the pivotal moment of his quest: will he slay his father and accede to power by the same corrupted route? Or will he transcend his father's inflated ego and seek greatness through compassion? This is the fundamental dilemma of the sacred warrior.

◎◎

EPISODE 5:
ATONEMENT WITH THE FATHER

Mwindo journeyed back from the underworld, exiting from the *kikoka* fern with his father and triumphantly arriving in Tubondo. Reunited with his aunt Iyangura, he recounted his adventures for her. Iyangura sought a public apology from her brother, but first she made a special request of Mwindo:

"My son, shall we go on living always in this desolate village alone, without other people? I, Iyangura, want you first to save all the people who lived here in this village; only when they have been resuscitated shall I ask Shemwindo to confess how he acted toward you and the evil he perpetrated against you. You, my son, are the eternal savior of people."

For three days, Mwindo resurrected those who had fallen in the battle for Tubondo. He beat his conga over the bones of the dead, and miraculously they arose, resuming precisely the activity they had been engaged in at the time of their death.

After the inhabitants of Tubondo had been resurrected, Iyangura asked Shemwindo to call together all the people, and those three radiant stars—Mwindo, Shemwindo, and Iyangura—appeared to the pleasure of the assembled crowd.

Turning to his father Mwindo beckoned: "Now you, my father, it is your turn. Explain to the chiefs the reason why you have had a grudge against me; tell the chiefs so that they may understand."

Sweat rose from Shemwindo's body, shame welled up in his eyes. He uttered his confession in quivering tones, broken by a spitting cough:

"All you chiefs," Shemwindo stammered, "I don't deny the evil that I have done against my son; indeed, I passed a decree that I would kill all male children. I tried many times to kill this child, but each time, instead of harming him, I only made him stronger. I fled to the underworld thinking I would be safe, but my son set out in search of me; he came to take me away from the abyss of evil in which I was involved. I was at that time withered like dried bananas. And it is like that I arrived here in the village of Tubondo. So may the male progeny be saved. My son has let me see the way in which the dark sky becomes daylight and given me the joy of witnessing again the warmth of the people and of all the things here in Tubondo."

After that Iyangura spoke: "You, Shemwindo, together with your counselors and nobles, acted badly. If it were a counselor from whom this plan of torment against Mwindo had emanated, then his throat would be cut here in the council. You discriminated against the children, saying that male children were bad and female children were good. You did not know what was in the womb of your preferred wife, what you were given by Sheburungu, but you saw it to be bad."

Iyangura turned to the counselors and nobles, concluding her remarks: "Shemwindo has committed a heinous deed. If the people of Tubondo had been exterminated, Shemwindo would have been guilty of exterminating them."

Finally, Mwindo stood up and with great compassion said, "I, Mwindo, man of many feats, the little-one-just-born-he-walked, I am not holding a grudge against my father; may my father not be frightened, believing that I am still angry with him; no, I am not angry with my father. What my father did against me and what I did against my father, all that is already over. Now let us examine what is to come, the evil and the good. If either of us starts quarreling again, it is he who will be in the wrong, and all the elders here will be the witnesses of it. Now, let us live in harmony in our country, let us care for our people well."

Full of shame and repentant, Shemwindo wished to cede his throne to his son. He voluntarily stripped himself of the trappings of kingship, giving them to Mwindo; then he blessed Mwindo and left on a self-imposed exile to a mountain retreat. After his enthronement, Mwindo proclaimed that now he had become famous, and would never act like his father. ◎◎

This "father quest" is the engine driving most of the major recorded African epics—such as those of Sundiata (also known as Son-Jara)[5] and Ozidi,[6] as well as of Mwindo. With the heroes of these other tales, as with our Mwindo, the themes of revenge and replacement of the father-king are prominent. But Mwindo's choice of atonement with his father after vanquishing him sets this myth apart from the others, where the warrior-son simply replaces the father-king through force. Mwindo's is a nobler response to the thorny problem of plotting the course of one's life.

For how *are* we to proceed with the conduct of our life? Do we choose the security of succeeding in Father's footsteps? This is often the path of least resistance, the path frequently demanded by family and society. Or do we risk adventure beyond the safety of what has already been accomplished and what is already known? This is the untested way, the more arduous yet potentially more rewarding path of the hero-warrior in quest of Father.

Mwindo's journey is along this untested way, a way of heroic enterprise, of an authentic life lived in response to the dictates and demands of one's own conscience, which often leads beyond the pale of the group. This is a path of creative engagement with life where one is willing to brave the chaos of the unknown, while others take shelter in the ordered way of things; where one creates a path through the darkest part of the forest, while others see only the obstacle of the trees and stand fast.

Many traditional African societies clearly understood the importance of the hero who would break the established rules. "They know that they depend upon the individual who resists the pull of the established social order," declares ethnographer Charles S. Bird, speaking about the hero in Mande society, "just as they depend upon the individuals who do not resist; they know that they require the individual who will change things, even if these changes are potentially destructive."[7]

Encoded in the *Mwindo Epic,* then, is a sophisticated, long-standing African approach to the interdependence of the needs of the individual and those of the group. This approach, particularly in regard to spiritual concerns, contrasts with that of oriental or occidental mythology. In oriental mythology, the accent is principally on the group and not the individual; in the Eastern tradition, for example, the guru, or spiritual teacher, single-handedly directs the spiritual quest of his devotees. While the guru may lead the group in a radical way, each individual is implored to follow the guru's dictates rather than his or her own.

Mythological traditions unique to the West, on the other hand, focus principally on the individual to the exclusion of the group. Joseph Campbell, for instance, identifies this accent on the individual repeatedly in the Arthurian romances.[8]

In the midst of these opposing tensions, then, African mythology strikes a balance between the individual and the group, emphasizing neither to the exclusion of the other. Perhaps an aphorism cited earlier best captures this integration: "I am because we are, we are because I am."

So we find Mwindo cast between the established order of his father, and his destined heroic adventure into the unknown. In the end, he has reconciled himself with both.

Yet even this compassionate atonement with his earthly father does not bring Mwindo's spiritual journey to completion, for a final revelation of the Father awaits him: realization of the Father as the heavenly mystery, the divine unknown, at the hands of the gods themselves.

EPISODE 6:
A FINAL JOURNEY AMONG THE GODS

Many days after his ascension to the throne, Mwindo had a terrible craving to eat some wild pig meat, so he sent the Forest People* to hunt for a fresh pig. Following the trail of a red-haired pig, they encountered Kirimu the Dragon, master of the deep forest. He appeared to them in horrific form, a huge animal with a black hide, seven heads, seven horns, seven eyes, teeth like a dog, a huge belly, and the tail of an eagle.

Kirimu devoured the Forest People, whereupon it then fell to Mwindo to save Tubondo from the beast's reign of terror. Mwindo fearlessly met the monster in battle; then just as Kirimu was about to swallow him whole, Mwindo unleashed his conga and slew the dragon instead. The people rejoiced at the sight of this plentiful supply of fresh meat and were even more pleased when, once the dragon was cut open, all those whom he had ever swallowed were released unharmed from his belly.

But it so happened that Nkuba, the lightning hurler, had made a blood pact with Kirimu. When he inhaled the odor of his dead friend carried on the wind, tears came to his eyes. "What shall I do with this Mwindo?" Nkuba said to himself.

"If I make him suffer up here among the gods, then perhaps he will learn and I can return him to earth to his village again," he mused. "If Mwindo had known I had exchanged blood with Kirimu, then he would not have killed my friend. If he had known, yet still killed Kirimu, I would kill Mwindo right here and now without ever returning him to his country. But he is safe because he did not know that Dragon was my friend."

Nkuba descended for Mwindo and said, "I have come to take you, my friend; I want to teach you because I am very displeased with you since you dared to kill Dragon, who was my friend. You must know this time that you have done wrong."

Still Mwindo showed no deference or fear toward Nkuba, though all the people of Tubondo were stricken with terror, believing their chief was lost forever.

Mwindo sang taunts of his greatness to Nkuba while the pair

---

*The original translation referred to "Pygmies," a pejorative term now in disuse.

climbed slowly up into the air. "I have rescued you many times from many dangers," Nkuba reminded Mwindo. "Still you sing so arrogantly. Do you think that you are now equal to me?"

Once in the celestial realm, Mwindo experienced cold weather and icy winds. And there was no house! They lived as nomads, never settling in one spot. Nkuba seized Mwindo; he climbed with him up to Mbura the Rain. When Rain saw Mwindo, he told him, "You, Mwindo, you never accept being criticized; the news about your toughness, your heroism, we surely have heard the news, but here, there is no room for your heroism." Rain fell upon Mwindo seven and seven times more; he had Hail fall upon him, and he soaked him thoroughly. Mwindo thought to himself, "This time I am in trouble in a big way."

Nkuba then lifted Mwindo up again and had him scramble across to Mweri the Moon's domain. When Moon saw Mwindo, he pointed at him: "The news has been given us of your pride, but here in the sky there is no room for your pride." Then Moon burned Mwindo's hair.

Nkuba lifted Mwindo up again; he went with him to the domain of Kentse the Sun. When Sun saw Mwindo, he burned him with his heat. Mwindo lacked all means of defense against Sun; his throat became dry; thirst strangled him; he asked for water. The gods said to him, "No, here there is no water for you; now we advise you to grit your teeth and to put your heart on your knee."*

After Sun had made Mwindo sustain these pains, Nkuba lifted Mwindo up and brought him to the domain of Kubikubi the Star. When Star saw him, he too echoed the words of the other gods: "The news comes that you are a great hero, but here there is no room for your heroism." Star ordered the Rain and Sun and Moon to come, and all of the assembled gods—Nkuba, Mbura, Mweri, Kentse, Kubikubi—delivered Mwindo a message in unison:

"We have respect for you, but just that much; otherwise, you would vanish right here. You, Mwindo, you are ordered to go back; never a day should you kill an animal of the forest or of the village or even an insect like a centipede or a water spider. If one day we learn that you have begun killing such animals, you will die and your people will never see you again."

They pulled his ears seven times and seven more, saying, "Understand?" And Mwindo said, "Yes, I understand." They also admonished

---

*To sustain intense suffering and resist crying, the Nyanga gnash their mouths against their knees.

him: "Nkuba will oversee your behavior and comportment; if you stray from our commands Nkuba will report to us, and that day he will seize you instantly, without even a moment to say farewell to your people."

Finally, after one year of wandering in the abode of the sky, Mwindo was allowed to return home. He assembled all his people and told them of his ordeal: "I, Mwindo, the little-one-just-born-he-walked, performer of many wonderful things, I tell you the news from where I have visited in the heavens. When I arrived in the sky, I met with Rain and Moon and Sun and Star and Lightning. These five gods forbade me to kill the animals of the forest and of the village, saying that the day I would dare to touch a living thing in order to kill it, that day my life-fire would be extinguished; then Nkuba would come to take me without my saying farewell to my people and my hope of return would be lost forever."*
He also told them, "I have seen in the sky things I cannot divulge."

Mwindo then passed good laws for his people, saying,

May you grow many foods and many crops.
May you live in good houses and a beautiful village.
Don't quarrel with one another.
Don't pursue another's spouse.
Don't mock the invalid passing in the village.
Accept the chief; fear him; may he also fear you.
May you agree with one another, harboring no enmity nor too
*   much hate.*
May you bring forth tall and short children; in so doing you
*   will bring them forth for the chief.*

Mwindo's fame grew and stretched widely; it spread to other countries from which people came to pay their allegiance to him. And among children, none was thought bad; whether males or females, whether able or disabled, they were not rejected. For Mwindo realized there was nothing bad in what God has given to humankind. ◎◎

Mwindo's frighteningly austere celestial exile is reminiscent of the spiritual journeys of the ascetic mystics of the East. His ego is thoroughly demolished; then, with the transformation accomplished, the gods return him to the earth no longer a warrior-king but a sacred

---

*To this day, Nyanga chiefs are forbidden to partake in the hunt.

warrior, an enlightened leader to whom the greatest of mysteries has been revealed. "I have seen in the sky," he reports to his followers, "things I cannot divulge."

Mwindo dies, the myth tells us, as a secular warrior and king, but he is reborn as a sacred warrior and world redeemer. Prohibited, under penalty of instantaneous annihilation at the hand of the thundergod, from participating further in the round of secular life, he can neither eat meat nor partake in the kill. In his character as lawgiver, he reminds us of Moses returning with the Ten Commandments from forty days in exile on a mountaintop with Yahweh, the Hebrew God. And his legend echoes themes found in the figures of the Christ, the Hindu *jivanmukti*, the Buddhist boddhisatva, and the Chinese goddess of compassion, Kuan-yin (Kwannon in Japan). All are enlightened ones who, out of compassion for humanity, return to show others the path to spiritual fulfillment and illumination.

6

THE WAY OF THE
MASTER ANIMALS

*At heart he was a hunter, not of big game but of greater
meaning.*

LAURENS VAN DER POST ON THE SAN HUNTERS
OF SOUTHERN AFRICA

Where hunting was the way of life, the master animal was revered.
Salmon, buffalo, lion, bear, whale, antelope—all these master animals
represented a sacred, informing presence to those societies for whom
they were also the master source of food. The relationship between
human beings and these master animals was not simply one of predator and prey, for in traditional hunting societies it was believed that
the animal appeared and offered itself willingly. By killing it, the
hunter assisted the spiritual journey of the animal so it could once
again return to become nourishment for humankind. This was the sacred covenant between a divine presence that died and was resurrected, and humanity, which partook of its body and blood—a
covenant strengthened by the traditional sentiment that there was ultimately only one Life, though expressed in myriad forms. In other
words, the life of the hunter and that of the animal were not separate
but alternate reflections of the same life source. And because the master animals were seen to travel so regularly between the world of the
living and the world of the spirit, they were venerated as "bridges"

between these two worlds, to be used by shamans and priests who ventured into the realm of the spirit for the health and well-being of individuals and the group.

Animals appear with great regularity in the myths of traditional Africa; in fact, African mythology is too frequently associated exclusively with folktales about "animals that talk," like "How the Leopard Got Its Spots," or "The Talking Monkey," or stories about "Anase the Spider." In many of these folktales, as they have been handed down through the ages, the mythic wisdom is buried deep under the entertaining value of the tale; we are left only with a moral at the end of the story to remind us that there is something more here than what pleases the ear. Often it is possible to penetrate the enchanting veneer of an animal tale and discover the vestiges of the wisdom source from which it was fashioned: the "spider's web" as a metaphor for the World Axis that connects humanity to divinity as we have already seen; the "leopard's spots created by human handprints" symbolizing the deep identification of human life with all life; the "talking monkey" as an informing, though unruly, part of our own psyche. Sometimes the tale is so marvelously constructed that there is no doubt of its greater mythic import. The BaRonga of southeastern Africa, for example, have a myth about "The Miracle Worker of the Plains"—a phrase they use to describe their master animal, the African plains buffalo—that speaks in an elegant way to the sacred covenant between human society and the master animals[1]:

◎◎ A long time ago there was a couple who had successfully married off their daughter and, with the bride-price she commanded, felt they could then pay for the marriage of their son. But none of the local women appealed to him, and he set off from his village in search of a wife. This young man traveled far from his home into a region unknown to him; there he spied a group of young women and among them one whom he desired as a wife. He approached the village elders with his request and simultaneously produced the required bride-price, for he wished not to undergo the formality of returning home and having his parents return to this village with the bride-price and then conduct his wife to him.

The parents of this young woman consented to these somewhat unusual arrangements and reminded their daughter to be good to her inlaws and new husband. Then they offered her a younger daughter to help with the household chores, but the newly wedded daughter refused, saying, "No, I do not want her to help me with my tasks. Instead, please let me take the buffalo of our country, the Miracle Worker of the Plains. He will be my servant."

"How could you ask for such a thing?" her parents cried. "You know our life depends upon him. In this village, we treat the buffalo well; he is fed and looked after. You would not know how to take care of him in the strange country where you are going. He would be overworked and underfed; he would starve and die, and then we would all perish along with him."

The daughter said nothing but just gathered her belongings—a pot of herbal roots, a horn for bleeding, a small knife for making incisions, and a gourd filled with fat. Then she set out with her husband on the long journey. But the buffalo followed them, though he was visible only to her. Her husband was not aware that the Miracle Worker of the Plains was accompanying them home. ◎◎

In this initial episode, the defining moment comes when the young girl's parents protest her asking for the buffalo as a servant. Here the sacred covenant is reaffirmed: the master animal is not meant to serve humans, as the young girl desires. Rather, a mutual relationship is to exist between the two: the village takes care of him, and he takes care of them by assuring the supply of buffalo for the hunt. The life of the master animal and the life of humans are intertwined and dependent on this arrangement. The myth also informs us that the master animal is more than just a physical presence; it is his supernatural potency, a force invisible to the uninformed, that makes him sacred. The young woman knows how to behold this sacred presence, but will she also know how to tend to it now that it has joined her on her life journey?

◎◎ The husband and wife arrived back at his village to joyful cries of welcome. "Well," said the elders, "the women in this village were not good enough, so you struck out to find your own. Still you are welcome in your home. Just remember, you chose according to your own will. Should this choice bring you problems down the road, you will have no reason to complain."

Now the man wished his new wife to know the plot of land that she would help farm, so he took her into the fields and pointed out the boundaries to her. She committed everything he showed her to memory; then on the way back turned to him and said, "Oh, I must have lost my necklace in the fields; you go ahead, I'll go back to look for it."

Her husband walked back to the village while she returned to the fields; actually, she had not lost her necklace but needed an excuse so she could escape to see the buffalo. As her husband had with her, the woman pointed out the boundaries of their farm plot to the buffalo, and she also directed him to the nearby forest, where he could hide if need be.

And so whenever this woman wanted water, she simply placed a pot down by the edge of the field, and the buffalo ran with it to the water hole and returned promptly with it filled to the brim. If she needed wood, the buffalo would charge through the forest, breaking dead trees with his horns as he ran, thus providing her with all the wood she desired. When fields needed clearing, the buffalo would pull a hoe and prepare the required acreage. Everyone in her husband's village was amazed at how rapidly she accomplished these tasks, though no one suspected she had a miracle helper.

For many days, the buffalo helped his mistress, but she never gave him any food to eat, for there were but two plates in her household, one for herself and one for her husband. Now, in the village she came from, where the buffalo was well cared for, a separate plate was always set for the Miracle Worker of the Plains, and he was always provided with enough food to eat. The buffalo continued to clear fields, fetch water, and carry wood for the woman, though with each passing day he grew weaker and weaker and felt wave after wave of hunger pangs. ◎◎

The reverence of the young woman's village in approaching the master animal contrasts sharply with her own indifference. The reference in this myth to setting a separate plate for the buffalo is well known in cultures throughout the world. Similar practices were observed in the rituals of the "bear cult" that spread throughout Eurasia beginning as early as 6000 B.C.E. and continuing, in the case of the Ainu people of Hokkaido, to the present day. In Finland, Lapland, Siberia, and across the Bering Strait to North America, bears, the master animals of these various peoples, were ritually sacrificed and the lifeless bodies then fed food for their spirits' journey home. Excavations of Paleolithic sites in the Swiss Alps, for instance, have found cave bears buried with the long bones of the legs inserted into their open jaws.[2]

The BaRonga myth is similar to those that guided the ritual hunting of the master animal throughout ancient times, and Joseph Campbell suggested that in this approach to the master animal lie the most ancient roots of humanity's mythological and spiritual wisdom.[3] Some way had to be found to address the guilt and remorse associated with humankind's unavoidable participation in this most basic and horrific aspect of life—namely, that life lives through killing other life. The psychological leap that made this possible was the belief that death was not the end of life but one stage in a transformation that brings forth life again. And this is the idea that the young woman in the BaRonga myth seems unable to grasp, for she allows the buffalo to starve nearly to death before offering him this alternative:

◎◎ "Tonight," she said to the buffalo, "when no one can see you, go into the fields and take some beans from my plot, and from the others as well. But don't take too much from any one location so no one will notice any of her crop is missing."

The buffalo was unable to remain invisible while eating, so he followed his mistress's instructions and waited until night, then ate some beans from several plots. When the women arrived in the fields the next morning, they began shouting, "Hey, what happened to our plants? A wild beast laid them to waste; we can still smell his scent."

The young woman, however, assured the buffalo he would not be caught and urged him to go on stealing beans from the fields. With each passing day the other women became increasingly angry at the loss of their beans, and called their husbands to post an armed guard at night. Since the young woman's husband was an excellent marksman, he hid in the bushes behind his fields one evening to wait for the marauding beast.

"What kind of buffalo is this," exclaimed the man, on seeing the Miracle Worker from his blind. "I have never seen one like it before. This is certainly a strange animal to be roaming these parts."

He sighted down the length of his rifle and fired. The bullet penetrated the skull of the buffalo, and the Miracle Worker of the Plains rolled over once, then collapsed dead.

The man joyously announced his success to the rest of the village, but as everyone else set out with knives and baskets to cut up the buffalo, the young woman grew sick. She followed the others to the carcass, sobbing and crying. "What's wrong with you?" the others inquired.

She would not answer but insisted on being given the buffalo's head to carry back to her home. Placing the head inside a shed where she kept her pots, the young woman forbade anyone to disturb her. Then she took out the items she had brought from her village. She poured the herbs into a pot of boiling water and made incisions on the skull of the buffalo where the bullet had entered. Next, she placed the bleeding horn into the incisions and sucked and sucked until fresh blood started to flow. Then she exposed the area to the medicinal steam and soothed it with a covering of fat. Finally, she sang this song:

> Ah, my father, Miracle Worker of the Plains,
> they told me: you would go through the deep darkness;
> that in all directions you would stumble through the night,
> Miracle Worker of the Plains;
> you are the young wonder-tree plant, grown out of ruins,
> which dies before its time, consumed by a gnawing worm.
> You made flowers and fruit fall upon your road, Miracle
> Worker of the Plains!

As she finished, the buffalo's head began to shake, its body was restored, its forelegs and hind legs grew back, and it raised itself to stand. . . .

But just at this moment the woman's husband approached the shed demanding to know why she was staying out there into the wee hours of the night.

"Leave me alone," she replied angrily. But no sooner had she said that than the buffalo head dropped to the ground, wounded and dead as before.

Again she prepared her medicines and treated the buffalo's wound, again the animal came to life, and as it was about to stand, again her husband ran to the hut demanding to know why she stayed off by herself. By the time the woman prepared the medicines a third time, morning had broken, and the buffalo's wounds had progressed beyond her powers of repair. She asked to be left alone while she went to the lake to bathe. Then on her way back she told the others that she had met someone from her village who had been sent to call her home to her ailing mother. Of course, this, too, was a ruse, but she convinced her husband that she should leave immediately lest her mother die.

On her way home, all she could do was sing the song of the Miracle Worker of the Plains. When she arrived at her village, she announced that the buffalo was dead.

"We told you," they all said. "But you insisted on taking the buffalo with you, and now you have killed us all."

Shortly thereafter, her husband, who had followed his wife to the village, also arrived amidst jeers of "Murderer! Murderer!"

"Certainly I have killed a buffalo," he said, not understanding what had happened, "but that is no reason to call me a murderer."

"Yes," they said, "but this was no ordinary buffalo; he was your wife's assistant. He cleared your fields, he drew your water, and he gathered your wood. Your wife did none of those things, our buffalo did."

Then the man turned to his wife in shock. "Why did you not tell me? If I had known these things, I would never have killed that animal."

"It is too late now," the others stated. "All of our lives depended on him."

And then the people of this village began to cut their own throats. "Ah, my father, Miracle Worker of the Plains!" a young woman called out as she was dying.

"You shall go through darkness!" were the last words of the next person.

"You shall stumble through the night in all directions!" said the next.

"You are the young miracle-tree plant that dies before its time!" uttered the one who followed.

"You made flowers and fruit fall upon your road!" said the last to die.

Even the little children were killed. "Why should we let them live," the others said, "since they would only suffer from this great loss?"

The stunned man returned home and told the others in his village what had occurred. "By shooting the buffalo," he said, "I killed them all."

"Perhaps you should have listened to us," the elders admonished him. "We suggested a fine wife for you to marry, but instead you chose one based on your own desire. Now look at the result." ◎◎

It is possible, of course, to read this myth as a failure of the young man to heed the warnings of his elders; then we would interpret it as exhorting its listeners not to break rank with tradition—but this is just a subplot. The essence of the myth is more likely to be discovered in the song of healing sung to the buffalo and at the death of the villagers, for it reaffirms the sacred covenant.

The song informs us that when the buffalo is first killed, its spirit has not fully departed its body; it is "stumbling through the night," wandering in the deep darkness between the worlds of the living and the dead. Eventually the master animal will die, but only to be resurrected, like a "young wonder-tree plant" growing "out of ruins."

The life cycle of the buffalo is thus equated with the life cycle of the individual. For in societies like the BaRonga, when a person first died, they were said to enter an existence somewhere between the living and the dead. And when they had fully crossed over to the world of the dead, it was in preparation for rebirth.

A remarkably similar companion myth to "The Miracle Worker of the Plains" existed among the Blackfoot of North America. It too addressed the sacred covenant between human and animal society, and because the North American bison was their master animal, it also featured a buffalo of the plains.

When a herd of buffalo refused to stampede over a cliff to their death,* a young woman surveying the situation called to them, saying she would marry one if the others would jump. She did marry an old bull but eventually wanted to return to her village. Her father attempted to rescue her, but he was trampled to death. When she brought her father back to life with magic, the old bull was impressed. He gave her a song to teach the others before venturing out to hunt buffalo. From that point on, the buffalo medicine dance and song were performed to align tribal life with the rites through which the animals slain each year were returned to life.[4]

The Blackfoot woman kept the sacred covenant alive, while the BaRonga woman did not.

How High Is the Sea?

What a marvelous sight it must have been to behold Klara, an elderly African woman, on her hands and knees, bowing in reverence before a praying mantis.

"Please, how low is the sea?" she whispered. Mantis looked straight ahead, then suddenly pointed its two front feet down toward the ground.

"Please," she continued in devout tones, "how high is the sea?" To which Mantis raised his long front legs toward the sky.

Eager to tame Mantis in a similar manner, the young white boy tried a similar approach with the next mantis he saw, but there was no response. In frustration, he pushed its forelimbs in the desired direction with a blade of grass.

---

* This was a traditional way of hunting buffalo, by rounding them up and then driving them over a precipice to their death.

With a fierce gaze, the African woman snatched the grass from the young lad's hand and promptly whisked him away. Laying her hand on her heart, she proclaimed, "We never tease Mantis. We never ask anything of the Mantis for fun. We never ask unless we ask it here from the heart."[5]

Mantis is at the heart of San* sacred wisdom, as the most beloved incarnation of the San creator-god, /Kaggen. In fact, an early legend has Mantis riding the primeval sea at the beginning of creation, perched at the center of a prodigious, half-open white flower; the sea here represents that infinite ocean from which the universe in all its manifest forms (symbolized by the flower) arises and back into which it dissolves. This symbol of the godhead at the center of a flower is well known: in Christianity the rose encloses the Virgin in whose arms rests the child Christ, and in Hinduism and Buddhism, the Brahma or Buddha sits at the center of the lotus.

"How low is the sea?" It is down there, the murky depths that support the roots of the flower resting on its surface; there lies the life-sustaining, all-nourishing power of the abyss.

"How high is the sea?" It is up there, the divine heights from which rain the heavenly waters, anointing and nourishing the spiritual rebirth of life below.

With Mantis thus resting in the center of the World Flower, Klara's first question refers symbolically to the physical birth of humankind, the material conception of the world; her second question, then, refers to the spiritual rebirth of humanity and the world.

Joseph Campbell reminds us that the flower as a symbol can refer either to the "flowering of the universe," or the "opening of an individual's consciousness."[6]

Flower and mantis mirror each other, for as a flower unfolds, so too does the mantis in three stages from chrysalis to larva to winged being. Here we also have a familiar motif, usually symbolized by a butterfly, that depicts both the three modes of human consciousness (unconsciousness, waking consciousness, ecstatic consciousness) and the three realms of being (realm of the underworld abyss, realm of humanity, realm of divinity). And in the unique characteristic of the

---

* "San" is the preferred term for people also known as Bushmen. San are all but extinct from the southern African continent; the only surviving group are the Ju/'hoansi (also known as the !Kung) who inhabit the Kalahari Desert. When referring to these people as a group—both the Ju/'hoansi and the now extinct southern bands—I use the term "San." Ju/'hoansi is also my preference over the more familiar !Kung, for the former term is what these Kalahari San call themselves.

mantis—that the female consumes the male after he has impregnated her—is a reflection of the grand round of creation. "The invisible beginning and the fateful end made the image [of Mantis] complete in the mind of the [San]," writes Laurens Van der Post. "It said in terms of living experience and behavior that creation is not only birth but death as well, that through the death of what is, life on earth is born again to become more of what it is meant to be."[7]

The Dead and Resurrected Master Animal

Because Mantis represents the transformative potential of life, myths about him often reveal him either shape-shifting into other animals or creating other animals out of nothing. When not involved in these endeavors, Mantis transforms back into an ordinary human, a San who must go about life's daily tasks. A favorite transformation of Mantis is into an eland, that large African antelope with spiraling horns that is the master animal of the San hunt.

Elands hold a central position in both the physical and spiritual

Figure 9. San rock art painting of the Eland Bull Dance. The large figure in the middle is the young woman who has just experienced her first menses; figures with sticks are males, symbolically holding the horns of an eland.

nourishment of San society. Young boys are considered men when they kill their first adult eland with bow and arrow; they are seated on the skinned carcass and scarified with a broth made of the eland's fat. Thus, the hunter is thoroughly identified with the prey; his body is the eland's body.

At their first menstruation, young San girls are isolated in a hut, and after most of the men have departed the compound, the women perform the female initiation ritual known as the Eland Bull Dance (see Figure 9). Here, too, is a strong association between the eland and the pubescent girl; they are both referred to by the same name. Later, a young suitor will hunt an eland and give its heart to his potential mother-in-law, while at the wedding the bride is anointed with fat.[8] Now her body is the master animal's as well.

Atonement to the sacrificed god, so he may come forth again as nourishment for humankind, is the sense of these rites, the San enactment of the sacred covenant between humans and the master animal. After all, Eland is portrayed in myth as Mantis's beloved first son. In one myth, when a group of Meerkats (small carnivores of southern Africa) killed the first Eland, Mantis called to the dead Eland, which did not come; then Mantis wept at the loss of his first begotten spawn. "Mantis does not love us if we kill an eland," said a San.[9] So these rites are meant to reestablish that cosmic order (meaning the receipt of the god's love) disrupted by the kill—but only so

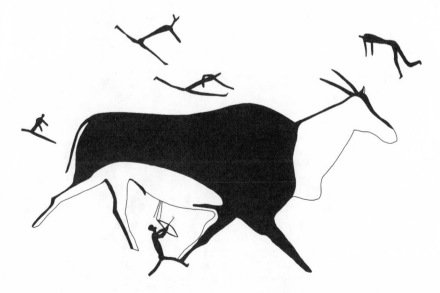

Figure 10. San rock art depicting an eland hunt.

that this order may once again be broken, for this is the inescapable, natural law of life feeding on life.

Master Animals and Shamanic Visions

Mantis is often depicted as a shaman and described as riding between the two horns of an eland, the supreme vehicle of shamanic power for the San. *Tcheni,* the Ju/'hoansi word for the sacred dance through which a shamanic trance is entered, is also a praise name for a dying eland, and the similarity between the master animal's death and the shaman entering a trance is quite startling. Both shake violently, stagger, lower their heads, bleed from the nose, sweat profusely, and ultimately, collapse unconscious.[10] San use the word *death* to describe shamanic trance, for in their words, shamans "die when they cross over into the spirit world."[11] Of course, we have seen this metaphor of death as an entrance to the spirit world in nearly every myth of the African hero we have already encountered; among the San, the myth is enacted as ritual.

Rock art clearly shows this relationship between the eland's death and the shaman's trance. David Lewis-Williams, of the University of the Witwatersrand in Johannesburg, the preeminent modern interpreter of San rock art, calls our attention to the similarities evident between the eland and the shamans in the painting shown in Figure 11.[12] First, note that three of the humanlike figures have heads with antelope features, while two of them have cloven hooves. As an eland dies, its muscles begin to weaken, its head drops, its forelegs give way, and its hind legs become crossed as it falters; from the response of its

Figure 11. San rock art of a dying eland, surrounded by shamans entering into trance.

autonomic nervous system, hair stands up throughout the body. One of the shaman figures, like the eland, is shown with hair standing erect over his body surface, and the figure holding the eland's tail has its feet crossed in emulation of the beast.

Qing, a southern San informant of the late nineteenth century, commented on such rock art scenes by observing the human figures had been "spoilt at the same time as the elands and by the dances of which you have seen paintings"—*spoilt* was Qing's word for describing the entrance of a shaman into trance.[13]

Traditionally, Westerners have viewed San art at best as an impressionistic representation of natural phenomena and at worst as the mere sketching of figures to pass the time. Many doubted its authenticity among the San, preferring to believe instead that the artwork was executed by foreigners; Erich von Daniken, the popular science fiction author, even went so far as to suggest an extraterrestrial origin. Current research, however, has convincingly demonstrated that this rock art did not concern alien visitors from outer space but San voyages to inner space. What is so remarkable is the existence of a record, etched in or painted on stone, that links San mythology and ritual practice to their exploration of supernatural states of consciousness available to them through trance. And some of this artwork, reports Lewis-Williams, approaches thirty thousand years of age when dated by modern scientific methods, providing us with the oldest existing pictorial accounts of the human spiritual quest.[14]

/Kaggen, as might be expected, is at the center of the mythology that supports the San trance phenomenon; according to the southern San, he created the trance dance:

Cagn [/Kaggen] gave us the song of this dance, and told us to dance it, and people would die from it [that is, go into trance], and he would give them charms to raise them again. It is a circular dance of men and women, following each other, and it is danced all night. Some fall down, some become as if mad and sick, blood runs from the noses of others whose charms are weak, and they eat charm medicine, in which there is burnt snake powder. When a man is sick this dance is danced round him, and the dancers put both hands under their armpits, and press their hands on him, and when he coughs the initiated put out their hands and receive what has injured him—secret things.[15]

Among the Ju/'hoansi, this trance dance is still enacted regularly throughout the month, and all members of Ju/'hoansi society participate. Dance and song are invested with a spiritual potency the Ju/'hoansi call N/um or ntum, a power released as the experience of fire in the bodies of the dancers. Ju/'hoansi women initiate this ritual celebration with the lighting of a central dance fire, then govern the tempo of the event through singing the "song of the dance," polyrhythmic clapping, and shaking rattles around the feet of the male dancers. After several hours of singing and dancing, some men begin to approach a rapturous state; an inner spiritual journey commences, described by a Ju/'hoansi shaman in the following way to anthropologist Richard Lee:

> [Ju/'hoansi] medicine [N/um] is put into the body through the backbone. It boils in my belly and boils up to my head like beer. When the women start singing and I start dancing, at first I feel quite all right. Then in the middle, the medicine begins to rise from my stomach. After that I see all the people like very small birds, the whole place will be spinning around and that is why we run around. . . . You feel your blood become very hot just like blood boiling on a fire and then you start healing.[16]

Another trance dancer described the experience to anthropologist Marguerite Biesele:

> When people sing, I dance. I enter the earth. I go in at a place like a place where people drink water. I travel a long way, very far. When I emerge, I am already climbing. I'm climbing threads, the threads that lie over there in the south. I climb one and leave it, then I climb another one . . . and climb another. . . . And when you arrive at God's place you make yourself small. You have become small. You come in small to God's place. You do what you have to do there. Then you return to where everyone is, and you hide your face. You hide your face so you won't see anything. You come and come and come and finally you enter your body again. All the people who have stayed behind are waiting for you—they fear you. You enter, enter the earth, and you return to enter the skin of your body.
> And you say "he-e-e-e." That is the sound of your return to your body. Then you begin to sing. The ntum-masters are there

around. They take powder and blow it—Phew! Phew!—in your
face. They take hold of your head and blow about the sides of your
face. This is how you manage to be alive again. Friends, if they don't
do that to you, you die. . . . You just die and are dead. Friend, this
is what it does, this *ntum* that I do, this *ntum* here that I dance.[17]

Reading these firsthand accounts of the inner spiritual journey familiar to the San, I am reminded of the descriptions given by the great
Hindu master of the nineteenth century, Ramakrishna, of the spiritual force or current called *kundalini* and of that rapturous state
known in the Orient as *samadhi* (the spiritual traveler's arrival at
"God's place"):

> One feels the sensation of the Spiritual Current to be like the move-
> ment of an ant, a fish, a monkey, a bird, or a serpent. Sometimes the
> Spiritual Current rises through the spine, crawling like an ant.
> Sometimes, in samadhi, the Soul swims joyfully in the ocean of di-
> vine ecstasy, like a fish. Sometimes, when I lie down on my side, I
> feel the Spiritual Current pushing me like a monkey and playing
> with me joyfully. I remain still. That Current, like a monkey, sud-
> denly with one jump reaches the Sahasrara [an area at the top of the
> spinal column]. That is why you see me jump up with a start. Some-
> times, again, the Spiritual Current rises like a bird hopping from one
> branch to another. The place where it rests feels like fire.
>   Sometimes the Spiritual Current moves up like a snake. Going in
> a zigzag way, at last it reaches the head and I go into samadhi. A
> man's spiritual consciousness is not awakened unless his Kundalini
> is aroused.[18]

While Hindu and Buddhist adepts wrote about their experience
of spiritual awakening, many millennia before them San shamans of
southern Africa committed memories of their ecstatic encounters to
painted and engraved images on rocks and cave walls. Lewis-
Williams has demonstrated how the often strange images of San rock
art are readily understood as the revelations of shamans about their
adventures in the spirit world. He compared both statements made
by the San themselves and scientific studies of individuals undergoing
trance with results that shatter many preconceived notions about
these mythic images.

Figure 12. A shaman with lines of spiritual force (*N/um*) entering his body.

Figure 12, for example, shows a shaman as *N/um,* the spiritual potency, probably of an eland, is entering his body. While the painting suggests a shaman in flight, the bent-over posture is more akin to the doubled-over position assumed by a trance dancer as he or she* begins to experience *N/um* entering through the stomach; the streaming lines are then not so much moving away from the shaman as entering him, except for the two black lines, which are most likely the shaman's perception of elongated arms, trailing behind. We also see antelope horns, an antelope cap, cloven hooves, and raised hair on this shaman, confirming the rendering of an eland's death as a metaphor for the shaman's trance; the master animal of the outer hunt now becomes the spiritual master of the inner way.

Flying sensations, like those experienced by many people in sleep, have also been reported by individuals in various forms and stages of trance. Many San paintings show shamans in flight, like the two

Figure 13. Rock painting of two swallow-tailed shamans in flight.

---

* In the present day, more Ju/'hoansi shamans are female than in previous times.

swallow-tailed images in Figure 13, reminding us of Ramakrishna's description of the "Spiritual Current" causing him to feel like a bird.

One of the strangest sensations I've experienced from long periods of sitting meditation are "somatic hallucinations," in which parts of my body feel foreshortened or inexplicably elongated while my eyes are closed. Such hallucinations of the body, reported among experimental subjects in the laboratory, are also well known among San shamans in trance, who represent them in rock art as humanlike forms with elongated body parts, as in Figure 14.

Lewis-Williams has described the many other portrayals of the rhapsodic state of shamanic trance in San rock art, from the underwater journeys of shamans transformed into fish to the spontaneous generation of visual hallucinations of dots, lines, curves, and other shapes known to modern-day neuroscientists as *entoptic phenomena*. And these images have not only been matched to the reports of other societies around the world where shamanism is still practiced today, but also confirmed in the laboratories of neuroscientists studying trance.

What is equally exciting is the evidence that the San have provided for the stages of development of human spirituality in general and of African sacred wisdom in particular. Here is an unbroken connection between myth, ritual, and human spirituality

Figure 14. Shamanic image of perceiving an elongated body in trance.

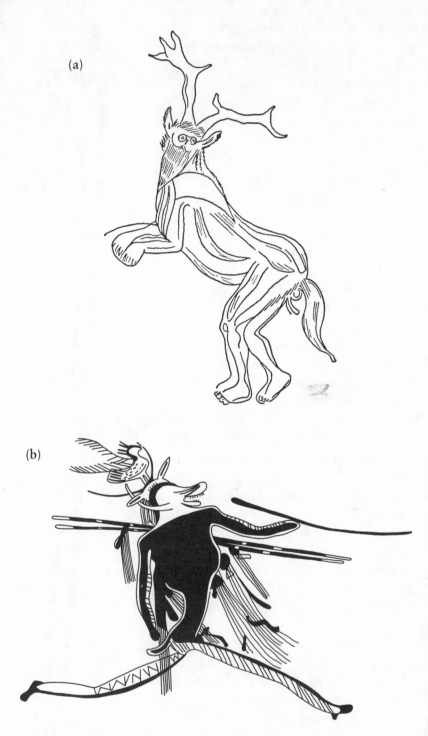

Figure 15. Paleolithic shamans: (a) *The Sorcerer of Trois Frères*, Ariège, France; and (b) the shaman of southern Africa, Cape Province, South Africa.

of great antiquity. Here are some of the earliest depictions of the great themes of human spirituality that still exist today: the dead and resurrected god; the quest of the spiritual hero and heroine; the experience of enlightenment upon achieving the godhead. And these themes are not just the motifs of a tale we may analyze, whose origins, history, and manner of recording we may still question; these themes have been preserved for us to behold in or on stone in Africa, some for as long as thirty millennia. The hero with an African face not only has a place among the world's great mythologies but that place *is* carved in stone.

Finally, these findings about the San suggest that the other sites of Paleolithic rock art throughout the world need also be considered in a new light. Until the ancient mystery behind San rock art was unmasked, the caves of Europe were thought to contain the oldest examples of the visionary art of shamans; this is no longer true. The age of the rock art in Lascaux, France, location of the most famous European caves, has been reckoned only to about 17,000 B.C.E.; there, too, images of the bull or the stag may be seen serving as the master animal of that locale and time. Of a similar age, in the Pyrenees, is perhaps the most well-known prehistoric image of a shaman, *The Sorcerer of Trois Frères,* and it is truly astounding how similar this European shaman is to the equivalent rock images of San shamans, though some of the latter may have been produced hundreds of generations earlier. When such European and African renderings are juxtaposed, as in Figure 15, both stand out as complex and enigmatic, humanlike while also composed of different animal forms. Both shamans follow the way of the master animals they embody in this rock art on a journey that reveals not only the rewards of the hunt but the bounty of the human soul.

7

THE GODDESS
IN AFRICA

Holy Mother Earth
She who guides those who live upon Her,
She whose laws the people of the Ibo follow,
Living in the honesty and rightness
that are the ways of the Goddess Ala;
it is She who brings the child to the womb
and She who gives it life,
always present during life
and receiving those whose lives are ended,
taking them back into Her sacred womb,
"the pocket of Ala."

PRAISE SONG TO THE GODDESS ALA,
FROM THE IBO OF NIGERIA

Is the Goddess lost in Africa? Evidence of her ancient reign, twenty thousand years ago or more, is forever engraved on rock walls and sculpted in stone figurines throughout what were the population centers of primitive Europe and Asia; faceless statuettes announce her fecundity: ample breasts, full hips, a pregnant belly. Throughout the world, from present-day France to China, this Goddess figure has been unearthed—but not in Africa, not here in humanity's womb.

These celebrated stone figurines, most no more than several inches tall yet all bearing a like design, have been heralded as commemorating the height of the World Age of the Goddess, when the Feminine was the revered and informing principle of humankind. It is as if the ancient artisans, though thousands of miles apart, crafted the Goddess's image from some ideal already known. And it is to these icons that a generation of modern women have now turned, seeking spirituality beyond the cloisters of inherited, patriarchal religious systems from East and West. Yet as I turn the pages of so many popular books on the Goddess, I cannot help but notice their silence on Africa.

Leo Frobenius was a lone voice offering an answer to these disparities in the account of the Goddess in Africa. She was not missing, he suggested boldly in 1927, but had been that very ideal the others had beheld—only her African roots had long since been forgotten. Frobenius proposed that the earliest Goddess figurines had actually been fashioned in Africa, the pattern then migrating with the human diaspora from Africa to Europe and beyond. But these African images had been carved of wood, not of stone, and so could not withstand the ravages of time.[1]

In Search of the Goddess in Africa

The search for the Goddess in Africa begins with an understanding that the Goddess is not simply the feminine face of God. *God* is a word with Indo-European origins in the Sanskrit root *gheu,* meaning "to invoke" and "to pour, to offer sacrifice." Here, the allusion is both to the invocation of the names of divinities and the rituals of libation and sacrifice to them.[2] The word *God* does not inevitably imply a "Supreme *Person*"; rather it is a reference to the Absolute, the Eternal—the ground of being whose ultimate nature is forever beyond the scope of rational human thought, that unending source from which the phenomenal world around us arises and into which it passes away. God is by definition beyond definition, beyond name, and beyond categories: Nyame, "the fathomless Spirit" known to the Ashanti; Njambi-Kalunga, "the God of the unknown" of the Lunda; Endalandala, "the Unexplainable," according to the Ngombe; Ngai, "the Unknown," as uttered by the Masai. God is also beyond human form—neither male nor female, neither young nor old. The Shona describe God as simultaneously "Father, Mother, and Son."[3]

So the mere reference to God as he or him, she or her, removes us from this realm of the Absolute and places us in the realm of duality and distinction that God is, by definition, beyond. It is regrettable, then, that many religions, particularly Christianity, Judaism, and Islam, have chosen to affix God's sex as male, for this bears false witness to the majesty of God's mystery, and its negative impact on women has been well documented by many authorities on female spirituality. However, it would be equally regrettable, and false, to attempt to balance the historical account of a male God by affixing God's sex as female and then using the term *Goddess*. For the Goddess is a wonder in her own right, not to be equated with the Absolute—the formless, sexless, transcendent vision of God.

What, then, of the Goddess? And how is she to be found in Africa? After studying both male and female initiation rites among the Ndembu of Central Africa in the 1950s, the English anthropologist Victor Turner concluded that Ndembu culture was founded on "a female or maternal principle pervading society and nature."[4] This definition begins to get at the nature of the Goddess, perhaps best understood as an archetype: a primordial image dwelling within us that finds expression in our feelings and actions, our beliefs and behaviors—from the artifacts we create and the myths we craft, to the worldviews we hold dear, to the manner in which we act in the world toward ourselves and others. A "woman with her baby," notes Joseph Campbell, "is the basic image of mythology."

> When one can feel oneself in relation to the universe in the same complete and natural way as that of the child with the mother, one is in complete harmony and tune with the universe. Getting into harmony and tune with the universe and staying there is the principal function of mythology.[5]

So through the Goddess the individual participates in the great mystery of being, at the level of the cosmos, the earth, the society, and the self.

But the Goddess in African mythology is frequently hidden. One major reason lies in how myths of the Goddess in Africa were originally collected, recorded, and interpreted. As we've already noted, the earliest written accounts of orally transmitted African myths did not come from professional mythologists, anthropologists, or ethnographers; rather they were provided by missionaries, explorers, and adventurers. Almost all were men, almost all were Christian, and almost all had biases and motives through which their recording of African myths were filtered. Christian dogma predisposed them to find a Supreme Creator who was male, even when the local African account may have suggested otherwise.

"However anxious a missionary may be to appreciate and to retain indigenous social and moral values, in the case of religion he has to be ruthless," said Diedrich Westerman, the German professor of African Languages and Cultures in a lecture on "Africa and Christianity" in 1935. "He has to admit and even to emphasize," Westerman continued, "that the religion he teaches is opposed to the existing one and the one [traditional African religions] has to cede to the other."[6]

Nyame, the Akan or Ashanti divinity, is a case in point: R. S. Rattray, the British political officer turned anthropologist, referred to Nyame or Onyame exclusively as male, the supreme "Sky God" of the Ashanti; after him many followed suit without questioning this interpretation.[7] Eva Meyerowitz, however—neither male nor Christian—found Nyame exclusively as the Akan Goddess, "the one supreme deity without beginning or end. . . . The substance or body of Nyame, in her aspect of Moon- and Firmament-goddess, is envisaged as fire; the life-giving spirit or power that animated the fire and caused the birth of the universe is called the *kra* [vital force]."[8] Geoffrey Parrinder, in a third account, takes a somewhat ambivalent position between these two: "Nyame of Ashanti is sometimes said to be both male and female," he writes, with the moon representing the feminine aspect of this deity and the sun the male aspect. "The female element created men with water," Parrinder goes on, "and the male sun shot its life-giving fire into human veins."[9]

Male, female, or androgynous? A similar ambiguity occurs with many other principal African deities: Nzambi of the BaKongo; Nana Buluku and Mawu-Lisa of the Fon; Odudua and Obatala of the Yoruba; Obosom, also of the Akan; and Nalwanga of the BaSoga, to name but a few. And I have the distinct impression after sifting through this literature that the European authorities on African sacred wisdom, particularly the older authorities, insisted and imposed simplicity on what they found, even when such simplicity was unwarranted.

No, the Goddess is not missing in Africa,

Figure 16. Androgynous deity, a Dogon wood figure from Mali.

though she has often been driven into hiding by those incapable of beholding her through the multitude of her forms. In fact, a haunting myth about the Goddess in hiding comes from the Soninke of the African Sahel—that semidesert southern fringe of the Sahara stretching from Senegal in the west to the Nile in the east. The high point of Soninke culture was around 500 B.C.E., and from the fourth to the twelfth century C.E., troubadours of the Sahel performed the *Dausi*, an epic about this earlier heroic period. Much of the *Dausi* has been lost, in large part due to the destructive influence of Islam on traditional African culture. *Gassire's Lute*, which follows, is one of the better-preserved selections from the Soninke *Dausi*.[10]

Here we witness a story from the early days of European intrusion into Africa, prior to Islam and Christianity, for the cities and peoples mentioned in this fragment bordered the famed "Chariot Road"—that thousand-mile trans-Sahara passage stretching from near Tripoli, on the Mediterranean Sea, to Gao, on the Niger River (see "A Map of the People and Myths of Africa," p. xvi). This is the road traveled as early as 1000 B.C.E. by the Nigretai, the Libyan charioteers esteemed for their beautiful black skins (see Chapter 1) and superb horsemanship. But it was also the desert conveyor of a new transportation technology into sub-Saharan Africa, the horse-drawn chariot, and with it a new machine of war and conquest. In 19 C.E., the Roman legate Cornelius Balbus pursued a military campaign along the Chariot Road, conquering every city from the Mediterranean to the Niger. And the new patriarchal values on which such bloody conquests were founded drove the Goddess into hiding, as the Soninke myth suggests:

◎◎ Four times Wagadu* stood there in all her splendor. Four times Wagadu disappeared and was lost to human sight: once through vanity, once through falsehood, once through greed, and once through dissension. Four times Wagadu changed her name. First she was called Dierra, then Agada, then Ganna, then Silla.† Four times she turned her face: once to the north, once to the west, once to the east, and once to the south. For Wagadu, whenever men have seen her, has always had four gates: one to the north, one to the west, one to the east, and one to the south. Those are

---

*Wagadu is both the name of the Soninke Goddess and the name of the legendary city of the Fasa (Fezzan) people.
†These four names also refer to cities spread across the Sahel.

the directions whence the strength of Wagadu comes, the strength in which she endures no matter whether she be built of stone, wood, or earth or lives but as a shadow in the mind and longing of her children. For really, Wagadu is not of stone, not of wood, not of earth. Wagadu is the strength that lives in the hearts of men and is sometimes visible, because eyes see her and ears hear the clash of swords and ring of shields, and is sometimes invisible, because the indomitability of men has overtired her so that she sleeps.

Sleep came to Wagadu for the first time through vanity, for the second time through falsehood, for the third time through greed, and for the fourth time through dissension. Should Wagadu ever be found again, then she will live so forcefully in the minds of men that she will never be lost, so forcefully that vanity, falsehood, greed, and dissension will never be able to harm her.

Hoooh! Dierra, Agada, Ganna, Silla! Hoooh! Fasa! ◎◎

Listen to the ancient Sahel bards, accompanying themselves on lute, singing of the emergence and disappearance of Wagadu. Particularly compelling is the metaphoric use of Wagadu, at once a city yet always something more: a feeling in one's heart; the goddess of compassion and wisdom; the goddess of directions birthing order from the chaos prior to her; the divine feminine allure of splendor beyond base human pursuits. In this way, Wagadu is reminiscent of the ancient Indian goddess Desahai Devi,[11] who commands the four directions, or of Arduisur, the female deity of ancient Persia, from whose body four rivers flowed as symbols of the four cardinal points.[12] The remnant of the Sahel epic continues:

◎◎ Wagadu was lost for the first time through vanity. At that time Wagadu faced north and was called Dierra. Her last king was called Nganamba Fasa. The Fasa were strong. But the Fasa were growing old. Daily they fought against the Burdama and the Boroma. They fought every day and every month. Never was there an end to the fighting. And out of the fighting, the strength of the Fasa grew. All Nganamba's men were heroes, all the women were lovely and proud of the strength and the heroism of the men of Wagadu.

Nganamba had a son, Gassire, who daily longed for his father's demise. "When will Nganamba die? When will Gassire be king?" Every day Gassire watched for the death of his father as a lover watches for the evening star to rise. By day, when Gassire fought as a hero against the

Burdama and drove the false Boroma before him with a leather girth, he thought only of the fighting, of his sword, of his shield, of his horse. By night, when he rode with the evening into the city and sat in the circle of men and of his own sons, Gassire heard how the heroes praised his deeds. But his heart was not in the talking; his heart listened for the strains of Nganamba's breathing; his heart was full of misery and longing. Gassire's heart was full of longing for the shield of his father, the shield that he could carry only when his father was dead, and also for the sword that he might draw only when he was king.

Kiekorro, an old wise man then told Gassire that his vanity would lead him to pick up the lute, instead of his father's shield, and this would cause Wagadu to disappear. Gassire scoffed at him, not really understanding this prophecy. "Ah, Gassire, you cannot believe me," the old man said. "But your path will lead you to the partridges in the fields, and you will understand what they say, and that will be your way and the way of Wagadu."

Gassire continued fighting against the enemies of the Fasa and won many great victories. Then one day he wandered away from his army into the fields, where he heard the partridges sing as prophesied.

"Hear the *Dausi*! Hear my deeds!" The partridge sang of its battle with the snake. The partridge sang, "All creatures must die, be buried,

Figure 17. Fresco of a horned Goddess from the Tassili Mountains, in the central Fezzan, an area northeast of the Soninke, created during the period 8000–6000 B.C.E. Might her image be similar to that of the lost goddess Wagadu, of whom the Soninke bards sing?

and rot. Kings and heroes die, are buried, and rot. I, too, shall die, shall be buried, and rot. But the *Dausi,* the song of my battles, shall not die. It shall be sung again and again and shall outlive all kings and heroes. Hoooh, that I might do such deeds! Hoooh, that I may sing the *Dausi!* Wagadu will be lost. But the *Dausi* shall endure and shall live!"

Hoooh! Dierra, Agada, Ganna, Silla! Hoooh! Fasa!

Now Gassire was seduced by this promise of immortality and went straightaway to the old wise man. "Kiekorro! I was in the fields. I understood the partridges. The partridge boasted that the song of its deeds would live longer than Wagadu. The partridge sang the *Dausi.* Tell me whether men also know the *Dausi* and whether the *Dausi* can outlive life and death."

"Gassire, you are hastening to your end," said Kiekorro. "No one can stop you. And since you cannot be a king, you shall be a bard, and for this, Wagadu will be lost."

"Then Wagadu can go to blazes!" yelled Gassire.*

Hoooh! Dierra, Agada, Ganna, Silla! Hoooh! Fasa!

So Gassire had a smith make him a lute.† But the lute would not sing.

"I cannot do anything about it," said the smith. "The rest is your affair." Gassire said, "What can I do, then?" The smith said, "This is a piece of wood. It cannot sing if it has no heart. You must give it a heart. Carry this piece of wood on your back when you go into battle. The wood must ring with the stroke of your sword. The wood must absorb dripping blood, the blood of your blood, the breath of your breath. Your pain must be its pain, your fame its fame. The wood must no longer be like the wood of a tree but must be a part of your people. Therefore it must live not only with you but with your sons. Then will the tone that comes from your heart echo in the ear of your son and live on in the people, and your son's life's blood, oozing out of his heart, will run down your body and live on in this piece of wood. But Wagadu will be lost because of it."

Gassire said, "Wagadu can go to blazes!"

Hoooh! Dierra, Agada, Ganna, Silla! Hoooh! Fasa!

Gassire went back to the battle with his lute strapped to his back and his eight sons at his side. But each of the next seven days, one of his sons fell

---

* Gassire's original oath undoubtedly sounded less British, but it has been lost under layers of translation.

† Although the translation calls Gassire's instrument a lute it was more likely an oud, a stringed instrument that found its way from Africa through Europe as the precursor of the lute and modern-day guitar.

to the enemy's swords, and each of these days he carried his fallen son back home over his shoulder with blood dripping on the lute. The deaths of his sons made Gassire even angrier, and he pursued the battle out of his rage. Many of his army were killed. All the women wailed. All the men were angry.

Before the eighth day of the fighting, all the heroes and the men of Dierra gathered and spoke to Gassire: "Gassire, this shall have an end. We are willing to fight when it is necessary. But you, in your rage, go on fighting without sense or limit. Now, go forth from Dierra! A few will join you and accompany you. Take your Boroma* and your cattle. The rest of us incline more to life than fame. And while we do not wish to die without fame, we have no wish to die for fame alone."

The old wise man said, "Ah, Gassire! Thus will Wagadu be lost today for the first time."

Hoooh! Dierra, Agada, Ganna, Silla! Hoooh! Fasa!

Gassire and his last, his youngest, son, his wives, his friends, and his Boroma rode out into the desert. They rode through the Sahel. Many heroes rode with Gassire through the gates of the city. Many turned back, but a few accompanied Gassire and his youngest son into the Sahara.

They rode far, day and night. They came into the wilderness, and in the loneliness they rested. All the heroes and all the women and all the Boroma slept. Gassire's youngest son slept but Gassire was restive. For a long time he sat by the fire before falling asleep. Then, suddenly he jumped up and listened. Close beside him Gassire heard a voice, which rang as though it came from himself. Gassire began to tremble and he heard the lute singing. The lute sang the *Dausi.*

When the lute had sung the *Dausi* for the first time, King Nganamba died in the city of Dierra; when the lute had sung the *Dausi* for the first time, Gassire's rage melted, and he wept. When the lute had sung the *Dausi* for the first time, Wagadu disappeared—for the first time.

Hoooh! Dierra, Agada, Ganna, Silla! Hoooh! Fasa! ◎◎

And Gassire thus learned that when vanity and fame are sought above all else, the goddess of compassion and true life forever eludes the seeker. For Gassire gave up his sons, his community, and his kingship in pursuit of his immortality, and lost Wagadu, the great Goddess, in return. One final time, the bards sing Wagadu's refrain:

---

* Most likely members of this tribe who were his servants.

◎◎ Every time that the guilt of man caused Wagadu to disappear, she won a new beauty that made the splendor of her next appearance still more glorious. Vanity brought the song of the bards, which all peoples imitate and value today. Falsehood brought a rain of gold and pearls. Greed brought writing as the Burdama still practice it today and which in Wagadu was the business of the women. Dissension will enable the final Wagadu to be as enduring as the rain of the south and the rocks of the Sahara, for every man will then have Wagadu in his heart and every woman a Wagadu in her womb.

Hoooh! Dierra, Agada, Ganna, Silla! Hoooh! Fasa! ◎◎

Alas, the songs of the ancient Sahel bards are now lost to the ages; the epic is incomplete, and we do not know the fate of Gassire, his sword, and his lute, or whether after exile he rediscovered Wagadu, only to lose her again. For only later do we learn of this Goddess in another surviving fragment of the *Dausi:* "No one knew where she was. Then she was found again. And then she was lost again and did not reappear for seven hundred and forty years."[13]

No, the Goddess in Africa is not lost, but she has, like Wagadu, receded to await our rediscovery of her. Perhaps when she is found this next time, as the Sahel bards foretold of Wagadu, she will live so forcefully in our minds that she will never be lost again.

Our Mother

We are so accustomed to saying, "Our Father" in reference to a supreme being that it comes as a refreshing surprise to discover this from the Ijo of southern Nigeria:

◎◎ Once there was a large field, and in this field stood an enormous iroko tree with large buttresses. One day, the sky darkened, and there descended on the field a large table, a large chair, and an immense "creation stone." And on the table was a large quantity of earth. Then there was lightning and thunder, and Woyengi, the Mother, descended. She seated herself on the chair and placed her feet on the "creation stone." Out of the earth on the table Woyengi molded human beings. But they had no life and were neither man nor woman, and Woyengi, embracing them one by one, breathed her breath into them, and they became living beings. But they were still neither men nor women, and so Woyengi asked them one by one to choose to be man or woman, and she made them so, each according to his or her choice.

Next Woyengi asked them, one by one, what manner of life each would like to lead on earth. Some asked for riches, some for children, some for short lives, and all manner of things. And these Woyengi bestowed on them one by one, each according to his or her wish. Then Woyengi asked them one by one by what manner of death they would return to her. And out of the diseases that afflict the earth they each chose a disease. To all of these wishes Woyengi said, "So be it."[14] ◎◎

The mythic Goddess in Africa, the Great Mother of Creation, is revealed here amidst three pervasive symbols of her provenance and power: the tree, the earth, and the stone. And it is exactly through such symbols that the Goddess's presence may be known in African sacred myth. Of these three—the tree, the earth, the stone—the last would seem most out of place, for stone is cold and hard and lifeless—attributes with which the Goddess is not normally associated. But in *The Great Mother*, his seminal work on the Goddess, Israeli psychologist Erich Neumann makes the definitive connection. In discussing the anatomy of the Goddess (the female body) as a symbolic vessel containing a sanctified universe, Neumann relates the Goddess's body to a mountain rising out of the primal waters of creation, and he notes that the womb of the Goddess is then represented in "such symbols as chasm, cave, abyss, valley, depths, which in innumerable rites and myths play the part of the earth womb that demands to be fructified . . . Accordingly, it is not only the mountain that is worshiped as the Great Mother but also rocks representing it—and her."[15]

Dominique Zahan, the French anthropologist, describes such African sacred stone sites as "elementary cathedrals."[16]

Such sacred rocks and stones representing the power of the Goddess are found throughout Africa. Malidoma Somé tells a modern-day story of "Goddess stones" that played a part in his reentry into Dagara society after spending years away in European schools. A meeting was convened at a shrine to the Earth Goddess to determine if this prodigal son should be received by the Dagara. The counsel of elders was seated upon six sacred stones.

Presently each of the six stones had a man on it. Each elder was assigned a stone to use until he died. Each time a stone was left empty by death, the chief of the earth shrine [priest of the Goddess] selected another man among the grandfathers and great-grandfathers of the community. The priest of the earth shrine is always succeeded at his death by the eldest of his sons from his first wife. So this circle had existed since time immemorial.[17]

In addition, the Kabre of Togo know certain rocks as "creation stones," bearing the imprinted footsteps of the first created humans; and the Mossi of Upper Volta install their king by having him take a seat on a series of stones between the city of his coronation and the city from which he will rule. The earthly king thus sits on a throne symbolic of the divine Goddess Mother, an image replicated in an Egyptian statue of the pharaoh Amun Ra sitting on the stone throne of the Great Goddess Isis, as though a child on the lap of its mother. Joseph Campbell noted the relationship between this Egyptian representation of the theme and a later Christian variant: "At Chartres Cathedral," he recalled, "you will see an image of the Madonna as the throne upon which the child Jesus sits and blesses the world as its Emperor. That is precisely the image that has come down to us from most ancient Egypt. The early fathers and the early artists took over these images intentionally."[18]

The Goddess and the Snake

◎◎ At first there was one God, Nana-Buluku; she was at the same time both male and female. Mawu came from Nana-Buluku. Mawu was one person but she had two faces: the first was that of a woman, whose eyes belong to the Moon. That face took the name of Mawu. The other was the face of a man, whose eyes belonged to the Sun, and it took the name of Lisa. Mawu directed night, while Lisa directed the day. This is why, when there is an eclipse of the moon or the sun, it is said that Mawu is having intercourse with herself, that Mawu and Lisa are engaged in making love. Since Mawu was both man and woman, she became pregnant. ◎◎

This is how the Fon of Dahomey begin their description of creation through Mawu, who is clearly an example of mythology's phallic Goddess.[19] Traditionally, Mawu-Lisa was honored in the four-day week of the Fon, recognizing the four days of her creation. On the first day, she gave birth to the lesser gods and goddesses, the *vodun,* and she created humans out of clay. On the second day, Mawu-Lisa made the earth habitable for life; on the third day, humankind received the gifts of sight, speech, and awareness; while on the fourth and final day, technology was conveyed to humanity. In this work, Mawu also had the assistance of Aido-Hwedo, the Great Serpent:

◎◎ Now, when the Creator made the world, she had Aido-Hwedo with her as her servant. Aido-Hwedo carried her in his mouth everywhere. We do not know if the world was there already. We know the earth was the first created, because the world is like a calabash. The top is put on last.

Wherever the Creator went, Aido-Hwedo went with her. That is why the earth is as we find it. It curves, it winds, it has high places and low places. That is the movement of the serpent Aido-Hwedo. Where Mawu and Aido-Hwedo rested, there are mountains, because the mountains were made by the excrement of Aido-Hwedo. That is why we find riches inside mountains.

Now, when the work was finished, Mawu saw that the earth had too much weight. There were too many things—too many trees, too many mountains, elephants, everything. It was necessary to rest the earth on something. So Aido-Hwedo was told to coil himself into a circle and rest as a carrying pad underneath the earth.

Now, when Aido-Hwedo stirs, there is an earthquake.[20] ◎◎

This powerful image shows the Goddess—Creatrix of all—being brought to her work of fashioning the world in the mouth of the serpent, symbolizing the vitality on which life rests. Wherever the serpent travels, life, or some principal feature of the world, is established; the same vital essence, then, weaves together all of creation into a single complex tapestry. It is not surprising that the Goddess, the Serpent, and Death often arrive simultaneously on the mythic stage; whether in the paradise of Eden or the purview of African mythology, they are all related forms. Periodically, the Serpent sheds the outer lining of its skin, as monthly the female sheds the inner lining of her womb; and the Serpent eating its tail (an image known as the uroboros; see Figure 18) represents the endless round of life begetting death, begetting life again. The Goddess, manifest in each female body, is the guarantor of this cycle.

Figure 18. Aido-Hwedo in the form of the uroboros from a bas-relief on the walls of the palace of King Gezo of Abomey.

The Goddess and the Snake also appear as the principal figures in a richly textured creation myth from the Wahungwe people of Zimbabwe[21]:

◎◉ Maori (God) made the first man and called him Mwuetsi (moon). He put him on the bottom of Dsivoa (a lake) and gave him a *ngona* horn filled with *ngona* oil. Mwuetsi lived in Dsivoa.

Mwuetsi said to Maori, "I want to go on the earth." Maori said, "You will regret it." Mwuetsi said, "Nonetheless, I want to go on the earth." Maori said, "Then go on the earth." Mwuetsi went out of Dsivoa and onto the earth.

The earth was cold and empty. There were no grasses, no bushes, no trees. There were no animals. Mwuetsi wept and said to Maori, "How shall I live here?" Maori said, "I warned you. You have started on the path at the end of which you shall die. I will, however, give you one of your kind." Maori gave Mwuetsi a maiden who was called Massassi, the morning star. Maori said, "Massassi shall be your wife for two years." Maori gave Massassi a fire-maker.

In the evening Mwuetsi went into a cave with Massassi. Massassi said, "Help me. We will make a fire. I will gather *chimandra* [kindling] and you can twirl the *rusika* [revolving part of the fire-maker]." Massassi gathered kindling. Mwuetsi twirled the *rusika*. When the fire was lighted Mwuetsi lay down on one side of it, Massassi on the other. The fire burned between them.

Mwuetsi thought to himself, "Why has Maori given me this maiden?

What shall I do with this maiden, Massassi?" When it was night Mwuetsi took his *ngona* horn. He moistened his index finger with a drop of *ngona* oil. Mwuetsi said, *"Ndini chaambuka mhiri ne mhiri."* ("I am going to jump over the fire.")* Mwuetsi jumped over the fire. Mwuetsi approached the maiden, Massassi. Mwuetsi touched Massassi's body with the ointment on his finger. Then Mwuetsi went back to his bed and slept.

When Mwuetsi wakened in the morning he looked over to Massassi. Mwuetsi saw that Massassi's body was swollen. When day broke Massassi began to bear. Massassi bore grasses. Massassi bore bushes. Massassi bore trees. Massassi did not stop bearing till the earth was covered with grasses, bushes, and trees.

The trees grew. They grew till their tops reached the sky. When the tops of the trees reached the sky, it began to rain.

Mwuetsi and Massassi lived in plenty. They had fruits and grain. Mwuetsi built a house. Mwuetsi made an iron shovel. Mwuetsi made a hoe and planted crops. Massassi plaited fish traps and caught fish. Massassi fetched wood and water. Massassi cooked. In this way Mwuetsi and Massassi lived for two years. ◎◎

Massassi, the Goddess of this first phase of creation, is identified as the morning star—the morning phase of the planet Venus during that portion of its orbit when it is seen as the brightest object in the heavens before the rising sun. As Virgin, Massassi's womb represents the world stage upon which the creation drama will play itself out. She is the matrix of the universe: nothing exists before her save divine will awaiting expression; she need not be penetrated but simply anointed for the round of creation to begin. With its drop of oil, the horn, of course, has phallic significance, but a *ngona* horn filled with oil also figures in many Zimbabwean myths where it turns out to be more important as a lunar symbol.

This association between the moon and the masculine aspect of creation may seem surprising at first, for frequently the moon is depicted as female, from the relationship between the lunar and menstrual cycles. But in this myth, Mwuetsi, much like the Chaga hero Murile, is symbolic of the Moon King, who reigns on earth, like the moon's light, then dies and is resurrected. We know from other Zimbabwean myths and the actual discovery of a *ngona* horn (see Figure

---

* This sentence is repeated many times in a melodramatic, ceremonial tone.

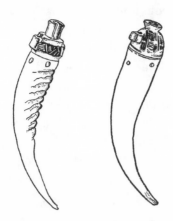

Figure 19. The Phallic Goddess in Africa. A pair of *ngona* horns from an antelope, found by German archaeologists and removed to the Afrika Archive in Frankfurt. The left one is male, the right female. From Frobenius (1968).

19) that the horn represents the two halves of a crescent moon—the thicker horn being female, the thinner horn male. The horn, then, is an androgynous symbol of creation, like the androgynous Goddess discussed earlier.

In the beginning of this myth, then, we have the motif of the phallic Goddess of creation. As in real life, the male, Mwuetsi, supplies the creative seed but afterward his job is largely done; the Goddess is the active creator: she swells with life, and she gives birth to the world. Her task done, the Goddess, in her initial form as the morning star, recedes from the world stage, her place to be taken by another:

◎◎ After two years Maori said to Massassi, "The time is up." Maori took Massassi from the earth and put her back in Dsivoa. Mwuetsi wailed. He wailed and wept and said to Maori, "What shall I do without Massassi? Who will fetch wood and water for me? Who will cook for me?" Eight days long Mwuetsi wept.

After eight days, Maori said, "I have warned you that you are going to your death. But I will give you another woman. I will give you Morongo, the evening star. Morongo will stay with you for two years. Then I shall take her back again." Morongo came to Mwuetsi in the hut. In the evening Mwuetsi wanted to lie down on his side of the fire. Morongo said, "Do not lie down over there. Lie with me." Mwuetsi lay down beside Morongo. Mwuetsi took the *ngona* horn, put some ointment on his index finger. But Morongo said, "Don't be like that. I am not like

Massassi. Now smear your loins with *ngona* oil. Smear my loins with *ngona* oil." Mwuetsi did as he was told. Morongo said, "Now couple with me." Mwuetsi coupled with Morongo. Mwuetsi went to sleep.

Toward morning Mwuetsi woke. When he looked over at Morongo, he saw that her body was swollen. As day broke, Morongo began to give birth. The first day Morongo gave birth to chickens, sheep, goats.

The second night Mwuetsi slept with Morongo again. The next morning she bore eland and cattle.

The third night Mwuetsi slept with Morongo again. The next morning Morongo bore first boys and then girls. The boys who were born in the morning were grown-up by nightfall. ◎◎

Star and crescent symbolically appear in this second phase of creation, as Mwuetsi receives the Goddess in her guise as Morongo, the evening star, the evening phase of the planet Venus. The Cosmic Mother is then impregnated, and through her, sentient beings are brought into the world. But the round of the Goddess is not over, for we then discover:

◎◎ On the fourth night Mwuetsi wanted to couple with Morongo again. But there came a thunderstorm and Maori spoke. "Let be. You are going quickly to your death." Mwuetsi was afraid. The thunderstorm passed over. When it had gone Morongo said to Mwuetsi, "Make a door and then use it to close the entrance to the hut. Then Maori will not be able to see what we are doing. Then you can couple with me." Mwuetsi made a door. With it he closed the entrance to the hut. Then he coupled with Morongo. Afterward Mwuetsi slept.

Toward morning Mwuetsi woke. Mwuetsi saw that Morongo's body was swollen. As day broke Morongo began to give birth. Morongo bore lions, leopards, snakes, and scorpions. Maori saw it. Maori said to Mwuetsi, "I warned you."

On the fifth night Mwuetsi wanted to sleep with Morongo again. But Morongo said, "Look, your daughters are grown. Couple with your daughters." Mwuetsi looked at his daughters. He saw that they were beautiful and that they were grown-up. So he slept with them. They bore children. The children that were born in the morning were full grown by night. And so Mwuetsi became the *mambo* (king) of a great people.

But Morongo slept with the snake. Morongo no longer gave birth. She lived with the snake. One day Mwuetsi returned to Morongo and wanted to sleep with her. Morongo said, "Let be." Mwuetsi said, "But I want to." He lay with Morongo. Under Morongo's bed lay the snake. The snake bit Mwuetsi. Mwuetsi sickened.

The next day it did not rain. The plants withered. The rivers and lakes dried. The animals died. The people began to die. Many people died. Mwuetsi's children asked, "What can we do?" His children said, "We will consult the *hakata* [sacred dice]." The children consulted the *hakata*. The *hakata* said, "Mwuetsi the Mambo is sick and pining. Send Mwuetsi back to Dsivoa."

Thereupon Mwuetsi's children strangled Mwuetsi and buried him. They buried Morongo with Mwuetsi. Then they chose another man to be *mambo*. Morongo, like Massassi, had lived for two years in Mwuetsi's Zimbabwe. ◎◎

In this creation myth, we observe the steps that must be taken in the progression from divinity to humanity, from the sole God (Maori) to the manifest world, from the One to the many, from the void to the plenitude, from the Immortal to the Mortal. This progression is brought about through the Goddess in her different forms: first the Virgin, bringing into the world the initial matrix, the bare set on which the drama of creation will unfold; then the Temptress, seducing her partner through guile and charm to bring forth life with her; then the Cosmic Mother who births through her mythic body all forms of living beings; and finally the Bearer of Death, consort of the Snake, who brings to her partner and her offspring the total acceptance of life and thus the complete surrender to death. With her work done and her message delivered, the Goddess, symbolically killed by her offspring, can recede from the drama of the world stage.

Humanity is then left to honor the cycle of life delivered to them by the Goddess: Mwuetsi is sacrificed and a new *mambo* chosen in imitation of the primordial ideal, which has been buried deep within humanity's collective psyche under the waters of Dsivoa. And what is this ideal? Simply put it is the prime directive of life: life consumes itself; through death comes eternal life; through mortality comes immortality.

We do know that this ideal was enacted in Wahungwe society: Wahungwe kings carried the *ngona,* and the Wahungwe practiced ritual regicide. In a version of this myth from the Wakaranga people, also of Zimbabwe,[22] the relationship between celestial bodies and the principal themes of death and resurrection is made explicit. The final recitation tells us that Mwuetsi arose from Dsivoa and now pursues

Massassi across the sky, attempting to regain the happiness of his first marriage. Here is the Moon in seeming pursuit of the planet Venus, mortality in pursuit of immortality, humanity in pursuit of the Goddess.

Red Buffalo Woman

Where the hunt provides the principal means of sustenance, the body of the Goddess is the field of the pursuit, whether forest or plain, while her fecundity is beheld in the ever-renewing supply of game to be stalked and killed. She willingly offers the lives of her issue to nourish the lives fed by the hunter, then willingly brings forth these lives again. The traditional hunter sees himself not as some modern-day bandit of the woods, out to plunder the bounty of the land, but instead as an agent of the Goddess's will. The hunter, then, must deeply identify with the Goddess. Such recognition of the life-regenerating power of the Goddess of the Hunt was found with the Thonga, mentioned previously, who consider the just-returned hunter too "hot" to enter normal society. He is then secluded in a manner normally reserved for menstruating women. Yoruba hunters, on the other hand, might identify with this Benefactress of the Forest through the legend of Red Buffalo Woman, one face of the Yoruba goddess Oya.

Uniquely adapted for the forest, the African buffalo presents a formidable challenge to the hunter: weighing almost seven hundred pounds with inward-curving horns two feet long, these beasts can slip agilely and silently into and out of thick woods; they are swift, sustaining speeds of thirty miles per hour on open ground; and they can fight fearlessly against their adversaries, whether human or other animals. Male buffalo are dark brown to black in color, but females are red, and herds of such African buffalo are led by senior females.

There is a strong association, then, between the buffalo and the Goddess in Yoruba society. Ethnographer Judith Gleason notes that Yoruba men find the red color of the buffalo cow attractive on women, and Yoruba women therefore use the color cosmetically.[23] But the buffalo is also a symbol of female reproduction and thus of the regenerative power of the Goddess. The striking resemblance between the buffalo's head and the female reproductive system has been the basis for this association between buffalo, bulls, or similarly horned animals and the Goddess for countless centuries throughout the world. When we add to this the fact that the shape of the horns is that of a crescent moon, we can see why these animals became potent symbols of the Goddess.

Marrying Buffalo Woman, then, represents the ultimate state of rapport between a hunter and this regenerating female power of the forest. This at least was the aim of Chief of Hunters, who went in search of a wife among the herd, one who would "shine brightly for him" like the light of the full moon that the Forest Goddess personifies[24]:

◎◎ He left on his evening hunt, staying out all night, but Chief of Hunters sighted nothing; he just lay on his platform up in the trees. Dawn came to the forest, and Chief of Hunters decided to wait a bit longer until it was light enough for him to make his way back home easily. All of a sudden he saw a buffalo cow approaching, looking right and left; seeing no one, she continued strolling majestically along the path. When she came to the base of a termite mound, to Chief of Hunters' great surprise, she began to remove her own skin—arm strips, leg strips, and the hide of her head. He watched her make a bundle of all this and stuff it inside the anthill. Then looking right and left again, and seeing no one, she changed herself into a beautiful woman. ◎◎

What a magnificent sight to behold: the Goddess unmasking to reveal her divinely human form; she is vulnerable now but eminently approachable in this transformed condition.

Chief of Hunters will have to plot his course with care:

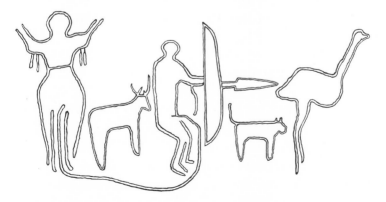

Figure 20. Paleolithic rock engraving depicting the connection of a hunter to the Mother Goddess via an umbilical cord. From Algiers.

◎◎ As Buffalo Woman headed off down the road toward the market, carrying locust-bean seeds for sale, Chief of Hunters waited until she was out of sight, then slipped down from his perch and sneaked over to where she had hidden her skin. He took up the bundle and made off home with it. Then Chief of Hunters went to market to buy some locust-bean seeds.

"Three shillings' worth of *irú*,* please," he said to Buffalo Woman, still in her beautiful human form. "Only I can't pay you just now," he uttered, pretending to search for his money. "Surely you wouldn't mind stopping by my house on your way home to collect what I owe you," he added.

"*Irú, irú,*" Buffalo Woman called out on her way back to the forest that evening, "who in this compound bought *irú* from me today?"

"Over here," said Chief of Hunters, stepping out of his house, "I purchased *irú* from you in the market this morning."

"I have come to collect my money," said Buffalo Woman.

"Very well," Chief of Hunters replied, then added, "but won't you come in for a moment?

"Here," he continued, "have something to eat before your journey." And he offered her some of the yam and some of the drink that he had sacrificed to Ifa.

Having eaten yam and drunk some wine, the beautiful woman felt very tired and sleepy. She fell into a deep sleep, and by the time she woke up, it was dark enough for her to leave without arousing suspicion among Chief of Hunters' neighbors. But when she reached the place she had hidden her skins, Buffalo Woman found them missing.

"Ai," she cried out, "Ai! Ai! What sort of thing is this?

"I looked right and left and saw no one," she recalled. "Who, then, could have taken them?" she mused. "It must have been the man who bought my locust-seed spice without paying," she realized. "I'd better go back and have a word with him."

When Buffalo Woman reached Chief of Hunters' house, she pleaded with him: "Please return those things you removed from my hiding place in the forest."

"I didn't see anything of yours," Chief of Hunters responded.

"You did," said Buffalo Woman. "Please, I beg you. Have pity on me, I implore you to return my things!"

"Marry me, then!" said Chief of Hunters abruptly.

Irú is a delicacy made of fried locust-bean seeds, a favorite offering food to Ifa. And Ifa is the ordering principle and world system of Yoruba cosmology, consulted as an oracle.

"I will," smiled Buffalo Woman. "Only you must promise never to mention to your other wives where you found me nor what it was you took from me," she admonished.

"Is that all?" said Chief of Hunters with surprise. "Well, then, I promise," he pledged.

And so it was that Chief of Hunters married Red Buffalo Woman.
◎◎

Earlier, we pointed out that the marriage of a hero to a goddess is to be understood not only in the conventional sense of a wedding of one individual to another but also in the spiritual sense of a sacred union of the individual with his or her highest spiritual striving. Buffalo Woman, Goddess of the Forest, is this spiritual ideal of Chief of Hunters; his superlative name implies that he has mastered not only the outer workings of the hunt but the inner dynamics as well, and he is therefore ready to achieve this highest revelation—namely, the realization of the Goddess, the motive force behind the cycle of predator and prey, life and death, to which he is so intimately bound. We know this, also, because Chief of Hunters is one manifestation of the Yoruba deity Ogun, the God of the Hunt. Buffalo Woman's immediate and unquestioning acceptance of his awkwardly timed marriage proposal further confirms Chief of Hunters' readiness for this ultimate boon; no tests or trials await him as he seeks the Goddess's hand. But winning the Goddess is not the end of the story; keeping her is the next challenge, and here Buffalo Woman will teach Chief of Hunters a lesson he will not soon forget:

◎◎ After several years, Buffalo Woman had given birth to four children by Chief of Hunters. One day, when he noticed his crop of red beans ready to harvest, he asked all his wives to come out into the fields to help. Now, his elder wives had never stopped asking where that "reddish" woman had come from. No relatives had arrived, not one, not once to visit her, nor had she ever been sent for by her family.

"What sort of a woman is this?" they thought. But Chief of Hunters refused to tell them.

One evening, however, they plied him with food and drink until he was no longer able to contain himself.

"Master, esteemed husband, father of the household, you owe it to us," his other wives began. "It's only proper that we should know the character of one with whom we are forced to associate," they continued.

"We are from good families—apparently she is not—but whatever her lineage we deserve to know. Don't you think it about time you told us?" they demanded.

"Can't you leave that poor woman alone?" Chief of Hunters boomed. "What's she to you?" he roared in his drunkenness. "Wasn't she that buffalo cow I saw taking off her skin out in the forest that day?" he slurred. "I bought *irú* from her and she came to collect her money. That's why I married such a buffalo, someone to confide in, someone to shine for me," he confessed in his stupor. "What do you skinny women know of the wonders of the forest anyway?" he went on. "Why shouldn't a hunter marry an animal? Now, does that satisfy you? Get off my back, I'm tired." And Chief of Hunters lapsed into a deep sleep.

"Hey, hey," the women gloated. "It's a good thing you told us now, isn't it?" they said to his deaf ears.

The evening before the harvesting of red beans was to begin, Chief of Hunters went to spend the night on his farm. His wives would join him the next morning. As soon as his wives arose, they stopped by Buffalo Woman's door.

"Are you ready?" they inquired.

"Not quite," she replied, for she was busy with her children.

"Hurry up!" goaded the wives. "The sun is up already. It's going to be a hot day."

"Please be patient," Buffalo Woman coaxed. "I'll be ready in a moment."

"Reddy, Reddy, come when you're ready," they taunted.

"We'll go on ahead," the wives sneered. "Take your own time, Reddy, just keep on chewing your cud. Your hide's in safekeeping up in the rafters, so count yourself fortunate, Red Woman!"

"Ai! Ai!" Buffalo Woman's stomach hit her back with the shock of it. As soon as her co-wives were out of sight, she sent her children out of the house, put her hands on her bag of magic power, then went to fetch water. Now she climbed up to the storage place under the roof, seized the bundle containing her hide, and began to soak it. Then Buffalo Woman put on her skin, bit by bit, over her calves, over her thighs, and over her arms. ◎◎

Buffalo Woman poses a significant threat to Chief of Hunters' other wives, for she personifies the wild, unknown, chaotic energies of the forest, and they stand for the domesticated, stable energies of society, the status quo. They can coexist only if they accommodate each other's vastly different requirements. Buffalo Woman proves herself capable of existing in their domesticated world, but the other wives are unable to handle her wildness.

It would have been customary for Chief of Hunters to mediate the domestic dispute among his wives; the abdication of this responsibility, through retreat to his bean fields, is really a worse mistake than being duped by his other wives into revealing Buffalo Woman's secret. Buffalo Woman, after all, was duped in a similar way by Chief of Hunters into marriage. But this is not a myth about maintaining domestic harmony; it is a myth about the choice between living a life committed to the authentic impulses of one's highest spiritual ideals (marriage to the Goddess) or living a life committed to society's status quo (marriage to the other wives). By withdrawing to his farm, Chief of Hunters fails to take a critical step on the path to an authentic life. For after shape-shifting back into her animal form:

◎◎ Buffalo Woman jumped down and ran through the town without touching or harming anyone, on her way to Chief of Hunters' farm. She ran into the first wife, and killed her, then the second wife, and killed her, and the same fate happened to the third. When her children saw her coming along the path, they began to run, crying, "Please don't hurt us!"

"See," Buffalo Woman said, stopping to pull the hide away from her cheek, "I'm your mother!"

"No, you're not, you're a buffalo," screamed the children. "Leave us alone! Won't you please go back to the forest?"

"Of course, it must be so," replied Buffalo Woman. "I am going back to the forest." But first she broke off a little piece of horn from her head. "Let me give you this," she told her children. "Whenever you want me to do something for you, just ask this. Call me properly, call Oya, for that is my name and I will always answer to it. Should anyone act with malice toward you, just let me know. Should you want anything— money, wives, children—just call on me, call Oya, Oya!

"Farewell, my children," she said for a final time, pulling the hide back over her face and setting off in the direction of her husband's farm.

Chief of Hunters saw her coming from a distance; instinctively he knew.

"Ai! Ai! My wives have ruined my life!" he cried.

Buffalo Woman would have killed him at once, but he began praising her. "Noble Buffalo, nothing stops you. You make your own road through the thicket. No undergrowth is too dense for you. Fighter, please don't kill this hunter simply for the sake of killing. It was he who fed you yam. It was he who gave you guinea-corn wine to drink. Please spare the hunter who hosted you, fighting bush-cow!"

Buffalo Woman was moved to pity.

"This day I am gone for good," she stated. "But I have left a piece of horn with my children. You too may call if you need me—that is, if you know how. Know that I am this sound—Oya! This form—Red Buffalo Woman. Know that I am this power."

Whereupon Buffalo Woman vanished into the forest. ◎◎

Corner an African buffalo and it will turn and run swiftly or else stand fast and mount an unrelenting fight; affront the Goddess inappropriately and she will respond in a swift and unrelenting way. In the death of the other three wives, we should not read revenge too quickly, for Buffalo Woman's response was not the simple vanquishing of foes. Here we gaze on yet another face of the Goddess—as the destroyer of unyielding forms, the smasher of vain, self-absorbed egos. Then in the next moment, upon encountering her children now afraid of her wild form, she lifts her mask for a final time to reveal her essential humanity; rest assured that though it was necessary for her to appear as the Great Destroyer, she has also never stopped being the bliss-bestowing Great Mother.

Even the children of the Goddess are no ordinary lot but are symbolic of us all, for the Goddess's offspring is humanity. And it is indeed a powerful scene when Buffalo Woman leaves her children with a snapped shard of her horn; this episode recalls the parting of another Buffalo Woman of myth, one known to the Lakota Sioux of North America. In this foundation myth of the Lakota, a beautiful young woman appears in a circle of elders, leaders, and people of the Black Hills in South Dakota. She teaches them seven sacred ceremonies and leaves them with a bundle, which when unwrapped reveals a sacred pipe to be smoked in honor of her revelations to the Lakota.

Horn and pipe are both sacred grails that lead back not just to the Buffalo Women who delivered them but to the message carried by these goddesses; that message, in the case of Red Buffalo Woman, is contained in the last few words spoken to her by Chief of Hunters: "Noble Buffalo, nothing stops you. You make your own road through the thicket. No undergrowth is too dense for you." So the

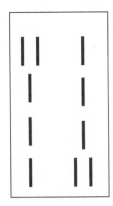

Figure 21. The Ifa sign known as Osa-Ogunda, associated with Red Buffalo Woman, which would be drawn in sacred powder by a *babalawo.*

horn of Red Buffalo Woman reminds us, as she reminded her children and Chief of Hunters, that her power can be ours when we need it; we need only call her name and follow her form, making our own road through the thicket of our lives, for no undergrowth is too dense for us to travel.

And should it seem that we are reading far too much into a simple African tale, then it might help to know that the legend of Red Buffalo Woman is told specifically as a healing narrative. When the Ifa oracle is cast, a process in which sixteen cowrie shells are thrown onto the ground like dice, should the person receive the sign known as Osa-Ogunda, this is the narrative that will be chanted by the *babalawo,* the Yoruba priest (see Figure 21 and Chapter 8 for a further description of Ifa). The afflicted person would thus be determined to be suffering from a condition of impotence and ineffectuality, possibly but not necessarily sexual, and the medicinal herbs given are called "fighting medicine," comprised chiefly of a plant known as "buffalo leaf," which is praised for its "big horns." But the whole purpose of this process is the development of a relationship with the Goddess.

"In developing a hunterly relation to the animal-goddess," observes Judith Gleason of this healing process, "the client will presumably acquire a more solid sense of self. Applying 'fighting medicine' to his body is only the beginning. Hopefully the story [of Red Buffalo Woman] will linger in his mind, calling him back to issues deeper than manifest symptoms. It all depends on his capacity for inner growth."[25]

The Legacy of the Goddess in Africa

We began this chapter with remarks about the "gap" in the archaeological record of stone artwork of the Goddess in Africa. I would
like to suggest here that perhaps even Frobenius did not venture far
enough in explaining this gap. We have seen the Goddess in Africa
through rocks, and trees, and snakes, and buffalo, among other
manifestations. Perhaps the appearance in Eurasia of these very
same forms of the Goddess, etched or carved in stone, were vestiges
of a more ancient time in Africa when it was wholly unnecessary to
create the Goddess out of stone because the Goddess was already beheld in the stone unadorned, already experienced in ritual, already
felt in the midst of the forest hunt. Then, as civilization increasingly
moved further and further away from a full mystical participation
with her archetypal form, perhaps the stone figurines of Eurasia
were fashioned from distant memories of this earlier age when, like
a babe and its mother, humanity was nestled in the bosom of the
Goddess. We do not know, but as Leo Frobenius said, it is a possibility worth keeping in mind.

We do know that much later than the stone figurines of Eurasia,
the Goddess of the North *was* born of the Goddess of the South, for
the Goddess in Africa was revered in parts of Europe. Isis, the Great
Goddess of Egypt, was worshiped throughout portions of Mediterranean Europe and the Near East right through the third century C.E.
Then, during the Italian Renaissance, attention turned to her again as
a brief period of metaphorical interpretation of Christianity flourished in some corners of Europe, spurred by new translations of the
Corpus Hermeticum (Greek writings on philosophy, theology, and
their relationship to Egyptian wisdom). Many artists of the day were
inspired by this amalgam of ideas from ancient Egypt and Greece.

On a recent trip to Rome, I visited the Vatican to see some of this
art, specifically the frescoes by the Italian Renaissance painter Pin-
turicchio in the Room of the Saints in the Borgia apartments off the
Sistine Chapel. To get past the security guards of this section of the
Vatican, then cordoned off to tourists, I posed as one of the pious
who had traveled all the way from America. Despite the ruse, I felt a
sincere reverence as I gazed on these frescoes. Several panels portrayed the myth of Isis and Osiris; and in one there was Isis (though
painted as a European) with Hermes and Moses standing before her.
These two represented two different approaches to the mythic wis-

dom of Africa: the Hermetic way of regarding such ancient wisdom as metaphor; and the Mosaic way of considering it outdated lore to be replaced by newer biblical truths. In the latter approach, the Goddess in Africa is lost to the ages, but in the former, she is revealed in all her glory. Standing there at the world center of the Mosaic path, I thought that if I listened devoutly, I might still hear the Goddess from Africa speak these words:

> I am Nature, the universal Mother, mistress of all the elements, primordial child of time, sovereign of all things spiritual, queen of the dead, queen also of the immortals, the single manifestation of all gods and goddesses that are. My nod governs the shining heights of Heaven, the wholesome sea-breezes, the lamentable silences of the world below. Though I am worshiped in many aspects, known by countless names, and propitiated with all manner of different rites, yet the whole round earth venerates me . . . and the Egyptians who excel in ancient learning and worship me with ceremonies proper to my godhead, call me by my true name, namely, Queen Isis.[26]

8

ORISHAS: MYSTERIES
OF A DIVINE SELF

If humanity were not, the gods would not be.

YORUBA PROVERB

Sitting in a Berkeley restaurant one evening in the mid 1970s, I struck up a conversation with a patron who introduced himself to me, then asked my name.

"Síva," I said, for in those days I used a name given to me in a naming ceremony by a spiritual teacher from India. Síva (pronounced as though there were an "h" after the "S") is the name of the great Hindu hero-deity, the god of death and transformation, the archetype of masculinity.

"Yes," said this fellow, "I know you. You are Shango, our Yoruba god. He has similar qualities."

We began talking about names, and I found myself narrating the story of another naming ceremony I underwent, only this time in Africa. Several years earlier, shortly before my eventful visit to the Elmina slave castle, I was in Kumasi, Ghana, walking down the street, when a group of men surrounded me, interested in the affairs of a young African American newly arrived in Africa.

"What is your name?" someone asked.

"Clyde," I replied.

"No," he said smiling, "what is your African name?"

"Why, I don't have one," I stammered.

When I lamented that I had no African name, he feigned shock and horror, then insisted that before continuing farther on my journey in Africa I should receive a name.

"Yes!" arose a collective cry. I needed an African name. What I thought at first would be a playful exercise quickly became a serious endeavor. I was whisked into an alley, a circle formed around me, and with little fanfare an impromptu initiation began. Different men called out possibilities while the others stared hard at me and asked pointed questions about my personality, my family, and my interests.

"No," one man dismissed a suggested name, "that is not a good name for him, he is not from a family of farmers."

"That name," interjected another, "does not fit his temperament."

This went on for nearly an hour, when finally one man asked on what day of the week I was born. In many parts of Africa, children receive a root name based on the day of their birth. As their life unfolds and their personality becomes established, additional names are added.

"I was born on a Tuesday," I told him.

"Ah, Kwabena," said the questioner.

"Mmmm," intoned the others.

"He does not feel like Kwabena to me" came an objection.

"What day did you come to Africa?" a voice called out next.

I had to stop to think, for it had been such a circuitous route due to missed airplane connections through Lisbon, Madrid, Zurich, and Rome. "Monday," I replied, "I first arrived in Africa on Monday."

"Kojo," said several men together.

"Yes," reiterated the self-appointed chieftain of this naming circle. "Your first name will be Kojo, a male child born on Monday," he continued. "When you first stepped onto this continent you were reborn in the spirit of Africa."

A similar process ensued until my second name was arrived at, Baako (Bah-ah-ko), which means the first male child in a family. So, Kojo Baako was the name I received amidst dancing, hugging, and much jubilation; and that is how I was known from then on in Africa.

• • •

The difference in naming practices between Africa and the West is noteworthy, for in the West we view names as facts given to us by our parents, rather than descriptors of the attributes we personify. A similar difference exists with reference to the idea of divinity or deity between Africa and the West, for in the West we regard deities as facts of life from which attributes proceed, rather than personifications of attributes found in nature and within ourselves. For example, in the West one speaks of a compassionate god, a being from whom compassion flows, while in the mythic wisdom of Africa, one speaks of a god of compassion, a personification of a force (in this case, compassion) that motivates all life, including our own.

These two different ways of regarding divinity give rise to two different ways of interpreting mythology, for where deities are considered to be facts, tales of those deities are understood historically, and where deities are viewed as personifications of source energies in nature and within ourselves, tales of those deities are understood symbolically. As facts, deities are worshiped and believed in primarily as entities outside one's self—"up there" or "down there," in a heaven or hell beyond human existence. But as symbols representing the source energies of life, deities are experienced as part of one's self: from birth to death, from hunger to anger, from love to pain, the forces that motivate us are themselves the gods and goddesses within us.

When divinity is understood in factual terms, even the symbols referring to divinity are arrested. In most of the Christian world, for example, the cross has one and only one meaning given in the historical event of Jesus' crucifixion. But that sole interpretation misses the opportunity of relating this symbol to more abiding issues of death and resurrection, compassion and suffering, that appear as active forces from moment to moment in our lives. It is customary in the West for divinity to be concretized by this sort of historical interpretation, while in the mythic traditions of Africa, divinity is released to participate in human life through interpretation in a symbolic, personal way.

One of the most robust examples of the symbolic interpretation of divinity occurs among the Yoruba of West Africa, who number about ten million in Nigeria, Dahomey, and Benin. The Yoruba pantheon, known as the *orishas,* is significant not only because of its central standing in Yoruba culture but also because the *orishas* have survived in the Americas, forming the vibrant core of such Afro-Caribbean and Afro–South American spiritual practices as Santeria, Macumba, Capoeira, and Candomblé, into which Christianity has been folded. Even in the United States, these practices appear, principally among Latino residents of urban barrios.

Most observers have applied Western standards in interpreting this unique aspect of African sacred wisdom; in other words, they see the gods and goddesses of the Yoruba pantheon as entities or forces, "beings of fact," capable of possessing those who address them through dance, song, drumming, and other ritual means. Contributing to such a view are the statements of Yoruba practitioners themselves, many of whom describe the various deities as "mounting" them or riding them like a "horse."

There is another approach, however, which is to view the *orishas* as one views all gods and goddesses in mythologically grounded cultures: as personifications of those archetypal energies that manifest in nature and within human life. Then the *orishas* are beheld not outside the individual but deep within; and the individual, through ritual address, possesses the gods and goddesses as a way of repossessing those essential, divine aspects of one's self. In *Myth, Literature, and the African World,* Nobel laureate Wole Soyinka, himself Yoruba, suggests just such an approach to understanding African mythology, calling these archetypal energies of the Yoruba pantheon "essence-ideals."[1]

Psychologist C. G. Jung had something similar in mind when he described his "archetypes of the unconscious," for Jung's archetypes are those "essence-ideals" of our unconscious that give rise to our conscious thoughts, feelings, and behaviors. Imagine such archetypes to be the DNA of our psyche, containing the basic blueprints of our psychic structure, the patterned proclivities of our personality, which are ultimately shaped by the circumstances of our upbringing and the experiences of our life. Jung thought that such archetypes are so fundamental to the human species that they were first formed in the very earliest stages of human development, millions of years ago, and like the basic structure of our bodies, they have undergone little significant change in the intervening aeons. So universal are these templates of the psyche that Jung suggested they exist not within the unconscious of each individual but in the shared, *collective unconscious* of humanity, rather like the common atmosphere in which we all live.[2]

"These patterns," writes Jungian psychologist Jean Shinoda Bolen, "can be described in a personalized way, as gods and goddesses; their myths are archetypal stories."

> And when you interpret a myth about a god [or goddess], or grasp its meaning intellectually or intuitively as bearing on your own life, it can have the impact of a personal dream that illuminates a situation and your own character, or the character of someone you know.[3]

It is in this way that we can understand and experience the *orishas.*

The Godhead Shattered

Before the pantheon came the plenitude; before archetypal forms came the primordial formlessness; before the many gods and goddesses came the one godhead, known as Orisa-nla.[4] In the beginning there was only this godhead, a beingless being, a dimensionless point, an infinite container of everything, including itself; and this uncreated creator was serviced by a slave known as Atunda. As Orisa-nla toiled away in a hillside garden, Atunda rebelled, rolling a massive boulder down the embankment, smashing Orisa-nla into a multitude of fragments. These fragments—and the number varies from 200 to 201, 400, 401, 600, 601, 1001, or more—became the Yoruba gods and goddesses, known as the *orishas.*

At first, it appears strange in this tale that the one who created everything is attended to by another being, Atunda, who is ultimately responsible for the first creative act. But Africans, you will recall, are fond of naming people for the qualities they possess, and here Atunda's name holds the key that unlocks the meaning of this brief tale of the origin of the orishas. For his name is actually a Yoruba word analyzable into three parts as *a-tun-da;* proceeding from right to left, we have *da,* to destroy and to create; *tun,* a prefix meaning again or anew (like the English prefix *re-*); and *a,* a prefix that makes a noun from what would have been the verb *tunda* (to destroy and create again). So, *atunda* means *"that which destroys and creates again."*[5]

The word *atunda* is also used regarding the principal divinatory approach to the *orishas,* known as Ifa, through which an individual may consult the pantheon as an oracle; this seeking of counsel is considered the equivalent of a death—a letting go of whatever situation or circumstance brought about the need for consultation—and then of a rebirth through the wisdom of the gods and goddesses provided by the oracle.⁶ Now, the message that this interpretation of Atunda's name suggests is that the primal cycle of destruction leading to creation, of death yielding new life, is the motive force that created the gods and goddesses, the archetypes of our own human consciousness.

Why then smash the godhead as if it were Humpty-Dumpty? Soyinka has cleverly suggested that Atunda did this so the gods and goddesses would then have some goal in life: returning to that wholeness from which they were dashed.⁷ Thus, a second portion of this spiritual formula of the Yoruba pantheon can be worked out: follow the gods and goddesses, engage the archetypes residing in your unconscious mind, through myth, ritual, prayer, dance, poetry, intuition, and other forms of meditation on them, and in this way you will be led back to original wholeness of the godhead as well. Then, finally, there is the revelation that the same cycle giving life to the gods and goddesses gives life to you, for Atunda's boulder rumbles through every moment of your life, if you have this awareness: in countless ways, you are continually being smashed only to be brought forth again in body, in mind, and in spirit.

Isn't it also interesting, given what we observed in the chapter on the Goddess in Africa, that a huge stone, not a thunderbolt or an arrow or a blade, was used to shatter the godhead? Atunda's boulder is the "creation stone," symbolic of the Goddess; even here, in the barest of tales, the Goddess rolls forth as the immanent and transcendent power that destroys and creates gods and goddesses, the archetypes of the unconscious, the templates of our conscious being in the world to which she then also gives birth.

At least several hundred shards exploded from the godhead—at least several hundred "vessels of sacred wisdom," for the word *orisha* literally means "one who has sunk a pot." Of these hundreds of *orishas,* a handful represent principal figures in the wisdom tradition of the Yoruba; it is their mythic biographies we wish to follow.⁸ A significant feature in the mythic tales of the Yoruba pantheon is that earth, not heaven, is the locale of their exploits. Unlike many myths of the spiritual quest, the Yoruba gods and goddesses come to earth from heaven seeking out humanity, rather than the other way around. This is reminiscent of the apocryphal Dead Sea Scrolls where Jesus, when asked about the kingdom of heaven, replied it was spread out in front of humankind, only they did not see it.[9] Through these accounts of the *orishas,* we can see that kingdom revealed before us—and meet the gods and goddesses, the saints and sages, within us.

Obatala and the Golden Chain of the Gods

◎◎ At the beginning of time, after the *orishas* had emerged from the godhead splintered by Atunda, there was no earth as we know it today, only a vast reach of water and untamed swamps. The *orishas* lived then in a place above the sky, a heaven land ruled by Olorun, the supreme *orisha,* also known as Olodumare, on whom many praise names are bestowed. Each *orisha* had attributes unlike the others'. Orunmilla, for example, the eldest son of Olorun, possessed the keys to sacred wisdom: the ability to peer into the future; to divine fate; and to understand the deepest mysteries of being. Obatala was a symbol of the power to create life. Then there was Eshu, who enjoyed his role as a trickster-god, playing with the elements of chance and serendipity; Eshu also commanded speech and language and was Olorun's interpreter as a result. Agemo, the chameleon, though not an *orisha,* attended Olorun as his servant.

Olokun was the only *orisha* who lived apart from the others. She reigned over the primal waters of the misty earth, a twilight domain with neither plant nor animal life. For many ages these two kingdoms, Olorun's above and Olokun's below, coexisted without conflict, for the other *orishas* were content to go about their days without paying much attention to the primitive realm below them.

Obatala, however, was not satisfied with this state of affairs; he believed that if land was raised from the watery domain of Olokun, then the *orishas* and other forms of life could inhabit the terrain. He approached Olorun with these concerns, and the supreme deity bid him undertake this great campaign to refashion the earth and introduce life into its barren environs. ◎◎

Thus with the universal stage set and the heavenly players poised for action, we are introduced to a cadre of principal Yoruba deities through which the first stage in the creation saga will unfold. A vintage mythological map is presented here with a male figure residing above and a female figure as the earth below, now on the brink of giving birth to life. Obatala, the motive force of this tale, is called King of the White Cloth, in part because white symbolizes seminal fluid, the creative potency of the male, which he is about to introduce into the feminine realm of Olokun. But Obatala is not certain how to go about impregnating the primal waters with land and life, so he first consults Orunmilla, the great seer.

◎◎ Orunmilla cast sixteen palm nuts on a divining tray, and from the pattern by which the nuts fell he read their meaning. After many such castings, and many readings, Orunmilla said to Obatala, "Go to the watery lands of Olokun by way of a chain of gold, being sure you carry with you a snail shell full of sand, a white hen, a palm nut, and a black cat as your companion. This is what the palm nuts tell us." ◎◎

Orunmilla is also known as Ifa, the name of the Yoruba system of divination that uses sixteen cowrie shells tossed on a sacred tray; 256 patterns are possible, depending on how the shells fall, heads up or down, and each pattern has several hundred verses of poetry associated with it that provide an interpretation. Thus, the same sacred forces that govern the mystery of the creation of life as a whole also govern the mystery of each individual human life; these forces are controlled by Orunmilla, the god and keeper of the sacred mysteries, and communicated to humanity through the divinatory system of Ifa.

◎◎ Obatala sought out a goldsmith to fabricate the sacred chain, but when he discovered he had not enough gold for the chain to reach the earth, he went from *orisha* to *orisha* collecting whatever gold they would donate to his effort. Still the goldsmith informed the god that the chain would not reach completely to the waters of Olokun.

"Make it anyway," commanded Obatala. "And melt down a few of the links to create a hook at the end."

So the chain of gold was made, and Obatala descended from the sky carrying a shoulder bag filled with the other required items—a snail shell of sand, a white hen, a palm nut, and a black cat. Halfway down this very long chain, Obatala began to feel himself leaving the light world of the *orisha* and slipping into the misty, twilight realm of Olokun. He continued on until he could hear the splash of waves, but just as the goldsmith had predicted, when he reached the bottom of the chain, he was still well above the waters. In limbo, he held onto the last link of the golden chain wondering what to do.

"The sand," whispered a voice from above. It was Orunmilla giving him instructions.

So Obatala took the snail shell from his satchel and poured the sand out of the shell.

"The hen," came the voice from above.

Next, Obatala pulled out the hen and let it drop onto the mound of sand he had just poured out. Immediately, the hen began to scratch at the sand, scattering it in all directions and thereby creating dry land; the hen's scratching was not uniform, so the sand formed high and low places, hills and valleys, mountains and ravines. After the hen stopped, Obatala let go of the chain and came to rest on solid earth, which reached for great distances in every direction. He called the place where he landed Ife.

Obatala built a house there and planted his palm nut, which quickly grew into a palm tree. The palm tree matured, and ripe palm seeds fell, giving rise to more trees so that now there was vegetation. Obatala lived at Ife for some time in this way, with only the black cat as his companion. ◎◎

We are treated to some classic symbols of mythology here, expressed in the local variations of the Yoruba: the golden chain as the World Axis communicating between heaven and earth; the palm tree as the World Tree, the nourishing, sheltering first symbol of life on earth; and the sand brought down by Obatala as the consecrated Holy Land. Ife, the original Holy City founded by Obatala in this myth, became an important center of sacred wisdom for the Yoruba and remains a city in Nigeria to this day, situated about a hundred miles northeast of the present capital of Lagos.

◎◎ Now when Agemo, the chameleon, climbed down the golden chain at Olorun's behest to check on Obatala, he found the *orisha* content but desirous of some light to warm and brighten the twilight land he now called home. When Olorun heard this news, he fully agreed that the lands below should have light, so he made the sun and set it in motion across the sky.

Obatala tired of just his cat as a companion, and one day determined that he should make men and women to share the earth with him. Working nonstop, he dug up bits of clay, which he fashioned into small figures, men and women, shaped like himself. Eventually, Obatala grew exhausted and thirsty from all this work and longed for some palm wine to refresh and rejuvenate him. So he paused from the task of making humans and drew the sap of a palm tree, which he let sit and ferment. Then he took a long draught of palm wine before returning to the task of creating human beings. But now Obatala had become drunk from the wine; his world had grown soft and slightly out of focus; his fingers had become unsteady. And some of the figures he next created reflected his impaired condition: they were albinos, cripples, hunchbacks, dwarfs, or deaf mutes. But in his drunken state Obatala failed to notice these deformities.

After creating a great many clay figures, Obatala turned again to Olorun and beseeched the supreme *orisha,* "I have created these clay figures to inhabit the earth, but they are without life. Only you, Olorun, have the power to bestow life on them. I ask that you give them this gift so I may live with them as my companions."

Olorun was pleased to comply with Obatala's wishes and breathed life into each clay figure created on earth. These newly created human beings saw Obatala's hut and began building huts of their own around his. In this way, the village of Ife grew up around the *orisha's* home.

When the haze of the palm wine wore off, Obatala looked around and, seeing all the malformed beings, realized what misery his drunkenness had wrought. His heart was filled with compassion and remorse. "Never," he said to himself, "never again will I drink palm wine. And I shall always be the protector of those who have been created with deformities and imperfections."

As the village of Ife continued to grow into a great city, Obatala longed more and more to return to his home beyond the clouds. One day he ascended back up the golden chain and arrived at Olorun's domain to a great celebration in his honor. When the other *orishas* heard him describe the land and people he had created below, many of them resolved to descend to the earth to live among humanity. They prepared for their departure with this code of conduct from Olorun: "As *orishas,* never forget that you are bound to the protection of even the lowliest of human beings. Always be open to their prayers, and offer them assistance when they are in need. Obatala, who first descended the golden chain to create this world of living beings, will retain dominion over all earthly affairs, but each of you will be given a unique role to fulfill among human beings. Exercise this trust and responsibility well."

The other *orishas* then left for the new land, while Obatala enjoyed a long period of rest, occasionally descending the golden chain to check on his creation below. ◎◎

We thus peer into the character of Obatala, the creator-god of the Yoruba, seen here as a compassionate, protective Great Father. Yet as we've suggested, the Yoruba pantheon symbolizes the vicissitudes of the human psyche, so the myth also squarely presents Obatala's human side, for he is drunk at the crowning moment of his glory. "The Yoruba assert straightforwardly that the god was tipsy and his hand slipped," observes Wole Soyinka, "bringing the god firmly within the human attribute of fallibility. Since human fallibility is known to entail certain disharmonious consequences for society, it also requires a search for remedial activities, and it is this cycle which ensures the constant regenerative process of the universe. By bringing the gods within this cycle, a continuity of cosmic regulation involving the worlds of the ancestor and the unborn is also guaranteed."[10]

This cycle of fallibility and remediation, itself a variant of the cycle of death and resurrection, regenerates not only the society and the universe but the individual as well. For human fallibility can now be viewed in godly terms, and godly remediation becomes a potential that all humans can realize in their lives. Even more of Obatala's character is revealed through other myths in the Yoruba cycle.

◎◎ Before heading off to visit his friend Shango, Obatala, King of the White Cloth, consulted with Orunmilla, supreme diviner of Ifa. After throwing the cowries and consulting the oracle, Orunmilla advised Obatala not to embark on the journey. "Great adversity, even death, may befall you," he told Obatala. That night Obatala's wife had a portentous dream as well: that Obatala's white cloth had been soiled so that even when it was washed, dark spots appeared on it after drying. She too pleaded with Obatala not to go.

But Obatala wanted to see his friend and insisted on making the journey. Orunmilla reluctantly advised him that though he might suffer greatly, should he wish to survive this trip he must never protest and never retaliate, no matter what was done to him.

Obatala departed for Shango's realm, and while on the way he met

Eshu, the trickster-*orisha*. Three times Eshu asked Obatala to help him lift a pot of oil, and each time the oil spilled on Obatala's cloth, but Obatala did not protest. With a soiled cloth he continued on the road to his friend Shango's realm and soon spied one of Shango's fine horses that had apparently run away. Unbeknownst to Obatala, Eshu had magically made the horse appear before him. Obatala caught the animal and was headed toward Shango's domain when some of Shango's servants suddenly appeared and took him for a horse thief. They apprehended Obatala and imprisoned him; still Obatala did not protest.

Obatala sat in prison thinking that surely someone would realize this grievous error and soon right the wrong. But many months passed, and no one came to his aid. During this time a great plague spread throughout Shango's kingdom; for seven long years rain ceased, crops failed, and women aborted.

Finally, out of great concern for his empire, Shango consulted the oracle. He was told by the *babalawo** that a holy person was languishing innocently in one of his prisons and that releasing him would stop the scourge. Shango left immediately to search his prison compounds and finally discovered Obatala in one of them. His white cloth was dirty, his beard was disheveled, and his skin was covered with dust, but still Shango recognized him as the King of the White Cloth. Though Shango was a great and proud ruler, he prostrated himself before Obatala like a common person, begging his forgiveness. Obatala was released, but he had created human beings, and it pained him to see them suffer. Though he had not brought it on, he lifted the scourge, and once again rain came, crops flourished, and women gave birth. ◎◎

Obotunde Ijimere, the Nigerian playwright, has wedded both these myths of Obatala into his play *The Imprisonment of Obatala,* where in one scene, a *babalawo* recites how the creator-god has now become the imprisoned god:

> *You drank the milky wine of the palm*
> *Cool and sizzling it was in the morning,*
> *Fermenting in the calabash*
> *Its sweet foam overflowed*
> *Like the eyes of a woman in love*
> *You refreshed yourself in the morning*

Babalawo is the Yoruba term for priest.

But by evening time your hands were unsteady,
Your senses were dull, your fingertips numbed.[11]

Obatala the Archetype

Through these tales, we see Obatala as creative, compassionate, merciful, and patient; one prepared to accept his lot; one who sidesteps conflict; protector of children and of the unfortunate or disabled members of society; benefactor of humanity; dedicated to friendship and the maintenance of the social fabric. As an archetype, Obatala represents the Good King, who fully embodies his *anima*, the feminine side of the masculine persona; he is not a god of war but of peace; he does not sow seeds of chaos and disorder, like Eshu, but creates harmony and order. Obatala, as a male deity, would be connected with those aspects of the masculine psyche that are often undervalued in modern society: sensitivity, caring, nurturing, feeling, self-sacrificing. Little wonder that when Obatala resurfaced on the other side of the

AREA	NIGERIA	CUBA	BRAZIL	HAITI	CHRISTENDOM
FORM OF WORSHIP	Yoruba Religion	Santeria	Candomblé	Vodun	Christianity
GROUP NAME	Orishas	Orixas	Orixas	Loas	Saints
	Olodumare/ Olorun	Oloddumare	Olodum	Gran Maître	
	Obatala	Obatalia	Oxala	Guede	Our Lady of Mercy, Our Lady of Mount Carmel
	Eshu, Elegba	Eleggua	Exu	Legba	Saint Simon, Saint Anthony of Padua
INDIVIDUAL FIGURES	Shango	Chango	Xango	Ogou Shango	Saint Barbara, Saint Jerome
	Ogun	Oggun	Ogum	Ogou	Saint John the Baptist, Saint George
	Oya	Oya	Oya	Erzulie	Saint Catherine, Saint Theresa
	Yemoja	Yemalia	Yemanja	Agwe	Our Lady of Regla, Mary of the Sea

Table 1. Principal correspondences between Yoruba tradition and its survival in the Americas.

Atlantic as a result of the slave trade, he was combined with Our Lady of Mercy and Our Lady of Mount Carmel. In this Christianized form, he was surreptitiously worshiped by African slaves throughout Central and South America and the Caribbean (see Table 1) as Our Lady of Mercy.

In Africa, Obatala's praise name, King of the White Cloth, indicates that he is a symbol of ritual, ethical, and spiritual purity. His shrines, worshipers, and priests are dressed in white; in his memory devotees still refrain from drinking the fateful palm wine, and a grove of palm trees may be consecrated as the symbolic site of Obatala's descent on the golden chain to create humankind.

In a December 1973 concert, the Philadelphia Orchestra's program embraced not only the music of the contemporary American composers Samuel Barber and Paul Creston but also the intense rhythms of the Yoruba, as the orchestra accompanied the acclaimed African-American dancer Arthur Hall performing his piece *Obatala*. The spirit of the King of the White Cloth lives on well into the present age.

Eshu, the Trickster-God

On his journey to Shango's, Obatala is assailed by Eshu, an *orisha* who often appears in the role of a trickster. But Eshu is a complex figure, whose principal association is as a messenger between the gods and humanity. It is through Eshu that the Ifa oracle is delivered to humankind, as the following myth tells:

◎◎ Once upon a time the gods and goddesses were hungry. They had not enough to eat from their sons and daughters who inhabited the earth, so they began to quarrel among themselves; some of them even went forth to try their hand at hunting or fishing, but still they could not obtain enough to sustain them. So Eshu took it upon himself to rectify this situation. First he consulted with the *orisha* Yemoja, the river goddess. She told him to give human beings something so good that they would always desire it. Eshu then asked Yemoja's husband, the *orisha* Orungan, what might be given to human beings.

"I know something that is so good that human beings will yearn for it," said Orungan. "It is a grand thing made of sixteen palm nuts. Get them, learn their meaning, and you will win the goodwill of humans again."

So Eshu went to this certain palm-tree grove, and there some monkeys delivered sixteen sacred palm nuts to him. But Eshu did not know what to do with this present, and the monkeys informed him that he would need to travel the world asking the meaning of these sixteen palm nuts. He would eventually hear sixteen sayings for each of the sixteen nuts, whereupon he should consult first with the other *orishas,* then tell human beings what he had learned.

The gods and goddesses were pleased to hear what Eshu had accomplished, and imparted their knowledge and will to humanity through the sixteen palm nuts he delivered to the earth below. Once human beings saw the evil that might befall them and then saw a manner of escape through offering sacrifices and consulting the palm nuts, the gods and goddesses no longer went hungry. Eshu went back to stay with Ogun, Shango, and Obatala, and these four *orishas* observed what humanity would do with this divine gift. And that is how Eshu brought Ifa to humankind. ◉◉

This is also how we can perhaps best appreciate the complexity of Eshu's character, as the deliverer of the wisdom of the gods to humanity and, in turn, as the deliverer of humanity's sacrifice to the gods. For the wisdom of the gods is an esoteric elixir, and the seeker of such knowledge must have a guide to its source; Eshu is that

Figure 22. Ifa divining bowl with images of Eshu, animals, and gods around the circumference.

Figure 23. Images of the trickster: the *orisha*, Eshu, from the planks and doors of Yoruba temples. After Arriens in Frobenius (1968).

guide. His face is carved on Ifa divining trays, where nuts or shells are cast to place humanity in contact with this sacred wisdom; a portion of every sacrifice offered belongs to him, for he is the *es-huona* ("Eshu of the way"), the opener of the path to the mysterious source of knowledge. And this source of knowledge, however it might be imagined or pictured, is ultimately found within oneself, for when the Ifa is consulted, the *babalawo* repeats the myths associated with the given pattern of the nuts or shells that are cast—the stories Eshu traveled around the world to collect—until one myth resonates with the circumstances of the seeker. It is there the answer lies.

But Eshu is also the notorious "bad boy" of the Yoruba pantheon, so vexing that even "Olodumare [Olorun], who made him, is now doubtful about his creation of Eshu."[12] Eshu's penchant for mischief is well illustrated in this classic tale.[13]

◎◎ Once there were two farmers who were the best of friends. Wherever they went they dressed alike, and their fields adjoined each other separated only by a path. Each morning Eshu walked this path wearing a black cap. But one morning Eshu decided to play a trick on the friends. First he made himself a cap of four colored cloths—black, white, red, and green—that appeared as a cap of a single color depending on the side from which it was viewed. He donned this hat, then took his pipe and stuck it not in his mouth as usual but at the nape of his neck, as if he were smoking from the back of his head. His staff, which he usually carried over his chest, he now slung over his shoulder from behind. Then he took off down the path separating the two friends, bidding them each a good morning, which they returned in kind.

On their way home, the farmers commented on the old man (Eshu) walking through their fields that day. "It was strange that he walked in a direction opposite to his normal route," said one. "I could tell from watching his pipe and staff, and he had a white cap on instead of his normal black cap."

"Are you blind, man!" retorted the other. "He had a red hat on, and walked in the direction he always walks."

"You must have drunk wine this morning, my friend," came the first's reply. "And it's dulled your senses."

"Be off with you," snorted the other. "You're making up lies to annoy me."

"You're the liar, not I!" cried the first.

Then one of the men went for his knife and slashed the other about the head. But the other man also drew his knife and wounded his assailant. Now both men ran bleeding into town, each pleading his case to the townspeople that the other was a liar.

In the meantime, Eshu went to the court of the local king who would adjudicate between these two aggrieved parties. When the two friends appeared, the king asked, "Well, what made you two best of friends fall out?"

"We could not agree about who went through our fields this morning," said one. "Normally, this man wears a black hat and always travels in the same direction," he continued. "But today he wore a white hat and walked in the opposite direction."

"Liar, liar," shouted the other man. "Why, it was plain to see the old man had on a red hat today and traveled in his usual direction!"

"Wait just a minute," interjected the king, before their argument reheated. "Who knows this old man?"

"It was I!" Eshu blurted out to the astonishment of all. He pulled out his hat and said, "Today, I put on this hat, which is red on one side, white on the other, green in front, and black behind. Then I stuck my pipe in the nape of my neck, and my staff on my back. When I walked," he went on, "it looked like I was traveling in one direction if you followed my feet and quite the other direction if you followed my pipe and staff.

"These two friends couldn't help themselves," Eshu confessed, "I made them quarrel. Sowing discord is my greatest delight." ◎◎

As a guide on the path to sacred wisdom, Eshu leads the individual, and the group, beyond what is obvious, for the domain of the ordinary, of surface appearances, is not the home of sacred wisdom.

Eshu, as the trickster, is able to crack the often tough veneer of the commonplace, as he did so effectively in this myth. In reality, no two people are as alike as the two farmers of this myth made themselves out to be, but it took Eshu's ruse to uncover the deeper truth beneath the external layer of conformity and uniformity they initially presented. So Eshu functions to break up old unproductive ways of being in deed or in thought, opening the way to reinvigoration of self and society. In a sense, he functions as both psychotherapist and sociotherapist.

Eshu the Archetype

As an archetype, Eshu is the "inner guide"—that part of ourselves capable of leading us to life-changing and life-sustaining insights and revelations. He is the transformer of old patterns that cause us to be stuck; the portion of our psyche ready to test limits and break bounds; a ruthless purveyor of our deeper truths, even when we would gladly confront something less. Eshu is also the "bad boy" or "bad girl" of our psyche, mischievous and naughty with all the attendant sexual connotations; he is frequently depicted as having a phallic-shaped haircut (see Figure 23), and his celebrations include joyful songs about his sexual deeds and mishaps. Sexuality is, of course, the great hidden motivator of men and women, and Eshu is intent on uncovering and exposing our relationship to this dynamic life force. Unlike Obatala, who works with this life force to shape human beings, Eshu is himself a personification of the life force of sexuality.

This aspect of Eshu as a personification of the life force extends into his role as solicitor of sacrifices, for sacrifice is more than just an "appeasement of the gods." To sacrifice a chicken, a goat, a cow is to take part actively and consciously in the elemental and sometimes grotesque cycle of life feeding on life for its survival. Elemental and grotesque himself, Eshu is a reminder of the part of us that will forever be connected to this cycle of life feeding on itself.

Finally, Eshu is the great mediator between the opposing forces of life. In negotiating among the gods, as he often does in Yoruba myths, he asserts balance, for example, between the compassion of Obatala and the aggressive warrior spirit of Ogun. And if these gods are within us, then Eshu represents the inner path that balances all the opposing tendencies of our own personality and that may require a force as willful and bent on shaking things up as the old man walking between the supposed best of friends. For the "Yoruba always remember that the restoration of order begins with a dissolution of false order," writes Robert Pelton, "passes through a phase of confusion, and ends with a 'new order,' which, in its depth, is a re-creation of the world. This memory focuses on Eshu, who brings to the surface hidden conflict and, once Ifa has spoken, knits together in true mutuality the relationships [inter- and intrapersonal] that forgetfulness, ignorance, passion, malice, or sheer routine have severed."[14]

Shango, the Revered Thunder Hurler

It is not hard to understand why Shango is one of the most revered and feared *orishas* among the Yoruba and why his cult has survived the ordeals of slavery to resurface in the Americas: his symbol is the thunderbolt; his sound, the roar of the storm. And it is truly one of those audacious synchronicities that as I seek to describe Shango's presence in the world, he is with me now. Though I live in an area where thunderstorms are rare, one rages on the horizon at this very moment. Miles of tranquil ocean, like a gently rippled mirror, lie in front of a dark, bluish-gray horizon; a low rumble travels by air and water and earth, entering me as an unsettling rhythm over which I have no control, an unearthly drumbeat that possesses all the cells of my body and causes them to shake and jump. Then suddenly there is a blinding stroke—one here, then there—lightning capering across this panoramic exhibition like flashing ballet dancers whose choreographed movements have been arranged to the awesome cadence of heavenly percussion.

Turning from my window to the notes of Leo Frobenius, written in 1913, I read his description of a dancer upon whom Shango has descended. In the shadows of a temple dedicated to Shango, a sonorous Bata drum swayed a group of dancers until suddenly one broke out of the whole and rushed the altar, grabbing an Oshe-Shango (a double-headed ax symbolic of the thunderbolt). This one dancer began jumping in a frenzy, moving in ways unlike the rest— the deity had "mounted" her and was "riding" her; now she embodied divinity in a manner supported by the Bata drummer, whose rhythms left those of the other celebrants to follow the one possessed. And the reveler danced through the streets, leading a procession of drums and bodies to her home where sacrificial rams, gifts, food, and drink were supplied to the group so they might partake, in symbolic measure, of the ecstasy and grace she knew. Yet this might not be the only thunderbolt that night, not the only flash of the god's favor, and should another one be so chosen, then the ensemble would proceed from dwelling to dwelling until the lightning strikes were through.[15]

The principal myth of Shango concerns his despotic rule over the ancient kingdom of Oyo, located approximately three hundred miles north of Ife:

◎◎ Shango was famous as a king passionately devoted to war and a master magician who possessed a potent medicine that caused a great fire to issue forth from his opened mouth. As king of Oyo, he had expanded the bounds of his empire through waging ruthless and relentless battles against neighboring kingdoms, but after one particularly hard-fought battle, two of his warlords, Timi and Gbonka, received greater acclaim for the victory than Shango, and this greatly angered the mighty king. What's more, many of his subjects grew tired of his brutal rule. So to rid himself of any pretenders to the throne, Shango insisted that the two commanders duel to the death. Gbonka won the first two contests, but in contempt of Shango's orders he mercifully spared the life of his friend Timi, further incurring Shango's wrath. Shango compelled the two to fight a third time, and in anger, Gbonka severed the head of Timi and delivered it mockingly to Shango's feet.

Enraged, Shango proceeded to deal Gbonka a painful death. A pyre was constructed, and Gbonka, still alive, was placed in the middle of it. With a mighty blast from his mouth, Shango set the heap ablaze. But after being consumed in the conflagration, Gbonka came to life again. An astonished Shango proclaimed, "What Gbonka can do, so can I. But I will no longer be a man, I will quit this world to become an *orisha.*"

Shortly thereafter, Shango retreated to the forest, carrying his sixteen cowrie shells, where he hung himself on an Ayan tree, from which two chains arose to convey him to his new abode beyond the sky. When others came to look for him, all that was found was his double-headed ax lying on the ground. "Shango has left the earth," they said, "and retired to the sky where he will forever be watching us and handing out swift justice to any who displease him." ◎◎

Here, once again, a god separates two friends, but in this story, the beguiling finesse of Eshu is supplanted by the brutal force of

Shango. Shango's excesses, on the battlefield and with his two commanders, are tempered only by the realization that the obedience of
Gbonka subjected this lieutenant to a law higher than that of the
earthly rule over which Shango already held sway—that is, the spiritual code of death and resurrection. But Shango's vice is also his
virtue; his indomitable will to wage war transforms into an equally
unconquerable desire to seek spiritual release, which he consummates
by hanging himself on the World Tree of spiritual enlightenment. This
relationship between war and spirituality is, in mythological terms,
well founded worldwide; the Indian Bhagavad Gita, for example, is a
comprehensive treatise on spirituality using the battlefield as a
metaphor for the human spiritual quest. The notion, in both India
and Africa, is that the unstoppable determination of a warrior is often required to conquer the challenges and overcome the obstacles on
the path to spiritual illumination. Shango demonstrates this unstoppable will. The difficulty comes in knowing when this very willfulness
is itself an obstacle to one's spiritual journey, as it had become for
Shango in the earthly realm. But we know that his efforts to hone his
vice into a virtue meet with some success, because when he meets
Obatala in prison, as told in the earlier myth, the great king of the
earth bows before the great *orisha* of the heavens.

Shango the Archetype

Shango presents us with the tenacious aspect of the human personality—one's will, determination, commitment. When applied to accomplishments in the world, Shango as an archetype shows up in those
who succeed in business, politics, the military, sports, or any arena
where competition and strong resolve are required. Shango represents
a "take no prisoners" attitude to life, often reacting before thinking
things through. When put to use for the sake of personal or social
transformation, Shango represents the energy that drives an individual to overcome the obstacles to a vexing life issue or to work dili-
gently for the sake of a worthy ideal or cause. Here, the danger is that
the negative aspect of a determined will can lead to zealous excess, as
the myths of Shango so often illustrate.

   Shango is the embodiment of masculinity, like Síva in the Hindu
pantheon; but Shango also has roots in the Goddess; not surprisingly
so too does Síva. Most Shango devotees are female, and many of the

male devotees dress as women in celebration of this god. In part, this comes from the sexual symbolism surrounding the rites associated with the *orishas,* for they are described as "mounting" those who fall under their influence. A similar sexual relationship is implied in many spiritual traditions; the Old and New Testaments, for example, often refer to God or Jesus as the "bridegroom," making humanity the "bride."

This female element of Shango is rooted in an even older veneration of the Goddess. For Shango's main symbol, the Oshe-Shango (see Figure 24) or double-headed ax, though an image of a thunderbolt, is also an ancient symbol of the Goddess found in Europe and Asia as well. Marija Gimbutas has demonstrated this symbol's European appearance as a stylistic representation of the butterfly, itself a manifestation "of the Goddess in whose hands was the magic transformation from death to life."[16] The labrys, as the double-headed ax is called, played an important role in the rites associated with the Greek goddess Demeter, and images of the labrys have been found on Minoan and Mycenaean pottery as early as the fourteenth and fifteenth centuries B.C.E.

On all the Oshe-Shango, the thunderbolt-labrys is attached to the head, for Shango is said to enter the body this way. Here, then, we have the thunderbolt, long symbolic of spiritual consciousness, entering the body through the portal of illumination, and this leads to the resolute pursuit of spiritual awakening, like Shango's own.

Some Buddhist sects celebrate a principal pantheon of five Buddhas known as the Mahāvairochana; among these figures, the Buddha of the eastern direction is called Akshobhya, which means "the one who cannot be moved." The primary quality of this Buddha is tenacity—but if this tenacity, say the Buddhists, is not directed toward spiritual illumination, it leads to obstinacy. The point is to accept, rather than eliminate, your vice, transforming it into your virtue. "Not a few who meant to cast out their devil," wrote Nietzsche, "went

Figure 24. An Oshe-Shango used by celebrants of the god.

thereby into the swine themselves."[17] If you're obstinate to begin
with, as Shango was, then don't give up that quality; redirect it toward a higher, more enlightening purpose. And what sign does Akshobhya, symbol of turning tenacity from vice to virtue, hold in his
hand? None other than the thunderbolt, Shango's symbol too, for
spiritual awakening is the aim of both these tenacious, divine figures.

Ogun, the Creator and Destroyer

Much is made of the theme of separation between humanity and divinity in African mythology (see Chapter 9); many myths portray a
time when the gods and goddesses walked among humanity, till some
rift tore asunder this idyllic relationship. Usually humanity is blamed
for the cleavage; some human act, some fall from grace, precipitates
the gods' departure, just as Adam and Eve are condemned for exiling
humankind from the blissful garden. After the fall, it is the task of humanity to reach out to divinity, to reclaim the lost treasure that is its
original birthright. Heaven may send representatives to the earth in
the form of gods, goddesses, saviors, saints, sages, angels, demons, or
other divine figures, but the purpose is always the same: to remind
humans of their lost divinity and inspire them to reach across the
abyss to reclaim it.

But with the *orishas,* the situation is uniquely turned the other
way around. Originally both divinity and humanity were contained
in the godhead, Òrisa-nla, the common primordial being shattered by
Atunda's stone. It was then the gods and goddesses who journeyed to
the earthly realm, for in their divine state they were incomplete, the
myths suggest, and needed to reembrace mortality to make them
whole. And Ogun was the *orisha* who forged the sacred path for the
return of divinity to humanity. There are many versions of the myth,
but its essential outline goes like this:

◎◎ When the *orishas* wished to return to the earth, their way of recon-
nection with humanity was blocked by a dense forest. Each *orisha* tried
to clear away the forest, but the tools they had, made of wood, stone, or
soft metal, were not equal to the task. Ogun journeyed deep into a
mountain, the womb of the earth, to retrieve the materials for making
iron, from which he fashioned implements capable of clearing the way.
After forging the sacred path, Ogun plummeted through the abyss to

earth and bade the other *orishas* follow. They joined him and beseeched him to be their king, but he refused, preferring to wander the earth unfettered, like the other *orishas*.

Ogun eventually came to the town of Ire and was welcomed by its residents, whom he assisted in waging battle against a formidable opponent. Out of gratitude the town elders offered him the crown, but again he refused, and this time he retreated to the seclusion of the mountains where he hunted and farmed. Over and over the people of Ire approached the mountain, hoping to persuade Ogun to become their leader. To dissuade the townspeople, Ogun descended from the mountain one day, dressed in warrior's clothes drenched from head to foot in blood; they fled upon sighting him, and he thought his message was finally delivered. But still they returned, appealing to him to appear in less terrifying garb, whereupon they would immediately salute him as general and king.

Finally, Ogun relented, quitting his mountain abode bedecked in palm fronds to enter Ire as king. Many battles he led, and many he won, till one day Eshu appeared during a pause in the fighting and offered the parched god a gourd of palm wine. Ogun found the palm wine to his liking and presently drained the full gourd. He then fought more magnificently than ever, rousting the enemy almost single-handedly. But in his stupor, he confused the combatants and slew not only the enemy but every one of those fighting under his command. Now his worst fear, the troubling thought that had kept him from the kingship earlier, was confirmed, and amidst this carnage Ogun stood all alone. Some say that Ogun then fell on his own sword, while others tell that he lived forever after in solitude and anguish in his mountain abode. ◎◎

It is certainly enticing to position Ogun midway between Shango and Obatala, and this would not be altogether incorrect, for Ogun embodies aspects of both these other deities: like Shango, Ogun is a relentless warrior who turns against his own subordinates, and like Obatala, Ogun's weakness for palm wine leads to his mishap. But Ogun encompasses far more; he is a coincidence of opposing forces. He blazes a trail for divinity to reunite with humanity but ultimately seeks isolation from both; he delivers iron to humanity, and it becomes the basis of creation (as in farm implements) and destruction (as in weapons); he has compassion for those he then ends up slaying.

Although only alluded to in this myth, Ogun is the quintessential forest hunter; we encountered him as Chief of Hunters in an earlier myth about Red Buffalo Woman. There, too, he embodied contradiction: intimately engaged in the cycle of life and death; identifying with both the sacred practice of the hunt and the profane demands of the husband. Then through other myths, poems, and praise songs, we learn that Ogun is a farmer, an artist, an inventor, "protector of orphans," "roof over the homeless," "terrible guardian of the sacred oath," and "lord of the road" to sacred wisdom. Wole Soyinka places him at the epicenter of Yoruba metaphysics. "Ogun's history," he observes, "is the story of the completion of Yoruba cosmogony; he encapsulates that cosmogony's coming-into-being in his own rites of passage."[18] Cosmogony, after all, is a cycle that depicts both the creation and the dissolution of the universe, the worlds, and all the forms they contain.

A telling moment in this myth of Ogun occurs when the people of Ire shrink from his appearance in blood-drenched robes. A similar instance, reported in another version of the myth, happens among the other *orishas* when after spending many days in the forest hunting game, Ogun appears before them with matted hair, wearing blood-soaked skins. They, too, recoil at the sight, stripping him of the title *oba* (king of the *orishas*) that they had previously given him. Ogun reminds the other deities that when they were in need of iron to clear their path, they pleaded with him to be king, but now they turn against him, uneasy because he is stained by the hunt.

This story delivers an exquisitely sophisticated message: to embrace life, you must also embrace death; to welcome creation, you must also welcome destruction; to be united with your highest aims, you must also be united with your lowest needs. It is typical, in the Christian thinking that pervades the West, always to seek the "good" (life, creation, spiritual aims) and shun the "bad" (death, destruction, worldly needs); but in this coincidence of opposites, Ogun points to a transcendent wisdom beyond the opposing pairs that daily confront human life. "There is a marked contrast here between West African and Western Christian modes of thought," ethnologist Sandra Barnes writes about Ogun.

> In the West, positive and negative—familiarly glossed as evil and good—can be divided into opposing parts and symbolized by Satan and God. In West Africa, positive and negative power is not separate. Power is singular, and therefore what we in the West see as dual and capable of being divided into two mystical notions cannot be divided in African thought.[19]

A similar mythic wisdom is also to be found in the East, particularly in Hinduism and Buddhism. In *The Mahabharata,* for example, Krishna, the Hindu god of war in this epic, tells Arjuna, the warrior-protagonist reluctantly preparing for battle, that to find peace of mind he must free himself of the desire for life or the fear of death, neither seeking pleasure nor running from pain, neither coveting health nor dreading illness. When one gets beyond these illusory opposites, the supreme deity informs Arjuna, then supreme bliss is the natural condition. And even within Western spirituality, this notion is found most prominently with the fifteenth-century German bishop Nicholas Cusanus who spoke of the joining of opposites as the highest state of spiritual revelation.

Ogun the Archetype

Ogun is that "dynamic center" of our psyche capable of containing, integrating, synthesizing, and even transcending the many opposing forces that operate within us. We all have an Obatala, Shango, and Eshu within our psyche—a compassionate, a destructive, and a trickster side of our personality—and we have a great many more aspects as well. We have only visited four principal *orishas,* yet each of the hundreds or thousands that exist could be linked to some facet of our being. Ogun represents that element capable of integrating all the others. There may be times when we need to proceed with the relentless determination of Shango, and other times when we need to shield that determination from others and present a more compassionate countenance like Obatala. One is not bad and the other good; it is more a question of whether these various aspects of our self operate from a center of control, and Ogun is that center.

The rituals associated with Ogun provide examples of him functioning as this "dynamic center." As the deliverer of iron to humankind, Ogun conveys a sacred presence to smelting and smithing; the blacksmith's forge, for instance, is considered to be a sanctuary in his honor and a refuge for anyone "metaphorically fleeing from Shango."[20] A hunter or warrior who has killed must undergo *Ogun wiwe,* "washing Ogun," a ritual in which the water used by a blacksmith is also used by the killer for several days until he is "cleansed of the killing" and able to reenter society.[21] And in Yoruba courtrooms even to this day, iron might be used to administer oaths instead of the Bible or Koran, as a symbol of trust in Ogun's power as "keeper of the sacred oath" and his ability to deliver balanced justice amidst contentious forces.

Ogun is present in so many human affairs, but he is also transcendent of them. He is the solitary god, the ascetic part of the human soul that recognizes, if only in fleeting moments, that there must be something more, something beyond the hurly-burly of life. "By incorporating within himself so many seemingly contradictory attributes," writes Wole Soyinka, "[Ogun] represents the closest conception to the original oneness of Orisa-nla."[22]

The Trickster's Hat

Perhaps it is the conniving of Eshu who so quickly prevents our further exploration of the Yoruba pantheon. Yet he at least leaves us with a precious parting gift: the four-colored hat he used to trick the two farmers. That hat, you will recall, was red on one side, white on the other, green in front, and black behind. Leo Frobenius was one of

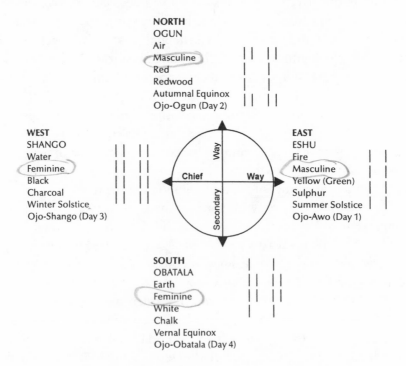

NORTH
OGUN
Air
Masculine
Red
Redwood
Autumnal Equinox
Ojo-Ogun (Day 2)

WEST
SHANGO
Water
Feminine
Black
Charcoal
Winter Solstice
Ojo-Shango (Day 3)

Chief

Way

Way

Secondary

EAST
ESHU
Fire
Masculine
Yellow (Green)
Sulphur
Summer Solstice
Ojo-Awo (Day 1)

SOUTH
OBATALA
Earth
Feminine
White
Chalk
Vernal Equinox
Ojo-Obatala (Day 4)

Figure 25. Eshu's Hat and the principal correspondences of Yoruba sacred wisdom.

the first outsiders to recognize it as more than a literary device; Eshu's hat is a summation of the cosmology represented by the *orishas* and contained in the Ifa, the sacred system by which humanity might receive this divine wisdom (see Figure 25).[23]

This integrated system is based on the counterclockwise motion of the sun through the four cardinal directions. Each compass direction is associated with a principal *orisha,* element, psychological aspect (Figure 25 just shows gender aspects, but there are many others), color, object from the earth, time of the year, and day of the week.

Each direction is also associated with a principal *odu* or Ifa sign, the marks that are drawn in sacred dust by a *babalawo* after casting the cowrie shells and that describe the pattern into which they fell. At the heart of this system is a cross uniting a horizontal axis known as the "Chief Way" with a vertical axis, the "Secondary Way"; these are the principal paths by which this mystery system is apprehended. Thus, based on this diagram, the principal Yoruba route to sacred wisdom is through bringing forth in one's life the archetypes represented by Shango and Eshu. The secondary path is through the archetypes expressed by Ogun and Obatala.

So, it seems, Eshu has fulfilled his role well, once again bringing to the surface what was hidden—in this case, the mythic wisdom of the Yoruba. For the trickster's hat is really a symbol, the key to a comprehensive mythic order that at once reclaims and rejoins the mysteries of the cosmos, the earth, and the social order with the mysteries of a divine self.

9

MYTHS AT THE BEGINNING AND END OF CREATION

We carry with us the wonders we seek without us:
There is all Africa and her prodigies in us.
SIR THOMAS BROWNE, *RELIGIO MEDICI*

A cacophony of sound during the day, city streets can recede into desolate silence at night. One evening I walked such a street, devoid of people, traffic, and noise, without the comings and goings that infuse the city with life. Mesmerized by this pause in the urban pulse, I was suddenly shocked by a disembodied voice calling out loudly, "Yo," then again in escalating tones, "Yo . . . yo." For a moment "Yo" hung in the air, resounding off sidewalks and building walls, looking for escape to the void from whence it came. I mused over the personal depths of this sound—a plaintive wail, a shrill exhortation, a moment's recognition? I would never know. Smiling to myself, I continued on, knowing the ancestors would be pleased. Through whatever fate this monosyllable had found its way into popular urban slang, I was certain that few who uttered it knew that Yo was spiritually gifted. The Bambara of Mali believe the universe begins and ends in the sound of Yo. So along with its echo down that urban corridor, I also heard the sound of the origins of creation itself.

From modern-day astrophysics, we learn:

In the beginning there was nothing, not even space or time existed.[1]

And from the ancient teachings of the Bambara[2]:

In the beginning there was nothing but the emptiness of the void (*fu*).

Astrophysics continues:

Then from a single point came a big bang, an explosion of immense proportions. Only faint glimmers of that explosion remain, detectable as a consistent level of background noise in the universe.

Bambara sacred wisdom answers:

The entire universe began from a single point of sound, the root sound of creation, Yo. Yo is the first sound, but it is also the silence at the core of creation.

Astrophysics goes on:

From that first eruption five to ten billion years ago, waves of energy rippled forth, birthing stars and planets and galaxies through raging, violent, thermonuclear explosions, then billions of years later bringing them to death in a similar way. These cosmic furnaces created atoms of carbon, oxygen, hydrogen, nitrogen, silicon, sulfur, iron, and the other elements; every atom of these elements in all living and nonliving things on earth today was once the matter of a galaxy, the substance of a star, the product of that first great explosion.

The Bambara put forth:

Emanations from this void, through the root sound Yo, created the structure of the heavens, of the earth, and of all living and nonliving things.

Then the cosmology of modern science and that of traditional Africa diverge. For astrophysics is content to address the physical origins of the universe, while the Bambara seek also to comprehend the origins of consciousness. They proceed with a belief that everything, including human consciousness, emanates from the root sound Yo:

"Yo comes from itself, is known by itself, departs out of itself, from the nothingness that is itself." All is Yo.³

From here on, the most appropriate comparison is to the mythological systems of the East. In the Upanishads, the sacred Vedic texts of ancient India, for example, we hear of a similar root sound, Om:

Om. This eternal Word is all: what was, what is and what shall be, and what beyond is in eternity. All is Om.⁴

The Bambara say:

Out of the void, the vibrations of Yo gave rise to *gla gla zo,* the highest state of consciousness. *Gla gla zo* ultimately manifested itself in the creation of human consciousness.

To which the Upanishads echo:

Supreme consciousness (Atman) is the eternal word Om. Its three sounds, A, U, M, are the first three states of consciousness, and these three states are the three sounds.⁵

Bambara teachings then refer back to the "silence" at the core of creation, distinguishing that "silence" from the "noise"—hence confusion—of the material world of created forms:

For those who know, therefore, there is silence at the core of the universe; from it all things continually spring forth. In the face of the noise of the material, social universe, the elders strive to return to the primal silence.⁶

The Upanishads echo the Bambara as they speak of Brahman—not the deity of the same name, but the divine mystery, the immanent and transcendent ground of being:

There are two ways of contemplation of Brahman: In sound and in silence. By sound we go to silence. The sound of Brahman is Om. With Om we go to the End: the silence of Brahman. The End is immortality, union and peace.[7]

Whether the universe emerges, then dissolves in a fiery, thermonuclear holocaust, in the vibrations of a cosmic sound, or through some other agency of becoming and passing away, this cosmogony—this human accounting for the beginning and end of creation—addresses a few basic themes: the origin and destiny of the universe, the birth and death of life, the arising and dissolution of human consciousness. The difference, then, between a scientific creation story and a mythological one is the former's reliance on observable fact and the latter's support in metaphorical truth; the problem rests not in their contrasting construction but in the ready temptation to interpret myth as scientific fact or to confuse science with mythological truth.

African creation myths are more than naive, primitive attempts to explain the phenomenal world. Rather, they grapple with the central questions for which all creation mythologies seek answers: How is form created from the formlessness prior to it? How is order established from chaos? How does the one break into the many? How does the void become the plenitude? How does the unmanifest give rise to the manifest? And ultimately, how is this sacred circle closed: the many returning to the one; form dissolving back into formlessness; order giving way to chaos; the plenitude disappearing into the void; the manifest yielding to the unmanifest. Or, in human terms, how do human life and human consciousness emerge through birth from the mystery preceding them, then dissolve through death back into that transcendent unknown? To these immense questions modern science offers answers no more valid than those proposed by the makers of African myth. And where science seeks a dispassionate relationship with objective knowledge, mythology offers an intimate rapport with subjective wisdom; for African creation myths are not merely to be consumed by the hearts of believers, the ears of listeners, nor the eyes of readers; they are to be *lived*.

African Genesis

A familiar motif is to be found in a creation myth from the Basari of northern Guinea[8]:

◎◎ Unumbotte made a human being. Its name was Man. Unumbotte next made an antelope, named Antelope. Unumbotte made a snake, named Snake. At the time these three were made, there were no trees but one, a palm. Nor had the earth been pounded smooth. All three were sitting on the rough ground, and Unumbotte said to them, "The earth has not yet been pounded. You must pound the ground smooth where you are sitting." Unumbotte gave them seeds of all kinds and said, "Go plant these." Then Unumbotte went away.

Unumbotte came back. He saw that the three had not yet pounded the earth. But they had planted the seeds. One of the seeds had sprouted and grown. It was a tree, and it had grown tall and was bearing fruit, red fruit. Every seven days Unumbotte would return and pluck one of the red fruits.

One day Snake said, "We too should eat these fruits. Why must we go hungry?" Antelope said, "But we don't know anything about this fruit." Then Man and his wife took some of the fruit and ate it. Unumbotte came down from the sky and asked, "Who ate the fruit?" They answered, "We did." Unumbotte asked, "Who told you that you could eat that fruit?" They replied, "Snake did." Unumbotte asked, "Why did you listen to Snake?" They said, "We were hungry." Unumbotte questioned Antelope. "Are you hungry, too?" Antelope said, "Yes, I get hungry. I like to eat grass." Since then, Antelope has lived in the wild, eating grass.

Unumbotte then gave sorghum to Man, also yams and millet. And the people gathered in eating groups that would always eat from the same bowl, never the bowls of the other groups. It was from this that differences in language arose. And ever since then, the people have ruled the land.

But Snake was given by Unumbotte a medicine with which to bite people. ◎◎

This tale, of course, parallels to a remarkable degree the story found in the third chapter of Genesis. Leo Frobenius collected this Basari myth at the beginning of the twentieth century and went to great lengths to document its existence prior to Basari contact with Christian missionaries. "It is important to know," writes Frobenius in 1924, "that as far as we know there has been no penetration of missionary influence to the Basari. . . . Many Basari knew the tale and it was always described to me as a piece of the old tribal heritage. . . . I have therefore to reject absolutely the suggestion that a recent missionary influence may lie behind this tale."[9]

The Mbuti people of the Ituri forest at the foothills of the Mountains of the Moon in the present-day Democratic Republic of Congo offer a similar account of creation:

◎◎ God made the first man and woman and put them into the forest. They had everything they could possibly desire; there was so much food that all they had to do was bend down and pick it up. God told them they should have children and that all humanity would live forever, and he let them do whatever they wanted, but he warned them: "Of all the fruit of the trees of the forest you may eat, but of the fruit of the *tahu* tree you may not eat." Both promised to abide by this prohibition.

The man was never interested in the *tahu* fruit, but while pregnant, the woman was overcome with an irresistible desire to eat it. She convinced her husband to steal into the forest and pluck the fruit, which he peeled and ate with her, hiding the peels under a pile of leaves. God, however, was not so easily fooled and sent a strong wind into the forest, which blew away the cover of leaves.

"You have broken your promise to me," reprimanded an angry God. "For this you will now learn what it is to work hard, to suffer illness, and to die. And the woman," he continued, "she will suffer even greater pain in the delivery of her children." ◎◎

Once again, the similarity of this myth to the story of Genesis is astonishing. I have reproduced this account from several variations collected independently over many years by Father Paul Schebesta,[10] the Austrian cleric-scholar, and Jean-Pierre Hallet,[11] the Belgian author and humanitarian, both of whom insist on its authenticity prior to Christian contact with the Mbuti, as did Frobenius with the Basari. In each of the original versions of this Mbuti myth, the principal themes remain unchanged: God initially creates humanity in the immortal, paradisiacal domain of the earth, then issues just one prohibition—not to eat the fruit of the *tahu* tree. The fruit is, of course, eaten (in all versions at the urging of the woman), and humanity is then made to experience the vicissitudes of mortal life.

We remember from the rendition of this creation episode in Genesis that God walks into the garden and, on seeing the first couple with fig leaves covering their genitals, inquires whether they have eaten the forbidden fruit. Adam blames Eve, and Eve blames the serpent (the Basari legend presents a similar chain of finger-pointing). Then God fears that humans have tasted of their divinity, becoming godlike through a knowledge of good and evil, and that they might next taste the fruit of a second tree—the Tree of Life—from which they would gain immortality. So God drives humanity from the rapturous abode, placing cherubim and an ever-turning, flaming sword as guardians of the way to the Tree of Life.[12] In this way, after the fall—after this separation of humankind from the godhead—the path to direct experience of divinity is closed to humanity; the only approach now is through appeasement of and atonement with Yahweh, this jealous father-god. This is, at least, the officially sanctioned Judeo-Christian understanding of the biblical creation scene.

Now every morning before the Mbuti retreat deep into the forest for the hunt, they address prayers of gratitude, dances, and joyful songs to the godhead, called by them "our Father." *"Ndura nde Kalisia, ndura nde Mungu,"* they say: the forest is the godhead, the forest is the creator himself.[13] The Mbuti do not regard the separation of humanity from God as a fall from grace; this separation is not Original Sin, as Christians would attest, but more akin to Original Blessing. And the elegant reason given for the Mbuti's joyous attitude toward God's removal from his creation is that with this separation human consciousness has the necessary distance to behold the beatific vision everywhere—much as we might back away from a masterpiece of art to appreciate fully the radiance it unleashes.[14] For the Mbuti honor a divinity that is everywhere felt, a sacred presence, notes anthropologist Colin Turnbull, who lived for many years among them, experienced from "not just the trees or stream, or the sky or the soil, but from the totality, down to the last grain of sand."[15]

And this African notion that divinity is to be found everywhere, while reminiscent of the Buddhist precept that "everything has Buddha-consciousness," is even mirrored within the discarded elements of early Christianity. The Dead Sea Scrolls were shown to contain references to the sayings of Christ that could only be interpreted in a symbolic manner befitting the Gnostic sects from which they arose. In the Gospel of Thomas, Jesus says of the divinity of creation, "It is I who am the all. From me did the all come forth, and unto me did the all extend. Split a piece of wood, and I am there. Lift up the stone, and you will find me there."[16] Then later, he responds to the question,

"When will the kingdom come?" "It will not come by waiting for it," he states. "It will not be a matter of saying 'here it is' or 'there it is.' Rather, the kingdom of the father is spread out upon the earth, and men do not see it."[17]

A shift of vision, then, is required to experience the bliss-bestowing presence of the divine. This shift occurs in what the Mbuti call *ekimi mota*: "intense," "hot," or "powerful" quiet; a "joy in one's innermost being, which is the goal of life for the Mbuti and which can only be expressed in joyful songs of gratitude to the forest deity, dances, and a deep-welling tranquility felt as one goes about one's daily tasks."[18]

Logos Africana—The Sacred Word in Africa

From the Wapangwa, who inhabit the northeast shore of Lake Malawi in Tanzania, an account of creation begins like this[19]:

◎◎ The sky was large, white, and very clear. It was empty; there were no stars and no moon; only a tree stood in the air and there was wind. This tree fed on the atmosphere, and ants lived on it. Wind, tree ants, and atmosphere were controlled by the power of the Word. But the Word was not something that could be seen. It was a force that enabled one thing to create another. ◎◎

The Word finds a similar position in the creation myth of the Mande where the god Faro, an archetype of future human beings, reveals the first thirty words to Simboumba Tanganagati, one of the original human ancestors who descended from heaven on a celestial ark, the myth recounts, along with all the animals and plants that would multiply on the earth. The first Word revealed by the god to humanity was *nko*, "I speak"; the second Word was linked to Faro's seminal fluid and the further birth of humankind.[20]

Then from Ogotemmêli, the Dogon elder, we learn that creation proceeded through divine words brought to the earth through twin creator-gods known as the Nummo; these words are symbolized in the fibers of skirts still worn in the mask ceremonies of the Dogon. "Thus clothed, the earth had a language," observed Griaule, the French anthropologist who spent his life among the Dogon, "the first language of this world and the most primitive of all time. Its syntax was elementary, its verbs few, and its vocabulary without elegance.

And as we've already seen, the Bambara, near neighbors of both the Mande and Dogon, also understand the universe as emanating from a Cosmic Word, whose vibratory sound is Yo.

For the Yoruba, the Cosmic Word was first Hòò, the unmanifested sound, impregnated by Olodumare with *ogbón* (wisdom), *ìmò* (knowledge), and *óye* (understanding), these three elements representing the most potent aspects of creation. Only after the *orisha* Èlà (often identified with Orunmilla) brought Hòò to earth was its creative potential available to humankind as Òrò, the manifest Cosmic Word.[21]

By endowing the Word with this power of creation, these African mythologies seek to answer *how* creation takes place. For it does not suffice to say "this god" or "that goddess" created the world; the ancient African sages also sought to know how. Embedded in these African accounts of the dawn of humanity and the world is a proposition of long-standing regard in human reckoning with the origins of life: that the eternal mystery, the ground of being, forever shrouded in silence, was once shattered by a cosmic sound. Thus, through this primordial Word, the one became the many; order was established where before there was chaos; form emerged from formlessness; the plenitude was extracted from the void; and the Word was thus made flesh.

Compilers of these African myths about the Word all attest to their pre-Christian origins, yet they are certainly to be compared with the more familiar Western gospel of John whose verses (John 1:1–14) concern the *Logos*, as the sacred Word is known in Christianity: "In the beginning was the Word, and the Word was with God, and the Word was God. The same was in the beginning with God. All things were made by him; and without him was not any thing made that was made. . . . And the Word was made flesh, and dwelt among us." And we know further that John, in thus consecrating the Word, borrowed his theological ideas from more ancient Greek, Hebrew, and Egyptian doctrines of creation.[22]

At the opening of this chapter we compared the sacred Word of the Bambara to that of Hinduism, for Yo and Om are equivalent addresses to the godhead. And it should not go unnoticed that even modern science holds a similar view, for what is the Big Bang if not the primordial sound, the Word that broke the silence of the cosmic void?

But let us now return to the Wapangwa tale, for there is more to learn about creation:

◎◎ The Wind, it seems, was annoyed with the tree, which stood in its way, so it blew until a branch snapped, carrying away with it the colony of white ants. When the branch finally came to rest, the ants ate all the leaves except one large one upon which they left their excrement. This excrement grew into a large heap and eventually into a mountain that approached the top of the tree of origin. Now in contact again with the primordial tree, the ants had more food to consume and waste to eliminate, from which they fashioned a huge object, the earth, with mountains and valleys, all of which touched the top of the tree of origin. ◎◎

Lest we turn away in disgust at the thought of a world created from the waste of ants—or laugh at the whimsy of it—we should remember that the Dogon proposed that an ancestor-god vomited the world into being, as did Mbumba,[23] the Kuba creator-god. And the supreme Egyptian god Re, identified with the sun, is described in an ancient papyrus as masturbating the world into being.[24]

Now the Wapangwa tree of origin is a curious tree, to be sure: the earth, so says the myth, is built from the ground up to rest against the top of the tree. Only a tree lying upside down in space could satisfy this image, and an inverted World Tree is yet another symbol from African mythology with a venerable history in mythology worldwide. "Happy is the portion of Israel," says the *Zohar*, the principal medieval text of the Kabbalah, "in whom the Holy One, blessed be He, delights and to whom he gave the Torah of truth, the Tree of Life. . . . Now the Tree of Life extends from above downward, and it is the Sun which illumines all."[25] Dante encountered such a tree on the sixth ridge in his visionary ascent of the world mountain of Purgatory, which he described as an inverted form of the forbidden tree originally in the Garden of Eden.[26] And the sense of this symbol is perhaps best rendered in a verse of the *Katha* Upanishad:

> The Tree of Eternity has its roots in heaven above and its branches reach down to earth. It is Brahman, pure Spirit, who in truth is called the Immortal. All worlds rest on that Spirit and beyond him no one can go.[27]

So this tree with roots in the eternal mystery puts forth leaves that represent the created world and all its forms. But the Wapangwa saga of creation has other universal symbols to offer, as well:

◎◎ One day the Word sent a terrible wind, and white frost appeared on the earth. Soon a warm wind followed, and the ice melted into water. The waters swelled and drowned the ants, and in the end flooded the whole earth, until no spot remained dry. In those days the earth was as large as it is now, and it was a desert of water. ◎◎

The legend of the Great Flood destroying the first created world is indeed another universal symbol of creation mythology. Faro, the Bambara creator who revealed the first Word to humanity, also brought forth a flood to cleanse the land of the impurity brought by his evil twin, Pemba; disappointed by humanity's shortcomings, the Sumerian-Babylonian gods sent a Great Flood against the world that only Ziusudra (Utnapishtim in Babylonia) and his wife survived; a similar fate was delivered by the Roman pantheon, with only Deucalion and Lyrra coming through unscathed to be the postdiluvian World Parents; and themes of the Great Flood are to be found among the Hindu of India, the Yao of China, the Chewong of Malaya, the Andean culture of South America, and, of course, in Judeo-Christianity. Just as the creation of the world through the secretion of the creator's bodily fluids is analogous to the virgin birth of the hero, the Great Flood provides an analogy between the death and resurrection of the mythic hero and the death and resurrection of the world; for the water that drowns the world is also the *aqua mater* of its rebirth. After the Wapangwan deluge, we learn that:

◎◎ One day the atmosphere brought forth beings that moved about in the air—they spoke and cried and sang. They settled on the earth and each created his own sound. Birds, animals, and men—each had his own cry.

There was little food. The animals wanted to eat the tree of origin, but men forbade them to do it. But when men saw that the animals did not obey, they called them into a valley and began a great war, attacking each other with sticks and stones. It was a terrible war. The wind blew powerfully and the water roared. Many died before the war was finally over. Some animals remained men's prisoners, others escaped to the forest. But the animals of the forest began to attack men and to eat them. So all evil came into the world—murder and eating one another. ◎◎

With the emergence of living beings on the world stage comes both the mystery, seen in the atmosphere bringing forth life, and the misery, for this creation also begets the horrific cycle of life forever feeding on itself, the requisite evil of living beings murdering and eating one another. This war of life continues, we are told:

◎◎ The very earth began to tremble and bits of it broke loose. Some of the pieces began to glow with heat as they whirled through the air. These were the sun, the moon, and the stars. The sun glowed most, because it broke off with fire. The moon and stars broke off without fire, but later they began to shine also through the light of the sun. For the sun's rays shone through them, as they are only thin, transparent disks.

When the war came to an end, many new things were created that still exist today: the gods, rain, thunder, and lightning. ◎◎

Here the myth makes the tantalizing proposal that our relation to the cosmos, the gods, and natural phenomena is principally a projection of the fundamental conflicts and needs of our own psyche, for the gods and the cosmos come into being after humanity and as a result of the turmoil induced by our coming to terms with the necessity of life feeding on itself. "The first men had no gods," we learn as the story proceeds, "but they found them after the great wars." This observation is then reminiscent of the Yoruba maxim, "If humanity were not, the gods would not be."

◎◎ In times of war men used to pray to the wind, trees, and other things for help. In those days men had more gods than today. Many people then prayed to thunder. When the war ended, a sheep was born with a long tail and a long pointed horn. It was so happy about the end of the war that it became mad. It started to jump and play and it hurled itself into the air. It floated along in the air and caught fire in the atmosphere. Since that time it causes thunder and lightning when heavy rain falls. It is said that this sheep finally killed the Word and thus became the God of the world. It ruled over everything: earth, moon, stars, sun, and rain, and was the god of thunder and lightning. ◎◎

This is an epoch-marking event signaling the final turn in the round of creation, for the sheep is a domesticated animal, raised to be killed, a symbol of humanity's conquest in the war of predators and prey—and this symbol is now worshiped as a god. Where once the Word was made flesh, now the flesh has been made the Word; earthly sustenance (the sheep) replaces spiritual sustenance (the Word) as the revered presence. Divinity seeks to bring an end to this sacrilege, we hear in the concluding scene of this myth; for when a god is consulted about forever ending the war between animals and men, humanity is told:

◎◎ "You men kept a sheep, you made war, and your sheep became mad—it flew through the air and it killed the Word, from which all things that adorn the world have sprung. Well, I am the younger brother of the Word. And I tell you, you were great, but because of the things you have done you shall be reduced, you shall be small until in the end your height shall not even be half of your present stature. And in the end your entire world shall be consumed with fire." ◎◎

So in the end, the Word returns the world to its source.

Mystical Participation in the Whole of Creation

From the individual, to the family, to the community, to the earth, to the cosmos—from the microcosm to the macrocosm, then back again—African creation myths are blueprints for human engagement in all orders of creation. The Bambara creation mythology of the silence broken by the cosmic Yo is then the basis of their meditation on this sacred syllable as a means of returning to the silence; the transcendent ground of the beginning and ending of being.

Nowhere is this mystical participation better evidenced in African mythology than with the Dogon, who live as neighbors to the Bambara. Theirs is an intricate and controversial story of creation, which says as much about mythology as it does about the contact between African and European culture. It was reported through conversations between the French anthropologist, Marcel Griaule, and his Dogon informant, Ogotemmêli[28]:

Ogotemmêli proceeded to weave a complex tapestry of Dogon beliefs, offering his insights into a hidden and long-standing cosmology. He began with the dawn of all things, when the one God Amma fashioned the earth from a lump of clay and flung it from him to its present position in space. When this lonely God looked upon the beauty of his creation—shaped as a woman on her back with arms and legs outstretched—he desired intercourse with her, and this is how life on earth came forth. Initially, twins were born. Known as Nummo, this pair became the demiurges of the drama—the secondary actors through which the creation saga unfolded.

Amma, according to Ogotemmêli, then created two human beings from lumps of clay flung to earth; male and female bodies emerged, but they lacked souls. So the Nummo drew an outline of the human soul on the ground—a man lying on top of a woman—and both the male and female bodies stretched themselves out along this symbolic form in order to obtain a human soul. In this way, Ogotemmêli noted, the human soul encompassed both masculine and feminine principles regardless of the gender of the human body.

As the Nummo went about ordering the chaos set in motion by Amma's initial procreative act, a pivotal event took place. One of the children of the first human couple was transformed into a snake that humanity subsequently killed; its body was eaten, but its head was buried. It then fell to Lébé, the oldest living man, to embark on a journey in pursuit of the special knowledge that lay buried along with this snake's head. He descended into the bowels of the earth where he met the snake's head, but above ground, the metallic sound of a smith's hammer on the anvil traveled through the earth and regenerated the snake, which devoured Lébé whole. As the snake continued to sway to the rhythm of the smith, it began regurgitating the bones of the hero, which had since been transformed into colored stones called *dogué*. These stones were spit out in a specific, significant shape—that of a human body.

The snake, Ogotemmêli whispered to Griaule, "swallowed the old man head-first, and brought up the *dogué* stones, putting them in the shape of the stretched-out body. It was like a drawing of a man picked out with stones."[29]

The old sage viewed this regurgitation of the human form as a seminal event in Dogon cosmology, tying together all aspects of Dogon mythological and spiritual beliefs. The human body, according to Ogotemmêli, was the blueprint for the organization and functioning of all levels of human society.

"He organized the world," Ogotemmêli concluded, "by vomiting the *dogué* stones in the outline of a man's soul."[30]

A single head stone, representing the godhead, was laid out, followed by eight principal stones representing the major joints of the body: pelvis and shoulders (male joints); knees and elbows (female joints). These joints symbolized the eight original ancestors. They

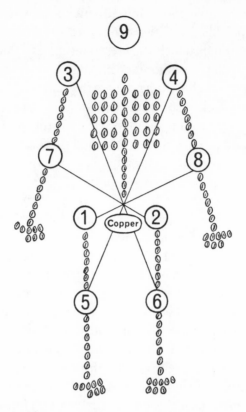

Figure 26. The Dogon world system revealed in the image of stones
spit out by a dead and resurrected creator-god.

also marked the transition of humans from a spiritual body (without
joints) to an earthly body (with joints). Next, the Nummo brought up
stones for the lesser bones: the ribs, spinal column, and long bones of
the extremities. Cowrie shells were used to indicate the fingers and
toes, arranged in the birth order of the eight original ancestors. Finally, the Nummo placed copper between the legs of this human
form.

For Ogotemmêli, the human body was thus a most sacred symbol
and seal: it symbolized the spirit, the Word made flesh, the covenant
between God and humankind. Ideally, he indicated, Dogon villages
were to be laid out in the shape of a body. Oriented in a north-south
direction, a village should appear like a human body lying faceup. At
the head of this body was the main square of the village, symbolic of
the primal field where Lébé died and was resurrected for the sake
of humanity. Located here were the village smithy (symbolic of the

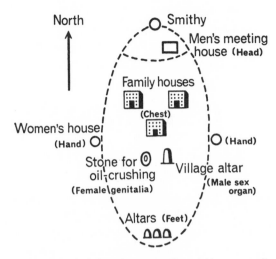

Figure 27. Ideal plan of a Dogon village, laid out, according to
Ogotemmêli, in the image of a human body.

seventh ancestor transformed into a snake) and the council of elders
(symbolic of Lébé, the oldest man). At both hands were houses
in the shape of wombs for menstruating women. Family houses were
the chest and belly of the village. Female genitals were represented
by the stone mortars women use to make oil from crushed seeds.
Next to these mortars was a phallic-shaped altar considered the foundation point of the village. And a Dogon village should be anchored
in the south by a set of communal altars.

Even within a Dogon house, Ogotemmêli continued, a similar
pattern, following the plan of a body, was to be repeated. Also built
on a north-south axis, the soil of the ground floor was symbolic of
the sacred earth that received and then resurrected Lébé. Dogon
houses should have a large central room that communicates with the
outside through a vestibule at the north end and from which store-
rooms proceed to the east and west. The vestibule represents the male
partner of the household, the main door is symbolic of a phallus, and
the communicating door is symbolic of a vulva. The main portion of
the house, as Ogotemmêli described it, represented a couple lying in
intercourse: the central and side rooms were the woman lying on her
back with outstretched arms; the ceiling was a man whose skeleton
was represented by the beams; and the four upright poles supporting
the ceiling were the couple's arms, the woman's arms supporting the
man whose hands rested on the ground.

This image of a conjugal couple was, of course, symbolic of the outline of the human soul originally traced on the ground by the Nummo to imbue humanity with the spark of divinity. Therefore, Ogotemmêli observed, children should be both conceived and delivered in this central womb of the house where they may then take possession of their soul.

Seeds for sowing should be placed under the bed, for in sexual intercourse men are considered to be introducing fertilizing rain onto the feminine ground. A couple in bed with a covering over them is also symbolically lying in the earthen grave of the dead and resurrected hero-ancestor, Lébé; the snake that spit him out gains metaphorical entrance to the house through the two sets of doors (male and female genitalia) at the north end. Just as Lébé was resurrected through the power of the Spirit serpent, so too shall seeds and children germinate from this same Spirit acting through the conjugal couple.

The body, that vehicle through which we participate in life, is here rendered and sanctified as the primary vehicle of mystical participation in the entire order of creation. At each turn—from the blueprint of a village, a granary, or a house, to the construction of drums, to the plan of the cosmos, to the act of lovemaking, to the conduct of commerce, to the performance of dance, to the journey of the soul after death—Ogotemmêli interpreted the human body as the principal divine oracle. It reveals the mysteries of life and the cosmos, represents the organization of human society, reasserts the relationship between human life and the earth, and reminds humanity of its seamless connection to divinity.

"What an enormous chapter could be written on African spirituality," wrote Dominique Zahan, "as revealed through its immediate foundation, the human body!"[31] Such a view of the sacredness of the human body and the original divine nature of humanity stands in sharp contrast to orthodox Christianity where, for example, we read in Saint Paul's Letter to the Galatians: "But I say, walk by the Spirit, and do not gratify the desires of the flesh. For the desires of the flesh are against the Spirit, and the desires of the Spirit are against the flesh; for these are opposed to each other, to prevent you from doing what you would."[32] And these Pauline sentiments were then reiterated in the fundamental Christian doctrine of original sin, here expounded in 426 C.E. by the theologian Saint Augustine, whose mythology could be contrasted nearly point for point with that of Ogotemmêli:

> As soon as our first parents had transgressed the commandment, divine grace forsook them, and they were confounded at their own wickedness; and therefore they took fig-leaves and covered their shame. . . . Then began the flesh to lust against the Spirit, in which strife we are born, deriving from the first transgression a seed of death, and bearing in our members, and in our vitiated nature, the contest or even victory of the flesh.[33]

What a contrast to the affirmation of the sacred accord of flesh and spirit expressed by Ogotemmêli and found throughout traditional African mythology. One wonders how different Western culture might be today without this deeply ingrained schism between body and spirit.

An African Trinity

◎◎ At the beginning of things, when there was nothing, neither man, nor animals, nor plants, nor heaven, nor earth. But God *was* and he was called Nzame. The three who are Nzame, we call them Nzame, Mebere, and Nkwa. At the beginning Nzame made the heaven and the earth and he reserved the heaven for himself. Then he blew onto the earth, and earth and water were created, each on its side.[34] ◎◎

Thus begins a myth from the Fang of Gabon, in which we are told in the beginning there was nothing but that God *was;* God, then, was the *"uncreated* creator"—a symbol of the transcendent mystery that preceded creation, the wholeness from which the fragmentation of creation emerges. Then God is given names and attributes, depicted here in the form of a Trinity. From this African Trinity we learn that God is both the transcendent and immanent ground of creation: as Nzame, God is, by definition, beyond and prior to creation, but God is also Mebere and Nkwa, representing the male and female aspects of creation, the ever-present duality through which the mystery of creation unfolds.

The opening of this myth also offers a sense that God's spirit is cast upon the earth, much as the spirit of the Hebrew Bible's creator "moved upon the face of the waters." In this Fang myth, God "blew onto the earth," and the relationship between *breath* and *spirit* is quite literally established from the Latin derivation of the word *spirit, spiritus,* meaning breath.

Creation then proceeds in a somewhat humorous way, with Nzame checking his progress with the other members of this African Trinity:

◎◎ Nzame made everything: heaven, earth, sun, moon, stars, animals, plants—everything. When he had finished everything that we see today, he called Mebere and Nkwa and showed them his work.

"This is my work. Is it good?"

They replied, "Yes, you have done well."

"Does anything remain to be done?"

Mebere and Nkwa answered him, "We see many animals, but we do not see their chief; we see many plants, but we do not see their master."

As masters for all these things, they appointed the elephant, because he had wisdom; the leopard, because he had power and cunning; and the monkey, because he had malice and suppleness.

But Nzame wanted to do even better, and working together, he, Mebere, and Nkwa created a being almost like themselves. One gave him force, the second sway, and the third beauty. Then the three of them said:

"Take the earth. You are henceforth the master of all that exists. Like us you have life, all things belong to you, you are the master."

Nzame, Mebere, and Nkwa returned to the heights to their dwelling place, and the new creature remained below alone, and everything obeyed him. But among all the animals the elephant remained the first, the leopard the second, and the monkey the third, because it was they whom Mebere and Nkwa had first chosen.

Nzame, Mebere, and Nkwa called the first man Fam, which means "power."

Proud of his sway, his power, and his beauty, because he surpassed in these three qualities the elephant, the leopard, and the monkey, proud of being able to defeat all the animals, this first man grew wicked; he became arrogant and did not want to worship Nzame. He scorned him:

Yeye, O, layeye,
God on high, man on the earth,

Yeye, O, layeye,
God is God,
Man is man,
Everyone in his house, everyone for himself!

God heard the song. "Who sings?" he asked.
"Look for him," cried Fam.
"Who sings?"
"Yeye, O, layeye!"
"Who sings?"
"Eh! It is me!" cried Fam.

Furious, God called Nzalan, the thunder. "Nzalan, come!" Nzalan came running with great noise: boom, boom, boom! The fire of heaven fell on the forest. The plantations burned like vast torches. Foo, foo, foo!—everything in flames. The earth was then, as today, covered with forests. The trees burned, the plants, the bananas, the cassava, even the pistachio nuts, everything dried up; animals, birds, fishes, all were destroyed, everything was dead. But when God had created the first man, he had told him, "You will never die." And what God gives he does not take away. The first man was burned, but none knows what became of him. He is alive, yes, but where? ◎◎

Fam is created in the image of God and given the essential qualities of the Trinity: power, mastery, and beauty. He is told he has life like the creators, too—eternal life, that is—and he is given dominion over the earth. But then comes the turning point of the myth, for this first human being is unable to integrate these heavenly boons, instead giving way to the demands of his ego. In retaliation, Nzame unleashes an apocalyptic thunderbolt destroying the earth and driving Fam into hiding; the second phase of creation has ended, and a third begins to unfold:

◎◎ But God looked at the earth, all black, without anything, and idle; he felt ashamed and wanted to do better. Nzame, Mebere, and Nkwa took counsel, and they did as follows: over the black earth covered with coal they put a new layer of earth; a tree grew, grew bigger and bigger, and when one of its seeds fell down a new tree was born; when a leaf severed itself, it grew and grew and began to walk. It was an animal, an elephant, a leopard, an antelope, a tortoise—all of them. When a leaf fell into the water it swam; it was a fish, a sardine, a crab, an oyster—all of them. The earth became again what it had been and what it still is today. The proof that this is the truth is this: when one digs up the earth in certain places, one finds a hard black stone that breaks; throw it in the fire and it burns. ◎◎

So creation proceeds once again; the scorched earth is fertilized by the gods, and the tree that grows from this hallowed ground sheds leaves that become the animals and plants, rekindling life on earth. By now this is a familiar mythic symbol: the Cosmic Tree, the World Tree, the Tree of Life.

◎◎ But Nzame, Mebere, and Nkwa took counsel again; they needed a chief to command all the animals. "We shall make a man like Fam," said Nzame, "the same legs and arms, but we shall turn his head and he shall see death."

This was the second man and the father of all. Nzame called him Sekume, but did not want to leave him alone, and said, "Make yourself a woman from a tree."

Sekume made himself a woman, and she walked, and he called her Mbongwe.

When Nzame made Sekume and Mbongwe, he made them in two parts—an outer part called Gnoul, the body, and the other that lives in the body, called Nsissim.

Nsissim is what produces the soul; Nsissim is the soul—it is the same thing. It is Nsissim who makes Gnoul live. Nsissim goes away when man dies, but Nsissim does not die. Do you know where he lives? He lives in the eye. The little shining point you see in the middle, that is Nsissim.

> *Stars above*
> *Fire below*
> *Coal in the hearth*
> *The soul in the eye*
> *Cloud smoke and death.*

Sekume and Mbongwe lived happily on earth and had many children. But Fam, the first man, was imprisoned by God under the earth. With a large stone God blocked the entrance. But the malicious Fam tunneled through the earth for a long time, and one day, at last, he was outside! Who had taken his place? The new man. Fam was furious with him. Now he hides in the forest, waiting to kill the couple, or under the water, waiting to capsize their boats.

> *Remain silent,*
> *Fam is listening,*
> *to bring misfortune;*
> *remain silent.* ◎◎

The Trinity decide that they will create a man like Fam but, as Nzame says, "we shall turn his head and he shall see death." Fam, the original man, was created like the gods, and gods do not really live because gods do not really die. Because he has been made to embrace death, Sekume, the newly created man, is also made to embrace life. The challenge of discovering immortality in the face of mortality is then presented to Sekume in two ways. First, he is allowed to make a woman, Mbongwe, from a Cosmic Tree. This preserves the classic counterpoise between death and sex, for sex is the manner by which one generation begets the next, thus assuring their genetic immortality.

But a second path is also given, a turning within to discover what is immortal. Sekume and Mbongwe are given both a mortal body (Gnoul) and an immortal soul (Nsissim), and they are told to find the soul by looking to the light within the eye. In other words, through the eye of inner vision they can find the light of immortality dwelling within.

Nsissim is also translated as "shadow," and the myth proposes the existence of both atoned (soul) and unatoned (shadow) forces within the human psyche. Fam, initially banished to the underworld, manages to escape and live on in the forest and underwater, a malevolent force dangerous to any who dares venture in these realms. Forests and water are universal symbols of the human unconscious, and the creatures lurking there represent the danger and the dynamism of this inner realm. So a note of caution is sounded to humanity in its pursuit of the sacred: travel within to find the gemstone of immortal consciousness, but beware of the unreconciled forces you will encounter on this inner quest.

10

CLOSING THE
SACRED CIRCLE

The wise aim at boundaries beyond the present; by their
struggle they transcend the circle of their beginning.

AFRICAN PROVERB

The sacred circle, the cosmogonic round, the wheel of the arising and passing away of the created world and all its manifest forms is like a symphonic composition arranged in three movements: prelude, crescendo, and finale; emergence, fulfillment, and dissolution. Mythologies of the cosmogonic round trumpet the coming into being of humanity and the world as we know it from a transcendent ground of being; then they score the complex relationship between humanity, this ordinary world of space and time, and the great mystery of being; and finally they herald the dissolution of this phenomenal world back into the transcendent mystery from which it emerged.

When sung in the tones of African mythology, the cosmogonic round is not only an ode of the world, it is also a song of the soul. It notes the endless arising and passing away of the world as we know it, then asks us to listen even more closely to hear it as a metaphor for the creation and dissolution of the worlds within ourselves—the movement of human consciousness from birth, through life, and into death.

The Coming of Death

Death of the world, or death of the self, is the last phase of the creation cycle. Death appears in many African creation myths; in fact, one form of its entry into the world is so common that it has earned the name "the failed message." The basic story, told in many different variations, is quite simple: two creatures are sent to humanity; the first carries a message of immortality, the second of mortality, but the first message fails to get delivered. From the Khoi of Southwest Africa comes a simple and exemplary version of the tale[1]:

◎◎ The Moon, it is said, once sent an insect to men, saying, "Go to men and tell them, 'As I die, and dying live; so you shall also die, and dying live.' "

The insect started with the message, but while on his way was overtaken by the Hare, who asked, "On what errand are you bound?"

The insect answered, "I am sent by the Moon to men, to tell them that as she dies and dying lives, so shall they also die and dying live."

The Hare said, "As you are an awkward runner, let me go." With these words he ran off, and when he reached men, he said, "I am sent by the Moon to tell you, 'As I die and dying perish, in the same manner you also shall die and come wholly to an end.' "

The Hare then returned to the Moon and told her what he had said to men. The Moon reproached him angrily, saying, "Do you dare tell the people a thing that I have not said?"

With these words the Moon took up a piece of wood and struck the Hare on the nose. Since that day the Hare's nose has been slit, but men still believe what the Hare told them. ◎◎

Rather than a "failed message," I read in this myth and its variations a wonderful summary of the creation cycle and the human spiritual adventure as seen from the perspective of traditional African mythology: Every twenty-eight days the moon throws off death, in the form of the shadow cast upon it by the earth from the light of the sun, and is reborn into the fullness of the sun's light. The sun's light is constant (immortal), while the moon's light—a reflection of the sun's—dies and is reborn (mortal). Symbolically, then, the moon finds immortality through its mortality. And as the moon throws off the shadow of death to be reborn in the fullness of the sun's light, so too should humans throw off the veil of death to discover that consciousness which transcends death.

The failure of humanity to receive the moon's message adds a marvelous twist to this myth, for the hare is the trickster figure. By inaccurately delivering the moon's message, the hare serves as a lure to the spiritual quest; the challenge is to discover the intended message of the moon in *spite of what* the trickster says. And this message—the ability of human beings to find immortality through their mortality—informs the mythic wisdom of traditional Africa.

The Circle of the Spirit

Kongo civilization records the turning of the cosmogonic round in the compact symbology of an ideogram traced on the ground (Figure 28). Known as the *yowa,* this cross, which predates the intrusion of Christianity into central Africa, is the centerpiece of oath-taking and some ritual initiations. With solar disks at the ends of each cross arm and arrows suggesting a counterclockwise direction of motion, the cruciform represents the four stations of the sun's movement through the sky. Fu-Kiau Bunseki, a modern-day BaKongo interpreter of this symbol, observes, "The cross was known to the BaKongo before the arrival of Europeans, and corresponds to the understanding in their minds of their relationship to their world."[2] Bunseki goes on to note that when the symbol was used as the basis of ritual initiation into the Lemba healing society, the medicine man conducting the ceremony

would use the sun in order to expound his teaching [to the assembled initiates] about the earth and the life of man, following the sun through its course about the earth and thus pointing out the four stages which make up the cycle of man's life:

- rising, beginning, birth, or regrowth [right, east]
- ascendancy, maturity, responsibility [top, north]
- setting, handing on, death, transformation [left, west]
- midnight, existence in the other world, eventual rebirth [bottom, south].[3]

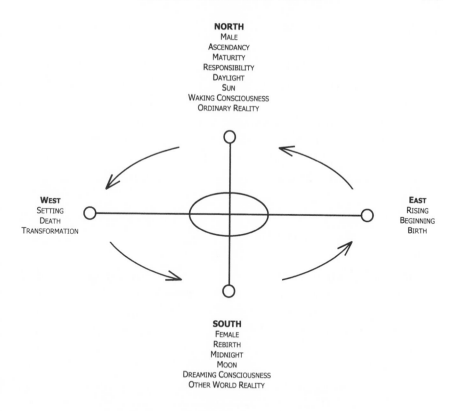

NORTH
Male
Ascendancy
Maturity
Responsibility
Daylight
Sun
Waking Consciousness
Ordinary Reality

WEST
Setting
Death
Transformation

EAST
Rising
Beginning
Birth

SOUTH
Female
Rebirth
Midnight
Moon
Dreaming Consciousness
Other World Reality

Figure 28. Yowa cross, symbolic of the Kongo cosmos and journey of the human soul. After Thompson (1983).

The central ellipse represents the mythic waters of Kalunga separating two worlds that are mirror images of each other: the ordinary world (Ntoto) and the "land of the dead" (Mputu). "Between these two parts, the lands of the dead and the living," writes Bunseki, "the water is both a passage and a great barrier. The world in Kongo thought is like two great mountains opposed at their bases and separated by the ocean."[4] This mythic symbolism is practically universal and very old. A Sumerian bas-relief from the period 2350–2150 B.C.E., for example, depicts the Sun-god climbing out of the sea and ascending the World Mountain to the summit, then returning back to the sea.[5]

Kalunga is the name by which the infinite sea of Kongo cosmology, the ellipse in the ideogram, is known, and it is the term used to describe the land of the dead to which this sea is both a barrier and a passageway. Kalunga is also the threshold crossed by captured

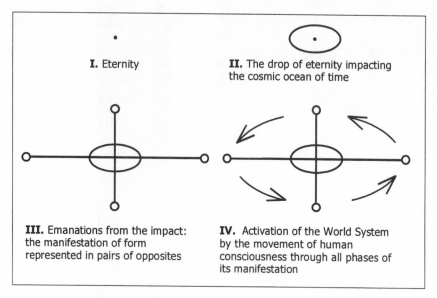

I. Eternity

II. The drop of eternity impacting the cosmic ocean of time

III. Emanations from the impact: the manifestation of form represented in pairs of opposites

IV. Activation of the World System by the movement of human consciousness through all phases of its manifestation

Figure 29. Stages in the cycle of creation represented in the Kongo cosmogram.

slaves entering the Middle Passage, and the land to which Sudika-mbambi, the Ambundu child-hero, journeyed to face death and later be resurrected by his twin brother (see Chapter 3). The Kongo cruciform, then, stands as an emblem of the hero's journey, and the formula of the heroic quest—departure, fulfillment, return—is equivalent to the solar voyage through the sky.

We unveil still another level of insight when we read this cosmogram not around the circumference but from the center to the periphery, like an oriental mandala of which it is surely an African counterpart.

Hindu and Buddhist mandalas are used as aids to meditation, helping the aspirant visualize, and thus understand in symbolic terms, the nature of the inward spiritual quest he or she is undertaking. Similarly, the *yowa* is an aid to meditation; an initiate into the Lemba society of healers contemplates it while standing in the middle of the cruciform pattern chalked on the ground. This signifies, according to Bunseki, "that he knew the nature of the world, that he had mastered the meaning of life and death."[6]

At the center of the *yowa* (Figure 29, stage I) is the point of the Absolute, of eternity—the symbolic representation of the transcendent mystery source prior to its manifestation in the known world. "*Yimbila ye sona,*" say the BaKongo: one must "sing and draw the point."[7] "They believe," says art historian William Farris Thompson, "that the combined force of singing KiKongo words and tracing in appropriate media the ritually designated 'point' or 'mark' of contact between the worlds [of divinity and humanity] will result in direct descent of God's power upon that very point."[8]

Thus, for the BaKongo, the World Axis or World Center is wherever it is drawn, celebrated through song, and assimilated into the consciousness of the spiritual pilgrim. The Bambara know this as the central point of emanation of the cosmic sound Yo—the " 'God-point' or God-'ball,' kuru, the phase of creation in which the divinity itself was still no more than a dimensionless being in a universe without coordinates."[9] Sudanese refer to this intersection of the cross arms as dagu, meaning the "initial point of departure" (creation), "giant head of the limit" (dissolution), and "the old man" (creator).[10] And in mystical readings of Christianity this axial point of the cross is described as the "sun door" through which divinity descends to humanity and humanity ascends to divinity, as did Jesus through his crucifixion.[11]

How can we picture the impact of the Absolute on the cosmic waters of creation (stage II)? Imagine, for example, that instant immediately after the pebble you have tossed into a calm pool has broken the surface of the water but before the wavelets, in an explosion of motion, begin rippling outward from the center of this impact. Or consider the moment just after one sperm has broken the outer casing of the ovum, uniting with the egg but not yet producing that tremendous explosion of growth and activity that ultimately gives rise to new life. Or think about that time before time billions of years ago, the nanosecond before the cosmic explosion of the Big Bang. This is the aspect of creation, so imperfectly rendered by any symbol, that is suggested by the dot in the middle of the ellipse of the Kongo cosmogram: the person within the fertilized egg; the oak tree within the acorn; the universe within a dimensionless point; the potential prior to its manifestation.

Kalunga, the cosmic waters represented by this ellipse, is the Water of Life, the yolk inside the egg, the amniotic fluid of the womb. This ellipse then symbolizes the feminine aspect that is the matrix of creation—the Cosmic Womb from which the whole of creation is born. Kalunga is the word also used to describe the entire lower half of the full cosmogram, which the Kongo consider female; the upper half is correspondingly male. And finally, kalunga is associated with death. In many African creation myths, death comes into the world simultaneously with the appearance of a woman, for when this cosmogram is read from the outside in, this Cosmic Womb of creation then becomes the Cosmic Tomb of dissolution—the closing of the sacred circle.

In the third stage of our unfolding of the Kongo cosmogram, we also have the manifestation of the world symbolized in pairs of opposites. This dualism is so basic to the created world and so fundamental to our experience as human beings that it is doubtful a mythological or cosmological system could exist that did not recognize it on some level, even if only at the most basic biological level of the duality of the sexes.

Finally, in the last stage of expansion, the Kongo cosmogram adds lines of motion to the arms of the cross, symbolizing the movement of the sun, the movement of life from birth to death to rebirth, and the movement of human consciousness. Now the stationary cross has been transformed into a dynamic cross, a mythological symbol of joy in antiquity and of sorrow in modernity: the swastika. For thousands of years this symbol, found in cultures around the world, reflected the original meaning of the Sanskrit words from which its name derived, *suas* (auspicious) and *tika* (mark)—until Nazi Germany ripped this meaning away, elevating it instead as a symbol of hatred and genocide. It is, of course, in the original sense of the word that we find this symbol embedded in the Kongo cosmogram. The cosmogram is that "auspicious mark" one must "sing and draw," welcoming divinity to walk among humanity, inviting each person to discover the god within and thus close the sacred circle.

The healing strength of the Kongo symbol was not lost even to the treacherous tides of history, for when the sacred circle was broken, through the horrors of a slave trade that wrenched Africans from their hallowed ground, the symbol survived to close the circle once again. It defied the Middle Passage, bearing the whip and the auction block, to resurface on the other side of the Atlantic where to this day it may be found throughout the Caribbean in mystical ground drawings; in the Afro-Cuban barrios of Havana, Miami, and New York as spiritual tracings on the undersurface of ritual vessels called *prendas;* and among African Americans in the American South, though in a more modified form, as charms for good luck, healing, and love.[12]

(a)

(b)

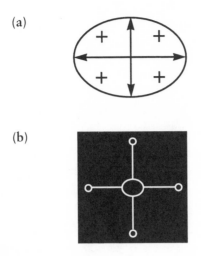

Figure 30. Survival of Kongo symbolism in the Americas: (a) Cuban ground drawing; (b) Afro-Cuban sign on the bottom of a *prenda*. After Thompson (1983).

The Journey's End

Now at the closing of this sacred journey through the mythic wisdom of traditional Africa, I find myself standing in the middle of a *yowa* I have traced in the sand. I am facing westward toward the ocean, the direction faced by millions of Africans pitched into the perils of Kalunga, the mythic direction of heroic transformation and infinite compassion, the direction of blackness and of the setting sun. If I listen intently, I can make out the ancestors' voices once again, rolling in echo upon echo, like the timeless motion of the waves. I am beginning to understand the message they had for me those many years ago. Once I thought the voices were meant to propel me to do and accomplish much in my life, in the face of their great sacrifice. Now I think they asked me only to know they had gone before; I need but follow the path of their own hero's journey and when I come upon my Middle Passage, find the strength to survive; when I come upon the demons of the dark night of my soul, find the courage to meet them in battle; and when I come upon that which would chain me down, find the mettle to struggle until I set myself free. For these heroes and heroines with African faces have now revealed the hero within me.

ENDNOTES AND PERMISSIONS

PREFACE

1. Kwame Gyekye and Kwame Anthony Appiah, two Ghanaians, feature most prominently in this debate with Appiah generally arguing against a pan-African perspective and Gyekye arguing for one. See Gyekye (1995) and Appiah (1992).
2. Adolph Bastian, C. G. Jung, and Joseph Campbell are among those who have pursued such an approach to mythology. Bastian, a German mythologist of the late nineteenth century, proposed that two forces were observable in mythology: *Elementargedanke*, "elementary ideas" common to all humanity, and *Völkergedanke*, "folk ideas" which were local, ethnic expressions of these universal motifs; Jung used this as the basis of his "archetypes" of the collective unconscious and Campbell took a similar starting point in his extensive work on mythology.

CHAPTER 1: VOICES OF THE ANCESTORS

1. For an excellent summary of the historical facts about the Middle Passage, see John Henrik Clarke's introduction in Tom Feelings's, *The Middle Passage* (New York: Dial Press, 1995).
2. I am following the convention of using a *K* to distinguish the civilization of the BaKongo people from the political entities, the two Republics of the Congo (People's and Democratic); and I am using the technically correct Bantu form of placing *Ki* in front of the name of the language, KiKongo, that is spoken by the BaKongo.
3. Wyatt MacGaffey, *Modern Kongo Prophets* (Bloomington: Indiana University Press, 1983), 136.
4. MacGaffey, *Modern Kongo Prophets*, 129–40.
5. MacGaffey, *Modern Kongo Prophets*, 136.

6. MacGaffey, *Modern Kongo Prophets*, 135–36.

7. Pierre Grimal Larousse, ed., *World Mythology* (London: Paul Hamlyn, 1965), 189–204.

8. The word *avesta* bears a striking resemblance to the Sanskrit word *sveta*, which is the Indo-European root of the modern word *white*.

9. See Martin Bernal, *Black Athena*, vol. 2 (New Brunswick, N.J.: Rutgers University Press, 1991), 92–93.

10. Since ancient Egyptian words have no vowels to guide their pronunciation, linguists have devised a coded spelling system that uses consonants and numbers. Bernal, *Black Athena*, 93.

11. The precise linguistic spelling is $\sqrt{(n)gr}$. Note, however, that with the addition of an *e* and an *o* to this root, we get the word *negro*. Bernal, *Black Athena*, 96.

12. As early as 600 B.C.E., for example, the Phoenicians, a Semitic people, had circumnavigated Africa in the service of the pharaoh Necho.

13. This is a paraphrase from John Mbiti, *African Religions and Philosophy* (Portsmouth, N.H.: Heinemann, [1969] 1990), 141.

14. Joseph Campbell, *The Hero with a Thousand Faces* (Princeton, N.J.: Princeton University Press, [1949] 1968), 3.

15. For an overview of current archaeological research about human origins in Africa, see Ian Tattersall, "Out of Africa Again . . . and Again?" *Scientific American* 276, no. 4 (1997), 60–67.

16. Adapted from Maria Leach, *Creation Myths Around the World* (New York: Crowell, 1956), 140–42, and Barbara C. Sproul, *Primal Myths: Creation Myths Around the World* (San Francisco: HarperCollins, 1979), 45–46.

CHAPTER 2: THE HERO WITH AN AFRICAN FACE

1. Joseph Campbell, following James Joyce, referred to this universal hero sequence as the *monomyth*. See Campbell, *Hero with a Thousand Faces*, 30.

2. Adapted from Henry Callaway, *Nursery Tales and Traditions of the Zulus* (Westport, Conn.: Negro Universities Press, [1868] 1970), 243–58.

3. Alice Werner, *Myths and Legends of the Bantu* (London: Frank Cass, [1933] 1968), 84.

4. From *A Treasury of African Folklore* by Harold Courlander (New York: Crown, 1975), 120–23. Copyright © 1996 by Harold Courlander. Reprinted by permission of Marlowe & Company.

5. See Kwame Gyekye, *An Essay on African Conceptual Thought: The Akan Conceptual Scheme* (Philadelphia: Temple University Press, 1995), 68–101.

6. Adapted from Hèli Chatelain, *Folk-Tales of Angola* (New York: Negro Universities Press, [1894] 1968), 85–97.

7. Amos Tutuola, *The Palm-Wine Drinkard* (New York: Grove Press, [1952] 1994), 214.

8. The original text indicates this fighting was done with guns, pointing to the creation or adaptation of this portion of the myth after the arrival of the Portuguese in Angola.

CHAPTER 3: MYTHS OF DEATH AND RESURRECTION

1. Adapted from Rev. E. Casalis, *The Basutos* (London: James Nisbet, 1861), 347–48.

2. Werner, *Myths and Legends of the Bantu*, 218.

3. Callaway, *Nursery Tales and Traditions of the Zulus*, 84.

4. Martin Luther King Jr., *Letter from the Birmingham Jail* (San Francisco: HarperSanFrancisco, [1968] 1994), 26.

5. King, *Letter from the Birmingham Jail*, 26.

6. MacGaffey, cited in Bolster, *Black Jacks: African American Seamen in the Age of Sail* (Cambridge: Harvard University Press, 1997), 65.

7. From *Myths and Legends of the Bantu* by Alice Werner, 70–76. Originally published in 1933 by Frank Cass & Co. Ltd.; reissued 1968. Reprinted by permission of Frank Cass Publishers, 900 Eastern Avenue, Ilford, Essex, IG2 7HH, England.

8. Leo Frobenius, *Schicksalkunde im Sinne des Kulturwerdens*, 127, translated and cited in Campbell, *The Masks of God: Primitive Mythology* (New York: Penguin Books, [1959] 1976), 166.

CHAPTER 4: THE SOUL'S HIGH ADVENTURE

1. From *Hero with a Thousand Faces* by Joseph Campbell, 69. Copyright © 1949 by Princeton University Press. Reprinted by permission of Princeton University Press.

2. Werner, *Myths and Legends of the Bantu*, 51–52.

3. From *Myths and Legends of the Bantu* by Alice Werner, 57–61. Originally published in 1933 by Frank Cass & Co. Ltd.; reissued 1968. Reprinted by permission of Frank Cass Publishers, 900 Eastern Avenue, Ilford, Essex, IG2 7HH, England.

4. Werner, *Myths and Legends of the Bantu*, 191.

5. Personal communication from K. Kajungu; also see Malidoma P. Somé, *Of Water and the Spirit* (New York: Putnam, 1994), 20.

6. Adapted from Courlander, *A Treasury of African Folklore*, 369–72, and other sources.

7. Adapted from Paul Radin, ed., *African Folktales* (New York: Stockmen Books, 1983), 73–78; Chatelain, *Folk-Tales of Angola*, 131–41.

CHAPTER 5: THE HEART OF THE SACRED WARRIOR

1. Dominique Zahan, *The Religion, Spirituality, and Thought of Traditional Africa* (Chicago: University of Chicago Press, 1979), 146–52.

2. Adapted from *The Mwindo Epic,* edited and translated by Daniel Biebuyck and Kahombo C. Mateene (Berkeley: University of California Press, 1969), with footnotes from the original translation. Copyright © 1969 by The Regents of the University of California. Included by permission of the University of California Press.

3. See Otto Rank, "The Myth of the Birth of the Hero" in *In Quest of the Hero* (Princeton, N.J.: Princeton University Press, [1909] 1990), 3–86.

4. See Campbell, *Historical Atlas of World Mythology,* vol. 1, pt. 2 (New York: Harper & Row, 1988), 244–48.

5. See John Williams Johnson, *The Epic of Son-Jara* (Bloomington: Indiana University Press, 1992).

6. See John P. Clark, *The Ozidi Saga* (Ibadan, Nigeria: Ibadan University Press, 1977).

7. Charles S. Bird and Martha B. Kendall, "The Mande Hero," in Ivan Karp and Charles S. Bird, eds., *African Systems of Thought* (Bloomington: Indiana University Press, [1980] 1987), 15.

8. See, for example, Campbell, *Transformations of Myth Through Time* (New York: Harper & Row, 1990), 209–60.

CHAPTER 6: THE WAY OF THE MASTER ANIMALS

1. Adapted from Radin, *African Folktales,* 229–34.

2. See Campbell, *Historical Atlas,* vol. 2, 154.

3. See, for example, Campbell, *Transformations of Myth,* 10.

4. George Bird Grinell, cited in Campbell, *Historical Atlas,* vol. 2, 234.

5. Recollections of his first experience of seeing a praying mantis as a child in southern Africa with his Bushman nurse Klara, in Laurens Van der Post, *The Heart of the Hunter* (New York: William Morrow, 1961), 163–64.

6. Campbell, *The Mythic Image* (Princeton, N.J.: Princeton University Press, 1974), 221.

7. Van der Post, *The Heart of the Hunter,* 167.

8. J. D. Lewis-Williams, *Images of Power: Understanding Bushman Rock Art* (Johannesburg, South Africa: Southern Book Publishers, 1989), 119.

9. Lewis-Williams, *Images of Power,* 120.

10. Lewis-Williams, *Images of Power,* 50–51.

11. Lewis-Williams, *Images of Power,* 50.

12. *Ibid.*

13. Lewis-Williams, *Images of Power,* 29.

14. Lewis-Williams, *Images of Power,* 20–21.

15. J. M. Orpen, "A Glimpse into the Mythology of the Maluti Bushmen," reprinted in *Folklore* 30 ([1874] 1919), 143–45.

16. R. B. Lee, cited in Lewis-Williams, *Believing and Seeing: Symbolic Meanings in San Rock Paintings* (New York: Academic Press, 1981), 81.

17. M. A. Biesele, cited in Campbell, *Historical Atlas,* vol. 1, 96.

18. Swami Nikhilananda, trans., *The Gospel of Sri Ramakrishna* (New York: Ramakrishna-Vivekananda Center, 1942), 829–30.

CHAPTER 7: THE GODDESS IN AFRICA

1. Leo Frobenius, *Das Unbekannte Afrika,* cited in Campbell, *Historical Atlas,* 40.

2. *Oxford English Dictionary.*

3. See Mbiti, *African Religions and Philosophy,* 45–46, for these and other African references to God.

4. Victor Turner, *The Forest of Symbols: Aspects of Ndembu Ritual* (Ithaca, N.Y.: Cornell University Press, 1967), 54.

5. Campbell, *Transformations of Myth,* 1.

6. Westerman, cited in J. B. Danquah, *The Akan Doctrine of God* (London: Frank Cass, [1944] 1968), 17.

7. See, for example, R. S. Rattray, *Ashanti* (Oxford: Clarendon Press, 1923).

8. Meyerowitz, cited in Marjorie Leach, *Guide to the Gods* (Santa Barbara, Calif.: ABC-CLIO, 1992), 54.

9. Parrinder, cited in Leach, *Guide to the Gods,* 54.

10. From *African Genesis* by Leo Frobenius and Douglas C. Fox (New York: Benjamin Blom, [1937] 1966), 97–110. Originally published in 1937 by Benjamin Blom, Inc.; reissued 1966.

11. See Martha Ann and Dorothy Myers Imel, *Goddesses in World Mythology* (Oxford: Oxford University Press, 1993), 257.

12. Ann and Imel, *Goddesses in World Mythology,* 319.

13. Ann and Imel, *Goddesses in World Mythology,* 111.

14. Adapted from Ulli Beier, ed., *The Origin of Life and Death: African Creation Myths* (London: Heinemann, 1966), 23–24.

15. Erich Neumann, *The Great Mother* (Princeton: Princeton University Press, [1955] 1963), 44.

16. Zahan, *Religion, Spirituality, and Thought of Traditional Africa,* 25.

17. Somé, *Of Water and the Spirit,* 185.

18. Campbell, *The Power of Myth* (New York: Doubleday, 1988), 179.

19. Adapted from multiple sources, principally Sproul, *Primal Myths,* 75–76, Melville J. Herskovits, *Dahomey, An Ancient West African Kingdom* (Evanston, Ill.: Northwestern University Press, 1967), vol. 2, 101.

20. Adapted from multiple sources, principally Herskovits, 1967, 113.

21. From *African Genesis* by Leo Frobenius and Douglas C. Fox, 215–20. Originally published in 1937 by Benjamin Blom, Inc.; reissued 1966.
22. See Beier, *The Origin of Life and Death*, 15–17.
23. Judith Gleason, *Oya: In Praise of an African Goddess* (New York: HarperCollins, [1987] 1992), 182.
24. Adapted from Gleason, *Oya*, 183–89.
25. Gleason, *Oya*, 190.
26. Robert Graves, *The Golden Ass* (New York: Farrar, Straus & Giroux, [1951] 1973), 264–65.

CHAPTER 8: ORISHAS: MYSTERIES OF A DIVINE SELF

1. Wole Soyinka, *Myth, Literature, and the African World* (Cambridge: Cambridge University Press, [1976] 1992), 1–2.
2. C. G. Jung, "Archetypes of the Unconscious" in *The Basic Writings of C. G. Jung*, Violet S. de Laszlo, ed. (New York: Random House, 1959). One difficulty I have with Jung's formulation of archetypes is his discrimination between the psyche of "primitive man" and that of "civilized man," implying contradictorily that while the archetypes are collective they somehow manifest differently in the "primitive" mind as opposed to the "civilized" mind. Such a distinction when applied to Africa, as Jung does, throws open a Pandora's box of racist and culturally biased interpretations of African sacred and mythic wisdom. See also Soyinka's similar and more extensive comments on this matter in *Myth, Literature, and the African World*.
3. Jean Shinoda Bolen, *Gods in Everyman* (New York: Harper & Row, 1989), 6–7.
4. At some later stage, Orisa-nla, which means "Great Orisha," was combined with the *orisha* Obatala. Originally the two were separate entities with Orisa-nla representing the primordial being. See Soyinka, *Myth, Literature, and the African World*, 152.
5. I am indebted to Professor Roland Abiodun of Amherst College, in Massachusetts, for this derivation.
6. My thanks again to Professor Abiodun for this insight.
7. Soyinka, *Myth, Literature, and the African World*, 27.
8. My sources for these myths of the *orishas* are many and varied. They include oral narratives heard from story-tellers, friends, and colleagues; and many different versions of a single myth found in printed text. Since I retold each myth by putting together what I had gleaned from all these various sources, I found it impossible to attribute the myths, except where noted, to a single source.
9. Thomas, verse 113, in James M. Robinson, ed., *The Nag Hammadi Library* (San Francisco: HarperSanFrancisco, 1990), 138.

10. Soyinka, *Myth, Literature, and the African World*, 18.

11. Ijimere, cited in Soyinka, *Myth, Literature, and the African World*, 20.

12. Robert D. Pelton, *The Trickster in West Africa* (Berkeley: University of California Press, 1980), 131.

13. Frobenius, *The Voice of Africa* (New York: Benjamin Blom, [1913] 1968), 240–43.

14. Pelton, *The Trickster in West Africa*, 138.

15. Frobenius, *The Voice of Africa*, 213–14.

16. Marija Gimbutas, *The Language of the Goddess* (New York: Harper-Collins, 1991), 275.

17. Friedrich Nietzsche, "Thus Spake Zarathustra," in *The Philosophy of Nietzsche* (New York: Modern Library, 1954), 70.

18. Soyinka, *Myth, Literature, and the African World*, 26.

19. Sandra T. Barnes, ed., *Africa's Ogun* (Bloomington: Indiana University Press, 1989), 19.

20. Barnes, *Ogun: An Old God for a New Age* (Philadelphia: Institute for the Study of Human Issues, 1980), 31.

21. R. J. Armstrong, cited in Barnes, *Africa's Ogun*, 33–34.

22. Soyinka, *Myth, Literature, and the African World*, 31.

23. Frobenius, *Voice of Africa*, 252–64.

CHAPTER 9: MYTHS AT THE BEGINNING AND END OF CREATION

1. For a description of the cosmology of modern astrophysics, see any textbook on the subject; for example, Robert Jastrow, *Astronomy: Fundamentals and Frontiers* (New York: John Wiley, 1977).

2. For a description of Bambara cosmology, see Zahan, *Société d'initiation Bambara* (Paris: Mouton, 1960) and *La Dialectique de verbe chez les Bambara* (The Hague, Netherlands: Mouton, 1963); Germaine Dieterlen, *Essai sur la religion Bambara* (Paris: Presses Universitaires de France, 1951); Evan M. Zuesse, *Ritual Cosmos: The Sanctification of Life in African Religions* (Athens: Ohio University Press, 1979); and Roy Willis, ed., *World Mythology* (New York: Henry Holt, 1993).

3. Zuesse, *Ritual Cosmos*, 154.

4. Juan Mascaró, trans., *The Upanishads* (London: Penguin Books, 1965), 83.

5. Mascaró, *The Upanishads*, 83. The Upanishads are referring to the three realms of ordinary human consciousness: waking consciousness (*A*), dreaming consciousness (*U*), and the consciousness present during deep, non-dreaming sleep (*M*).

6. Zuesse, *Ritual Cosmos*, 154.

7. Mascaró, *The Upanishads*, 102.

8. From *Historical Atlas of World Mythology*, vol. 1, by Joseph Campbell,

14, translated from *Volksdichtungen aus Oberguinea* by Leo Frobenius. Copyright © 1988 by Harper & Row Publishers, Inc. Reprinted by permission of HarperCollins. [Campbell incorrectly identifies another Basari people (from northern Togo) as the originators of this myth.]

9. Frobenius, cited in Campbell, *Historical Atlas,* vol. 1, 14.

10. Paul Schebesta, *Revisiting My Pygmy Hosts* (London: Hutchinson, 1936).

11. Jean-Pierre Hallet, *Pygmy Kitabu* (New York: Random House, 1973).

12. Genesis 3:22, 24.

13. Colin Turnbull, cited in Zuesse, *Ritual Cosmos,* 18.

14. Turnbull, cited in Zuesse, *Ritual Cosmos,* 20.

15. Turnbull, cited in Zuesse, *Ritual Cosmos,* 6.

16. Thomas, verse 77, in Robinson, *Nag Hammadi Library.*

17. Thomas, verse 112, in Robinson, *Nag Hammadi Library.*

18. Zuesse, *Ritual Cosmos,* 52.

19. Adapted from Beier, *The Origin of Life and Death,* 42–46.

20. Dieterlen, "The Mande Creation Myth," in *Africa* 17, no. 2 (London: Oxford University Press, 1957).

21. Roland Abiodun, "Composing Time and Space in Yoruba Art," *Word & Image* 3, no. 3 (July–Sept. 1987), 253.

22. J. Lebreton, "The Logos," in *The Catholic Encyclopedia* (New York: Robert Appleton Company, 1910), 328–30.

23. Leach, *Creation Myths Around the World,* 145–47.

24. Leach, *Creation Myths Around the World,* 19–20.

25. Beha Alotehka Zohar, cited in Campbell, *Mythic Image,* 192.

26. Dante, cited in Campbell, *Mythic Image,* 192.

27. Mascaró, *The Upanishads,* 65.

28. Over the years much has been attributed to the Dogon: visitation by extraterrestrial beings; prescientific knowledge of the existence of the binary stars Sirius A and B; and a culture steeped in esotericism well beyond the brief account presented in this text. Books have been written, films have been made, and a sizable tourist trade to Mali built on this material, but little confirmation of these reports has been obtained by anthropologists actually working among the Dogon. Most of these claims can be traced back to the French anthropologist Marcel Griaule and his Dogon informant Ogotemmêli. The suggestion has been made that Griaule's leading questions may have contributed to the answers he received. My own feeling is that Ogotemmêli's accounts are credible. Most likely he gave Griaule his own personal interpretation of Dogon cosmology, an interpretation that few were privy to and one that represented a deep understanding of Dogon sacred wisdom that died with elders like him. I also find it unnecessary to make African culture "exotic" (as in making it the site of UFO landings, the repository of paranormal knowledge, and so on) in order to find the beauty and value of its sacred wisdom. There is ample evidence among

the Dogon and other African cultures of their long-standing exploration of the "inner space" of the psychological and spiritual dimensions of humankind without the need to claim an "outer space" origin of their mythic insights. See Walter E. A. Van Beek, "Dogon Restudied," *Current Anthropology* 32, no. 2 (April 1991), for a good overview of this issue from many different points of view. My account of Dogon cosmology is compiled from Griaule, *Conversations with Ogotemmêli*.

29. Griaule, *Conversations with Ogotemmêli*, 50.

30. *Ibid.*

31. Zahan, *Religion, Spirituality, and Thought of Traditional Africa*, 55–56.

32. Galatians 5:16–18.

33. Augustine, cited in Campbell, *Hero with a Thousand Faces*, 148.

34. Adapted from Beier, *The Origin of Life and Death*, 18–22.

CHAPTER 10: CLOSING THE SACRED CIRCLE

1. Radin, *African Folktales*, 63.

2. Bunseki, cited in MacGaffey, *Modern Kongo Prophets*, 128.

3. MacGaffey, *Modern Kongo Prophets*, 128.

4. MacGaffey, *Modern Kongo Prophets*, 127.

5. See Campbell, *Mythic Image*, 77.

6. Bunseki, cited in William Farris Thompson, *Flash of the Spirit* (New York: Random House, 1983), 109.

7. Thompson, *Flash of the Spirit*, 110.

8. *Ibid.*

9. Zahan, *Religion, Spirituality, and Thought of Traditional Africa*, 26.

10. *Ibid.*

11. Campbell, *Hero with a Thousand Faces*, 260.

12. See Thompson, *Flash of the Spirit*.

BIBLIOGRAPHY

Abiodun, Roland. 1987. "Composing Time and Space in Yoruba Art." *Word & Image* 3, no. 3 (July–Sept.): 252–70.

Ann, Martha, and Dorothy Myers Imel. 1993. *Goddesses in World Mythology.* Oxford: Oxford University Press.

Barnes, Sandra T. 1980. *Ogun: An Old God for a New Age.* Philadelphia: Institute for the Study of Human Issues.

Barnes, Sandra T., ed. 1989. *Africa's Ogun.* Bloomington, Indiana: Indiana University Press.

Beier, Ulli, ed. 1966. *The Origin of Life and Death: African Creation Myths.* London: Heinemann.

Bernal, Martin. 1991. *Black Athena.* Vol. 2. New Brunswick, N.J.: Rutgers University Press.

Biebuyck, Daniel, and Kahombo C. Matene. 1969. *The Mwindo Epic.* Berkeley: University of California Press.

Bolen, Jean Shinoda. 1989. *Gods in Everyman.* New York: Harper & Row.

Bolster, W. Jeffrey. 1997. *Black Jacks: African American Seamen in the Age of Sail.* Cambridge: Harvard University Press.

Callaway, Henry. [1868] 1970. *Nursery Tales and Traditions of the Zulus.* Westport, Conn.: Negro Universities Press.

Callaway, Henry. 1885. *The Religious System of the Amazulu.* Springvale, Natal, South Africa: J. A. Blair.

Campbell, Joseph. [1949] 1968. *The Hero with a Thousand Faces.* Princeton: Princeton University Press.

Campbell, Joseph. [1959] 1976. *The Masks of God: Primitive Mythology.* New York: Penguin Books.

Campbell, Joseph. [1968] 1991. *The Masks of God: Creative Mythology.* New York: Penguin Books.

Campbell, Joseph. 1974. *The Mythic Image.* Princeton: Princeton University Press.

Campbell, Joseph. 1988. *Historical Atlas of World Mythology.* Vol. 1, pts. 1–2. New York: Harper & Row.

Campbell, Joseph. 1988. *The Power of Myth.* New York: Doubleday.

Campbell, Joseph. 1990. *Transformations of Myth Through Time.* New York: Harper & Row.

Casalis, Rev. E. 1861. *The Basutos.* London: James Nisbet.

Chatelain, Hèli. [1894] 1968. *Folk-Tales of Angola.* New York: Negro Universities Press.

Clark, John P. 1977. *The Ozidi Saga.* Ibadan, Nigeria: Ibadan University Press.

Courlander, Harold. 1975. *A Treasury of African Folklore.* New York: Crown.

Danquah, J. B. [1944] 1968. *The Akan Doctrine of God.* London: Frank Cass.

Dieterlen, Germaine. 1951. *Essai sur la religion Bambara.* Paris: Presses Universitaires de France.

Dieterlen, Germaine. 1957. "The Mande Creation Myth." *Africa* 17, no. 2. London: Oxford University Press.

Feelings, Tom. 1995. *The Middle Passage.* New York: Dial Press.

Frobenius, Leo. [1913] 1968. *The Voice of Africa.* New York: Benjamin Blom.

Frobenius, Leo. [1937] 1966. *African Genesis.* New York: Benjamin Blom.

Gimbutas, Marija. 1991. *The Language of the Goddess.* New York: HarperCollins.

Gleason, Judith. [1987] 1992. *Oya: In Praise of an African Goddess.* New York: HarperCollins.

Graves, Robert. [1951] 1973. *The Golden Ass.* New York: Farrar, Straus & Giroux.

Greenberg, Joseph Harold. 1966. *The Languages of Africa.* Bloomington, Indiana: Indiana University Press.

Griaule, Marcel. 1965. *Conversations with Ogotemmêli.* London: Oxford University Press.

Gyekye, Kwame. 1995. *An Essay on African Conceptual Thought: The Akan Conceptual Scheme.* Philadelphia: Temple University Press.

Hahn, Theophilus. 1881. *Tsuni- | | Goab: The Supreme Being of the Khoi-Khoi.* London: Trubner.

Hallet, Jean-Pierre. 1973. *Pygmy Kitabu.* New York: Random House.

Herskovits, Melville J. 1967. *Dahomey, An Ancient West African Kingdom.* Vol. 2. Evanston, Ill.: Northwestern University Press.

Jastrow, Robert. 1977. *Astronomy: Fundamentals and Frontiers.* New York: John Wiley.

Johnson, John Williams. 1992. *The Epic of Son-Jara.* Bloomington: Indiana University Press.

Jung, C. G. [1938] 1959. Violet S. de Laszlo, ed., *The Basic Writings of C. G. Jung*. New York: Random House.

Karp, Ivan, and Charles S. Bird, eds. [1980] 1987. *African Systems of Thought*. Bloomington: Indiana University Press.

King, Martin Luther, Jr. [1968] 1994. *Letter from the Birmingham Jail*. San Francisco: HarperSanFrancisco.

Larousse, Pierre Grimal, ed. 1965. *World Mythology*. London: Paul Hamlyn.

Leach, Maria. 1956. *Creation Myths Around the World*. New York: Crowell.

Leach, Marjorie. 1992. *Guide to the Gods*. Santa Barbara, Calif.: ABC-CLIO.

Lebreton, J. 1910. "The Logos," in *The Catholic Encyclopedia*. New York: Robert Appleton Company.

Leeming, David. 1994. *A Dictionary of Creation Myths*. Oxford: Oxford University Press.

Lewis-Williams, J. D. 1981. *Believing and Seeing: Symbolic Meanings in San Rock Paintings*. New York: Academic Press.

Lewis-Williams, J. D. 1989. *Images of Power: Understanding Bushman Rock Art*. Johannesburg, South Africa: Southern Book Publishers.

MacGaffey, Wyatt. 1983. *Modern Kongo Prophets*. Bloomington: Indiana University Press.

Mascaró, Juan, trans. 1965. *The Upanishads*. London: Penguin Books.

Mbiti, John. [1969] 1990. *African Religions and Philosophy*. Portsmouth, N.H.: Heinemann.

Neumann, Erich. [1955] 1963. *The Great Mother*. Princeton: Princeton University Press.

Nietzsche, Friedrich. 1954. "Thus Spake Zarathustra," in *The Philosophy of Nietzsche*. New York: Modern Library.

Nikhilananda, Swami, trans. 1942. *The Gospel of Sri Ramakrishna*. New York: Ramakrishna-Vivekananda Center.

Orpen, J. M. [1874] 1919. "A Glimpse into the Mythology of the Maluti Bushmen." Reprinted in *Folklore* 30: 143–45.

Pelton, Robert D. 1980. *The Trickster in West Africa*. Berkeley: University of California Press.

Radin, Paul, ed. 1983. *African Folktales*. New York: Stockmen Books.

Rank, Otto. [1909] 1990. "The Myth of the Birth of the Hero" in *In Quest of the Hero*. Princeton: Princeton University Press.

Rattray, R. S. 1923. *Ashanti*. Oxford: Clarendon Press.

Robinson, James M., ed. 1990. *The Nag Hammadi Library*. San Francisco: HarperSanFrancisco.

Schebesta, Paul. 1936. *Revisiting My Pygmy Hosts*. London: Hutchinson.

Somé, Malidoma P. 1994. *Of Water and the Spirit*. New York: Putnam.

Soyinka, Wole. [1976] 1992. *Myth, Literature, and the African World*. Cambridge: Cambridge University Press.

Sproul, Barbara C. 1979. *Primal Myths: Creation Myths Around the World.* San Francisco: HarperCollins.

Swantz, Marja-Liisa. 1970. *Ritual and Symbol in Transitional Zaramo Society.* Uppsala, Sweden: Almquist & Wiksells.

Tattersall, Ian. 1997. "Out of Africa Again . . . and Again?" *Scientific American* 276, no. 4 (April): 60–67.

Thompson, William Farris. 1983. *Flash of the Spirit.* New York: Random House.

Turner, Victor. 1967. *The Forest of Symbols: Aspects of Ndembu Ritual.* Ithaca, N.Y.: Cornell University Press.

Turner, Victor. 1968. *The Drums of Affliction: A Study of Religious Processes Among the Ndembu of Zambia.* London: International African Institute.

Tutuola, Amos. [1952] 1994. *The Palm-Wine Drinkard.* New York: Grove Press.

Van Beek, Walter E. A. 1991. "Dogon Restudied." *Current Anthropology* 32, no. 2 (April): 139–67.

Van der Post, Laurens. 1961. *The Heart of the Hunter.* New York: William Morrow.

Werner, Alice. [1933] 1968. *Myths and Legends of the Bantu.* London: Frank Cass.

Willis, Roy, ed. 1993. *World Mythology.* New York: Henry Holt.

Zahan, Dominique. 1960. *Société d'initiation Bambara.* Paris: Mouton.

Zahan, Dominique. 1963. *La Dialectique de verbe chez les Bambara.* The Hague, Netherlands: Mouton.

Zahan, Dominique. 1979. *The Religion, Spirituality, and Thought of Traditional Africa.* Chicago: University of Chicago Press.

Zimmer, Heinrich. [1946] 1992. *Myths and Symbols in Indian Art and Civilization.* Princeton: Princeton University Press.

Zuesse, Evan M. 1979. *Ritual Cosmos: The Sanctification of Life in African Religions.* Athens: Ohio University Press.

ART CREDITS

Dedication: Copyright © 1995 Tom Feelings.

Chapter 2 watermark, Chapter 3 watermark, Chapter 8 watermark, and Figure 24: © The British Museum.

Chapter 5 watermark, Chapter 6 watermark, and Figures 9, 10, 11, 12, 13, 14, and 15b: Courtesy of the Rock Art Research Center, University of the Witwatersrand, Johannesburg, South Africa.

Figure 2: The Metropolitan Museum of Art, The Michael C. Rockefeller Memorial Collection, Bequest of Nelson A. Rockefeller, 1979. Photograph © 1991 The Metropolitan Museum of Art. (1979.206.75)

Figure 4: The Metropolitan Museum of Art, Gift of Lester Wunderman, 1977. Photograph © 1982 The Metropolitan Museum of Art. (1977.394.15)

Figure 5: The Metropolitan Museum of Art, Edith Perry Chapman Fund, 1975. Photograph © 1985 The Metropolitan Museum of Art. (1975.306)

Figure 15a: From *Up from Eden: A Transpersonal View of Human Evolution* by Ken Wilber. Copyright © 1981 by Ken Wilber. Reprinted by permission of Quest Books, Wheaton, Illinois.

Figure 16: Photograph courtesy of Sotheby's.

Figure 22: Courtesy of Octopus Publishing Group Ltd./Horniman Museum London.

Figures 26 and 27: From *Conversations with Ogotemmêli* by Marcel Griaule. Copyright © 1965 International African Institute. Reprinted by permission of the International African Institute.

INDEX

Page numbers of illustrations appear in italics.

CLYDE W. FORD is a native of New York City and a graduate of Wesleyan University in Connecticut and Western States Chiropractic College. He received his professional training in psychotherapy from Synthesis Education Foundation and the Psychosynthesis Institute of New York.

While at Wesleyan, Dr. Ford won the Danforth fellowship for research in African and African-American history. He also helped found the Institute of the Black World at the Martin Luther King Jr. Memorial Center in Atlanta, then became one of the first students to attend that institute.

Dr. Ford has traveled throughout West Africa. He has taught Swahili at Columbia University, African-American history at Western Washington University, and somatic psychology at the Institut für Angewandte Kinesiologie in Freiburg, Germany. He has also served as editor of the *Brain/Mind Bulletin*, published by Marilyn Ferguson (author of *The Aquarian Conspiracy*). He is a founding member of the Northern Puget Sound branch of the National Association for the Advancement of Colored People (NAACP).

Dr. Ford's previously published books include *Where Healing Waters Meet: Touching Mind and Emotion Through the Body* (Barrytown, New York: Station Hill, 1989), *Compassionate Touch: The Body's Role in Healing and Recovery* (New York: Simon & Schuster, 1993) and *We Can All Get Along: 50 Steps You Can Take to Help End Racism* (New York: Dell, 1994). He has appeared on the *Oprah Winfrey Show* to discuss his work combating racism. His numerous articles have appeared in *Chiropractic Economics, Massage Therapy Journal, Massage Magazine, Hollyhock Review,* and *Journal of Manipulative and Physiological Therapeutics* (where his piece won the 1980 innovative-writing award). The twentieth-anniversary issue of *East West Journal* honored Dr. Ford's contributions in body-oriented therapeutics as one of the twenty important trends reshaping society.

Clyde Ford currently lives in Bellingham, Washington, where he writes, maintains a private practice, and enjoys mountaineering, sea kayaking, and cruising the waters of the Pacific Northwest.

Dr. Ford is the founding director of IAM, the Institute of African Mythology. For a schedule of the institute's programs, and to reach Dr. Ford regarding speaking engagements, please contact:

Institute of African Mythology
P.O. Box 3056
Bellingham, WA 98227-3056
Telephone: 360/758-7662
Fax: 360/758-2698
E-mail: cwford@premier1.net